FRENCH PHONOLOGY

Programmed Introduction
Instructor's Text

ROBERT SALAZAR

FOREIGN SERVICE INSTITUTE
DEPARTMENT OF STATE

WASHINGTON, D.C.

French Phonology
Programmed Introduction
by Robert Salazar

ISBN # 0-88432-803-1

This printing produced by Audio-Forum, a division of Jeffrey Norton Publishers, Inc.,
On-the-Green, Guilford, CT 06437

PREFACE

Introduction to French Phonology (Student's Manual) was developed by Robert Salazar over a two-year period during which he wrote draft materials, tried them out in class, and revised them to reflect the response of students and instructors. It is a little more than the name implies since it goes beyond matters of pronunciation to include explanations and drills on a few fundamental structures of French, particularly on the form and use of high frequency verbs. In its use at the Foreign Service Institute it serves as the initial syllabus for beginning students, preceding the *French Basic Course*. It is the exclusive syllabus for the first three to six weeks of full-time French instruction for beginning students. Mr. Salazar is a supervising linguist in this French section of the School of Language Studies.

The preparation of the textbook and the accompanying tape recordings was undertaken at the suggestion of Dr. C. Cleland Harris, Chairman of the Department of Romance Languages of the Foreign Service Institute. The manner of presentation was somewhat influenced by an unpublished programmed introduction to Polish written by Shirley Lowe at the Foreign Service Institute about 1966.

French instructors at FSI whose comments were particularly useful include Lydie Stefanopoulos, Chantal Clarke, Christine Schloesing, and Francoise Velez.

The preliminary versions were typed by Josette Howarth. Joann T. Meeks, a supervising linguist in the Department of Romance Language, read the text and made a number of helpful suggestions on the English explanations. Marianne L. Adams, Editor of FSI language publications, made useful editorial suggestions. Camera copy for the present edition was typed by Maryko Deemer of the School of Language Studies editorial office. The cover and title page were designed by John McClelland of the FSI Audio Visual Staff with the assistance of Joseph Sadote, Head of the unit.

Voice recordings play a central role in language instructional materials which are intended in any sense for self-study purposes. The tape recordings which complement the printed materials in this volume were voiced by Monique Cossard, Chairperson of the French language section, and the author, Robert Salazar. The recordings were made in the FSI language laboratory under the technical guidance of Jose Ramirez.

A companion volume *Introduction to French Phonology (Instructor's Manual)* contains directions and suggestions for the use of the materials presented in the student's manual.

James R. Frith, Dean
School of Language Studies
Foreign Service Institute
Department of State

INTRODUCTION TO FRENCH PHONOLOGY

Table of Contents

Preface.. iii

Introduction.. xii

Chapter One

PART 1

     Dialogue. (Laboratory)............................ 2

PART 2

    1. Accent "˜" over "ũ" and "ã." (Laboratory)... 19

    2. Silent final consonants. (Laboratory)....... 20

    3. Pronunciation of: "ou." (Laboratory)........ 20

    4. Hyphen in inversion verb-subject
        pronoun. (Laboratory)................... 21

    5. Pronunciation of vowels:
        é, ez, er, ai, est. (Laboratory)...... 21

    6. French syllable division. (Laboratory)...... 25

    7. Vowels: e, eu. (Laboratory)................. 26

    8. Preparation for class. (Homework)........... 29

    9. Reading exercises. (Classroom).............. 30

PART 3

     Tests. (Classroom and laboratory)................ 32

Chapter Two

PART 1

     Dialogue. (Laboratory)............................ 35

PART 2

    1. Question Forms. (Laboratory)............. 52
       Rising intonation with non-inversion.
       Rising intonation with inversion.

INTRODUCTION TO FRENCH PHONOLOGY

PART 2 (Continued)

    2. Statement/question. (Laboratory) 54

    3. Pronunciation of vowels:
       o, au, eau, ô. (Laboratory) 55

    4. Contrast of vowels oral/nasal:
       o, au, eau, on, om. (Laboratory) 58

    5. Liaison with "s." (Laboratory) 59
       Pronounced/not pronounced.

    6. Contrast of vowels oral/nasal:
       a/an, en, em, am. (Laboratory) 61

    7. Contrast between nasal vowels:
       on, om/an, en, em, am. (Laboratory) 63

    8. Vowel "e" first part. (Laboratory) 64

    9. Preparation for Class (Homework) 66

    10. Reading exercises. (Classroom) 69

PART 3

Tests. (Classroom and laboratory) 71

Chapter Three

PART 1

Dialogue. (Laboratory) 76

PART 2

    1. Intonation (questions)
       Question words/no question
       words. (Laboratory) 92

    2. Vowel "e" (silent). (Laboratory) 94

    3. Final consonant "r." (Laboratory) 98

    4. Pronunciation of "qu." (Laboratory) 99

    5. Pronunciation of "u." (Laboratory) 100

    6. Review. (Laboratory) 102

INTRODUCTION TO FRENCH PHONOLOGY

PART 2 (Continued)

    7. Preparation for Class (Homework).............. 104

    8. Reading exercises (Classroom)................ 107

PART 3

    Tests. (Classroom and laboratory)................ 110

Chapter Four

PART 1

    Dialogue. (Laboratory)........................... 120

PART 2

    1. Contrast: oui/ui (Laboratory).............. 137

    2. Apostrophe. (Laboratory).................... 138

    3. Mute "h." (Laboratory)...................... 140

    4. Pronunciation of final "x" (Liaison z). (Laboratory).............. 140

    5. Pronunciation of final consonants: c, f, l,.................... 141

    6. Review. (Laboratory)........................ 142

    7. Preparation for Class. (Homework).......... 143

    8. Reading exercises. (Classroom)............. 147

PART 3

    Tests. (Classroom and laboratory)................ 147

Chapter Five

PART 1

    Dialogue. (Laboratory)........................... 154

INTRODUCTION TO FRENCH PHONOLOGY

PART 2

1. Question forms with:
   Est-ce que ... (Laboratory) 171

2. Pronunciation of "r" between
   vowels. (Laboratory) 173
   Pronunciation of "r" after
   consonant. (Laboratory) 173

3. Nasal vowel "un." (Laboratory) 176
   Contrast: un/an/on/in

4. Il y a. (Laboratory) 178

5. "en" and "un" preceding vowel
   beginning words......................... 179

6. Pronunciation of "oi." (Laboratory) 181

7. "dix" in final position. (Laboratory) 182

8. Review. (Laboratory) 183

9. Preparation for Class. (Homework) 184

10. Reading exercises. (Classroom) 190

PART 3

Tests. (Classroom and laboratory) 193

Chapter Six

PART 1

Dialogue. (Laboratory) 198

PART 2

1. Pronunciation of "ill"
   (billet, bouillir). (Laboratory) 215

2. Explanation of s"'il vous plaît." (Laboratory) 217

3. Pronunciation of: "V<u>i</u>ent, D<u>i</u>eu." (Laboratory) 217

4. "e" continued. (Il ne sait pas/je ne sais pas)
   (Laboratory) 219

INTRODUCTION TO FRENCH PHONOLOGY

    5.   Numbers: 1, 2, 5, 9, 10, 18, 40, 50, 59.
           (Laboratory).............................. 222

    6.   Review. (Laboratory)........................ 223

    7.   Preparation for Class. (Homework).......... 224

    8.   Reading exercises. (Classroom)............. 228

PART 3

    Tests. (Classroom and laboratory)................ 231

Chapter Seven

PART 1

    Dialogue. (Laboratory)........................... 235

PART 2

    1.   Pronunciation of final "l." (Laboratory)..... 250

    2.   English meaning of "il." (Laboratory)....... 251

    3.   Pronunciation of written "ch." (Laboratory). 253

    4.   Pronunciation of the
           consonant "g." (Laboratory)............ 253

    5.   The negative form with
           "ne...pas." (Laboratory)............... 255

    6.   Review. (Laboratory)........................ 259

    7.   Preparation for Class (Homework)........... 260

    8.   Reading exercises. (Classroom)............. 265

PART 3

    Tests. (Classroom and laboratory)................ 267

Chapter Eight

PART 1

    Dialogue. (Laboratory)........................... 274

INTRODUCTION TO FRENCH PHONOLOGY

PART 2

1. Accents. The accent circonflêxe. (ˆ)......... 290

     The accent grave. (ˋ) (Laboratory) 290

2. The vowel "o" in words like
   "école" (Laboratory)................... 295

3. The "h" in words like: la hauteur.
   (Laboratory)........................... 296

4. Pronunciation of "seuil" "rail." (Laboratory) 298

5. Review. (Laboratory)....................... 300

6. Preparation for Class. (Homework).......... 301

7. Reading exercises. (Classroom)............. 306

PART 3

Tests. (Laboratory).........................308

Chapter Nine.

PART 1

Dialogue. (Laboratory).......................... 313

PART 2

1. The letter "s" between vowels. (Laboratory). 329

2. The vowel "e." (Laboratory)................ 331

3. Numbers: 1-2-3-4-5-6-7-8-9-10-18-40-50-59.
   (Laboratory).......................... 333

4. The verb "être" = to be. (Laboratory)....... 335

5. The verb "avoir" = to have. (Laboratory).... 336

6. Review. (Laboratory)....................... 337

7. Preparation for Class. (Homework).......... 339

8. Reading exercises. (Classroom)............. 344

INTRODUCTION TO FRENCH PHONOLOGY

<u>PART 3</u>

    Tests. (Classroom and laboratory)............... 346

Chapter Ten

<u>PART 1</u>

    Dialogue. (Laboratory).......................... 350

<u>PART 2</u>

    1.   The consonant "ç." (Laboratory).............. 366

    2.   The verb "aller" to go. (Laboratory)........ 366

    3.   Verbs ending in "er" like "déjeuner." (Laboratory).............. 368

    4.   Past tense, "passé composé." (Laboratory)... 372

    5.   Review. (Laboratory)......................... 376

    6.   Preparation for Class. (Homework)........... 377

    7.   Reading exercises. (Classroom).............. 387

<u>PART 3</u>

    Tests. (Classroom and laboratory)............... 389

INTRODUCTION TO FRENCH PHONOLOGY

INTRODUCTION

If you are willing to put in many hours of hard work reading, listening to, and imitating French sounds, words, and utterances, you can succeed in attaining a high degree of competence in French pronunciation and a basic knowledge of how French sounds correspond to the writing system.

The material that you are about to work with is divided into ten chapters. Each chapter has three parts.

- Part One: Presentation of a short dialogue for memorization.

- Part Two: Manipulation, correction, and reinforcement of the sounds presented in the dialogues involving a change of context, individual study, reading preparation and reading exercises.

- Part Three: Tests.

Part One usually consists of 140 to 150 frames dealing with the pronunciation of sounds contained in the dialogue. Each frame contains a task that you must accomplish before you are ready to move ahead to the next one.

You can learn Part One in about one hour in the language laboratory. That hour allows you to go over part one twice before entering the classroom for a check out session. Part Two will require another hour of laboratory work before you are ready to practice the language with your instructor. Part Three, Tests, are administered both in the laboratory and in the classroom.

Here is a list of activities that you will be required to perform in the language laboratory followed by the notation as it appears in the text.

- a. Listening only. ( )

- b. Listening and imitating. ( )x

- c. Reading French while listening to French. ( )

- d. Looking at English while listening to its French equivalent. (FR)

- e. Listening to French and then imitating French while reading French. ( )x

- f. Finding the solution to a problem or testing yourself. (answers are indicated in the left hand margin).

INTRODUCTION TO FRENCH PHONOLOGY

    g. Reading the sentence before your instructor does. x( )

Here are typical frames from Chapter One, Part One. The question mark shows that what you hear is a question.

For example:

    1. Listen to the following conversation in French.

        A: (?)
        B: ( )
        A: (?)
        B: ( )

    11. Listen and imitate this French word.

        ( )x ( )x ( )x

    22. Listen to the (R) right/(W) wrong contrast.

        (R)/(W) (R)/(W) (R)/(W)

    23. Which is the right one? Number 1 or number 2?

        (1)/(2) (1)/(2)

(2)

    89. Answer the following questions before your instructor answers for you.

        Instructor: (Q)
        You: _____( )

    91. This time you ask the question and listen to the answer.

        (begin)
        You: _____?
        Instructor: (A)

Since all frames are important, your interest in participating fully in all of them should be sustained from Chapter One through Ten. If at anytime you feel that you need more practice on previously introduced pronunciation items, you should stop your tape recorder, rewind your tape, go back to where you feel comfortable with your production, and begin again.

If upon completion of a particular frame you feel that that task was easy or even unnecessary, it probably means that you were on target--whether imitating, finding a solution to a problem, or reading. It means that the task was successfully completed and that you are ready to move to the next one. On the

INTRODUCTION TO FRENCH PHONOLOGY

other hand, if you do not share any of the feelings described above after having completed a task you need more work on that particular task.

Even though we have tried to simplify the description of selected material for oral production of the French sound system, we have introduced all the elements necessary for good pronunciation.

Where there are competing pronunciations, we have chosen to teach only one variety. We present both alternatives for listening but only one for repetition. The differences are minor and so very much a part of colloquial French, that many native speakers are not conscious of them. As we move along in our lessons, we will point out such variation in French sounds so that you will be aware of them when conversing or drilling with your instructors.

We hope that you will enjoy learning French in the classroom as well as in the language laboratory, and that you will acquire a useful level of proficiency by the time you are ready to leave for your assignment overseas.

INTRODUCTION TO FRENCH PHONOLOGY

Chapter One

PART 1

    Dialogue. (Laboratory)

PART 2

1. Accent "˜" over "ũ" and "ã." (Laboratory)
2. Silent final consonants. (Laboratory)
3. Pronunciation of: "ou" (Laboratory)
4. Hyphen in inversion verb-subject pronoun. (Laboratory)
5. Pronunciation of vowels: é, ez, er, ai, est. (Laboratory)
6. French syllable division. (Laboratory)
7. Vowels: e, eu. (Laboratory)
8. Preparation for class. (Homework)
9. Reading exercises. (Classroom)

PART 3

    Tests. (Classroom and laboratory)

Chapter One

Dialogue

A. Où allez-vous?   -Where are you going?

B. Je vais déjeuner.   -I am going to lunch.

A. Il est midi?   -It's noon?

B. Oui, il est midi.   -Yes, it's noon.

INTRODUCTION TO FRENCH PHONOLOGY

Part One

1. Listen to the following conversation in French.

    A: (?)
    B: ( )
    A: (?)
    B: ( )

2. Listen to the conversation again.

    A: (?)
    B: ( )
    A: (?)
    B: ( )

3. Listen to the rhythm of the sentences.

    A: (?)
    B: ( )
    A: (?)
    B: (B)

4. Listen to the rhythm of French again.

    A: (?)
    B: ( )
    A: (?)
    B: ( )

5. Listen again to the short conversation.

    A: (?)
    B: ( )
    A: (?)
    B: ( )

6. Now listen to the first sentence in the conversation.

    ( ) ( )

7. It's a question. Listen again.

    ( ) ( )

1.3

8. There are four syllables in the question. Listen.

   ( ) ( )

9. Now listen to the last syllable.

   ( ) ( )

10. This syllable is a French word. Listen.

    ( ) ( )

11. Listen and imitate this French word.

    ( )x ( )x ( )x

12. Listen and imitate.

    ( )x ( )x ( )x

13. This is the same word but its pronunciation is (W) wrong. Listen.

    (W) (W)

14. Listen to the (R) right/ (W) wrong contrast.

    (R)/(W)   (R)/(W)   (R)/(W)

15. This is the right (R) pronunciation.

    (R) (R)

16. Imitate the correct pronunciation. Keep the vowel short.

    ( )x ( )x ( )x

17. This is another French word. Listen.

    ( ) ( )

18. We'll place this new word in front of the one that you have repeated. Listen.

    ( ) ( )

INTRODUCTION TO FRENCH PHONOLOGY

19. Now, here are the two words pronounced almost separately.

    ( ) ( )

20. The vowels are short and clipped. Listen.

    ( ) ( )

21. These are the same words but the pronunciation is wrong. Listen.

    (W) (W)

22. Listen to the (R) right / (W) wrong contrast.

    (R)/(W)   (R)/(W)   (R)/(W)

23. Which is the right one? Number 1 or number 2?

    (1)/(2)   (1)/(2)

(2)

24. Here is the right pronunciation again. Listen

    (R) (R)

25. Listen and imitate the correct pronunciation.

    ( )x ( )x ( )x

26. Once more.

    ( )x ( )x ( )x

27. Look at the writing of the words you said and listen.

    allez-vous? ( )   ( )

28. Look at the writing again and imitate.

    allez-vous? ( )x ( )x ( )x

29. Notice that the last letter in the last word is not pronounced. Look and listen.

    allez-vou<u>s</u>? ( )   allez-vou<u>s</u>? ( )

1.5

30. Notice that the last letter of the first word is not pronounced either.

    alle<u>z</u>-vous? ( )   alle<u>z</u>-vous? ( )

31. Listen again and imitate.

    ( )x   ( )x   ( )x

32. Look at the writing, listen and imitate.

    allez-vous?   ( )x   ( )x

33. Once more.

    allez-vous?   ( )x   ( )x

34. Here is a new word. Listen.

    ( )   ( )   ( )

35. We'll place it in front of the words that you have repeated.

    ( )   ( )   ( )

36. Now the sentence is complete. Listen.

    ( )   ( )

37. This sentence is a question. Listen.

    ( )   ( )

38. Listen to the question and imitate.

    ( )x   ( )x   ( )x

39. Look at the words you have said and listen.

    Où allez-vous?   ( )   ( )

40. Look at the words again, listen and imitate.

    Où allez-vous?   ( )x   ( )x

1.6

INTRODUCTION TO FRENCH PHONOLOGY

41. The first and last syllables in the question have the same vowel sound. Listen.

    ( ) ( )

42. Look again at the question, listen and imitate.

    Où allez-vous? ( )x ( )x ( )x

43. This is a new word. Listen.

    ( ) ( )

44. This word has three syllables. Listen to the syllable division.

    ( ) ( ) ( )

45. The vowel in the second syllable is new. Listen to that syllable.

    ( ) ( ) ( ) ( )

46. Listen to the (R) right / (W) wrong contrast.

    (R)/(W)   (R)/(W)

47. Listen to the correct pronunciation of the vowel.

    ( ) ( ) ( )

48. Listen to another right/wrong contrast.

    (R)/(W)   (R)/(W)

49. Listen and repeat the correct pronunciation of the syllable.

    ( )x ( )x ( )x ( )x

50. Listen to the new word again.

    ( ) ( ) ( )

51. We'll say the vowels only. Listen.

    ( ) ( ) ( )

1.7

52. Now the word.

    ( ) ( ) ( )

53. This pronunciation is wrong. Listen.

    (W) (W)

54. Listen to the right/wrong contrast of that syllable.

    (R)/(W)   (R)/(W)

55. Here is the correct pronunciation again. Listen.

    ( ) ( ) ( )

56. Which is the correct pronunciation? Number 1 or Number 2?

    (1) (2) (1) (2) (1) (2)

(1)

57. The word containing the wrong pronunciation does not exist in French.

    (R)/(W)   (R)/(W)

58. Listen again. Which is the French word?

    (1) (2) (3)

(3)

59. Listen and imitate.

    ( )x ( )x ( )x ( )x

60. How many of the following are correct?

    ( ) ( ) ( ) ( )

(all)

61. Listen again. Are all of them correct?

    ( ) ( ) ( ) ( )

(yes)

INTRODUCTION TO FRENCH PHONOLOGY

62. Listen and imitate.

    ( )x   ( )x   ( )x

63. Listen again and imitate the rhythm carefully.

    ( )x   ( )x   ( )x

64. We'll place two more words in front. Listen.

    ( )   ( )   ( )

65. There are five syllables. Notice the rhythm.

    ( )   ( )   ( )

66. This is a right/wrong contrast of the first syllable. Listen.

    (R)/(W)   (R)/(W)   (R)/(W)

67. Here is the syllable again. Is the syllable correct?

    ( )   ( )

(no)

68. We'll say the sentence again. Is it right or wrong?

    ( )   ( )

(R)

69. Now, listen to the syllable division.

    ( )   ( )   ( )

70. Are the vowels in syllables two and three the same? Listen.

    (- - - - -)   (- - - - -)   (- - - - -)
    1 2 3 4 5   1 2 3 4 5   1 2 3 4 5

(yes)

71. Listen to the vowels in syllables one and four. Are they the same?

    (- - - - -)   (- - - - -)
    1 2 3 4 5   1 2 3 4 5

(yes)

1.9

10 INTRODUCTION TO FRENCH PHONOLOGY

72. Are the vowels in syllables one and two the same? Listen.

(- - - - -)   (- - - - -)
 1 2 3 4 5   1 2 3 4 5

(no)

73. Listen again. This time only the vowels will be pronounced.

( ) ( ) ( )

74. Listen and imitate.

( )x ( )x

75. Here is the sentence. Listen and imitate.

( )x ( )x ( )x

76. This is the sentence at normal speed. Listen.

( ) ( ) ( )

77. Listen to this (R)/(W) contrast in rhythm.

(R)/(W)   (R)/(W)

78. Listen to another (R)/(W) contrast.

(R)/(W)   (R)/(W)

79. Which is right? One or two?

(1)/(2)   (1)/(2)

(1)

80. Listen again. Is this Right or Wrong?

( ) ( )

(R)

81. Listen and imitate.

( )x ( )x ( )x

82. Imitate again.

( )x ( )x ( )x

1.10

INTRODUCTION TO FRENCH PHONOLOGY

83. Look at the writing of the words you have said and listen.

   Je vais déjeuner ( ) ( )

84. Here is the writing again with each syllable underlined. Look and listen.

   <u>Je</u> <u>vais</u> <u>dé</u> <u>jeu</u> <u>ner</u>   ( ) ( )
    1   2   3   4   5

85. Look at the writing. Determine whether the vowels in syllables 2, 3 and 5 are (S) same or (D) different.

   Je <u>vais</u> <u>dé</u>jeu<u>ner</u> ( ) ( )

(S)

86. Now look, listen and imitate.

   Je vais déjeuner ( )x ( )x ( )x

87. Listen and look at the meaning of the following exchange.

   A: ( ) "Where are you going?"
   B: ( ) "I'm going to lunch."

   Listen again to No. 87.

88. Listen to the exchange.

   A: (?)   B: ( )
   A: (?)   B: ( )

89. Answer the following question before your instructor answers for you.

   Instructor: (Q)
   You: _____ ( )

90. Try that again.

   Instructor: (Q)
   You: _____ ( )

91. This time you ask the question and listen to the answer.

   (begin)
   You: _____ ?
   Instructor: (A)

1.11

12 INTRODUCTION TO FRENCH PHONOLOGY

92. Again.

   (begin)
   You:_____?
   Instructor: (A)

   For more practice with this exchange go back to frame 89.

93. This is a new word. Listen.

   ( ) ( ) ( )

94. Notice that the vowels are the same in both syllables.

   ( ) ( ) ( )

95. Listen to the syllable-division.

   ( ) ( ) ( )

96. This is the same word pronounced at normal speed.

   ( ) ( ) ( )

97. Listen to the (R) right/ (W) wrong contrast.

   (R)/(W)   (R)/(W)   (R)/(W)

98. Listen to the correct pronunciation.

   ( ) ( )

99. Which is the right one? Number one or number two?

   (1) (2) (1) (2)

(1)

100. Here again is the correct pronunciation. Listen.

   ( ) ( )

101. Listen and imitate. Keep the vowels short.

   ( )x ( )x ( )x

1.12

INTRODUCTION TO FRENCH PHONOLOGY

102. Repeat No. 101.

    ( )x ( )x ( )x

103. We'll add two more words in front. Listen.

    ( ) ( ) ( )

104. It is a question. Listen.

    ( ) ( ) ( )

105. Listen again. Are all vowels alike?

(no)
    ( ) ( ) ( )

106. Listen to the syllable division.

    ( ) ( )

107. How many syllables are there?

(4)
    ( ) ( )

108. Which syllable is different from the others?

    (- - - -)   (- - - -)
     1 2 3 4   1 2 3 4
(2)

109. Listen again to the question and imitate. Keep the vowels short.

    ( )x ( )x ( )x

110. Here is the writing. Look and listen.

    Il est midi? ( ) ( )

111. Notice the three words which are spoken as if they were one. Look and listen.

    Il est midi? ( ) ( )

1.13

112. In fact, speakers of French divide the sentence into these syllables.

$\underset{1}{\underline{I}} \underset{2}{\underline{lest}} \underset{3}{mi} \underset{4}{\underline{di}}$? ( ) ( )

113. Listen again.

$\underline{I}$ $\underline{lest}$ mi $\underline{di}$? ( ) ( )

114. Look, listen and imitate.

Il est midi? ( )x ( )x ( )x

115. Look at the writing again and listen. Notice that in final position the underlined letters are not pronounced.

Il e$\underline{st}$ midi?midi? ( ) ( )

116. Look at the meaning of the question and listen.

It's noon? ( ) ( )

117. Look at the writing again and imitate the rhythm and syllable division.

Il est midi? ( )x   Il est midi? ( )x

118. Listen and imitate.

( )x ( )x ( )x

119. Listen to the following exchange.

    A: (?)
    B: ( )
    A: (?)

Listen again to No. 119.

120. Look at the writing of the exchange and listen.

    A: Où allez-vous? ( )
    B: Je vais déjeuner. ( )
    A: Il est midi? (·)

121. Listen and imitate.

> A: (?)x
> B: ( )x
> A: (?)x

122. Listen and imitate.

> A: (?)x
> B: ( )x
> A: (?)x

123. Answer your instructor.

> Instructor: (Q)
> You: _____
> Instructor: (Q)

124. Once more.

> Instructor: (Q)
> You: _____
> Instructor: (Q)

125. Ask the question.

> (begin)
> You:_____?
> Instructor: (A)
> You:_____?

126. Again.

> (begin)
> You:_____?
> Instructor: (A)
> You:_____?

For more practice with this exchange go back to frame 123.

127. Here is another French word.

> ( ) ( )

128. Look at the meaning of this word and listen.

> Yes. ( ) ( )

INTRODUCTION TO FRENCH PHONOLOGY

(1)
129. How many syllables does this word have?

    ( ) ( )

130. Listen to the (R) right/(W) wrong contrast.

    (R)/(W)   (R)/(W)

131. Listen again to the correct pronunciation.

    ( ) ( )

(2)
132. Which one is right? Number one or number two?

    (1) (2) (1) (2)

133. Is the following (R) or (W)?

    ( ) ( ) ( )

(R)
134. Listen and imitate the correct pronunciation.

    ( )x ( )x ( )x

135. Look at the writing of this word and listen.

    oui. ( ) ( )

136. Look, listen and imitate.

    oui. ( )x ( )x ( )x

137. We'll add three words that you know. Listen.

    ( ) ( )

138. Listen again.

    ( ) ( )

139. Listen and imitate.

    ( )x ( )x ( )x

INTRODUCTION TO FRENCH PHONOLOGY

140. Once more.

       ( )x ( )x ( )x

141. Listen to this short conversation.

       A: (?)
       B: ( )
       A: (?)
       B: ( )

142. Look at the writing and listen.

       A: Où allez-vous? ( )
       B: Je vais déjeuner. ( )
       A: Il est midi? ( )
       B: Oui. Il est midi. ( )

143. Listen and imitate.

       A: (?)x
       B: ( )x
       A: (?)x
       B: ( )x

       Repeat No. 143.

144. Look at the writing again and listen.

       A: Où allez-vous? ( )
       B: Je vais déjeuner. ( )
       A: Il est midi? ( )
       B: Oui. Il est midi. ( )

145. Listen and imitate each sentence carefully.

       A: (?)x
       B: ( )x
       A: (?)x
       B: ( )x

       Repeat No. 145.

146. Participate in the conversation. Answer your instructor.

>   Instructor: (Q)
>   You: _____
>   Instructor: (Q)
>   You: _____

147. Once more.

>   Instructor: (Q)
>   You: _____
>   Instructor: (Q)
>   You: _____

148. You ask the question.

>   (begin)
>   You: _____?
>   Instructor: (A)
>   You: _____?
>   Instructor: (A)

149. Again.

>   (begin)
>   You: _____?
>   Instructor: (A)
>   You: _____?
>   Instructor: (A)

150. Practice frames No. 141 to 149 several times.

End of Chapter One, Part One.

Report to your classroom.

INTRODUCTION TO FRENCH PHONOLOGY

Part Two

1.

<u>Accent "ˋ"</u> - accent grave over ù and à.

1. Read the following sentence before your instructor does.

    Où allez-vous?   x( )

2. Here is the first word of that sentence. Notice the accent "ˋ" above the letter "u". What does that word mean in English?

    où

    Student's answer: <u>where</u>

3. Used with the word "où", the accent "ˋ", has no pronunciation value. Look at those French words and listen.

    où, ou   ( )

4. Here is another pair of French words. One has the accent "ˋ". Listen.

    a, à   ( )

5. Look at these words again and listen. Do they sound different?

    a, à   ( )

    Student's answer: <u>no</u>

6. The accent "ˋ" is used to differentiate in writing and in meaning only between words 1 and 2. Which one means "where"?

    1. où
    2. ou

    Student's answer: <u>1</u>

1.19

INTRODUCTION TO FRENCH PHONOLOGY

2.

7. Read the following sentence again.

    Où allez-vous? x( )

8. Listen to the French.
   What does it mean in English?

    ( )

    Student's answer: <u>Where are you going?</u>

9. Here is the sentence in English. Say it in French.

    Where are you going? x( )

10. Say the last word of that sentence.

    x( )

11. Look at that word. Is the underlined letter pronounced?

    vou<u>s</u>

    Student's answer: <u>no</u>

12. In general many written final consonants are not pronounced. Look at the following words and listen.

    vous ( )   loup ( )   doux ( )

13. Read the following words before your instructor does.

    bout x( )   doux x( )   joug x( )   loup x( )

3.

Pronunciation of: "ou".

14. Here is a combination of two vowels. Those two vowels represent one sound. How do you pronounce it?

    ou x( )

INTRODUCTION TO FRENCH PHONOLOGY

15. Read the following words before your instructor does.

    nous   x( )
    joue   x( )
    mou   x( )
    doux   x( )
    vous   x( )

4.

Hyphen in inversion verb-subject pronoun.

16. Look at the following question in English, then say it in French.

    Where are you going? x( )

17. Say the last two words.

    x( )

18. Look at these two words. What is separating them?

    allez-vous?

    Student's answer: a hyphen

19. The hyphen is always used in an inversion verb-pronoun (question form). Look at the following and listen.

    a. allez-vous?   ( )
    b. voulez-vous?   ( )
    c. savez-vous?   ( )

5.

Pronunciation of vowels: é, ez, er, ai, est.

20. How do you pronounce the following word?

    allez x( )

21. Here is that word again. How do you pronounce the underlined letters?

    all<u>ez</u> x( )

1.21

22. Now, say this:

    ez   x( )

23. Read the following before your instructor does.

    Allez-vous?   x( )
    Voulez-vous?   x( )
    Savez-vous?   x( )
    Boudez-vous?   x( )

24. Read the following.

    Je vais déjeuner   x( )

25. Notice the pronunciation of the underlined syllables. Listen to the syllables underlined.

    Je vais déjeuner.   ( )

26. Do the vowels in the underlined syllables sound alike? Listen.

    Je vais déjeuner.   ( )

    Student's answer: yes

27. Does the combination "er" sound different from the combination "ez"?

    Student's answer: no

28. Does "é" sound like "er" and "ez"?

    Student's answer: yes

29. How about "ais"? Would you say that it sounds like "é", er, ez"?

    Student's answer: yes

30. There is no difference in pronunciation among the following. Look at number one, two and three and listen.

    é,   er,   ez   ( )
    1   2   3

INTRODUCTION TO FRENCH PHONOLOGY

31. And many speakers of French have the same pronunciation for all of these. Listen to number one, two, three and four.

    $\underset{1}{\text{é}}$, $\underset{2}{\text{ais}}$, $\underset{3}{\text{er}}$, $\underset{4}{\text{ez}}$ ( )

32. Yet, many speakers of French pronounce "ai" slightly differently from: é, er, ez. Listen to 1, 2, 3, 4.

    1. é   ( )
    2. er ( )
    3. ez ( )
    4. ai ( )

33. For the sake of pedagogical simplicity, 1, 2, 3, 4, above will share the same pronunciation throughout chapter one.
    Listen again and imitate.

    1. é   ( )x
    2. er ( )x
    3. ez ( )x
    4. ai ( )x

34. In the future, accept either of the following two pronunciations of "ai." Some French speakers use one; some, the other. Listen.

    1. Je vais   ( )
    2. Je vais   ( )

    Again.

    1. Je vais   ( )
    2. Je vais   ( )

35. Read the following words.

    a. vider x( )   vidé x( )   videz x( )   vidais x( )
    b. aller x( )   allé x( )   allez x( )   allais x( )
    c. saler x( )   salé x( )   salez x( )   salais x( )
    d. filer x( )   filé x( )   filez x( )   filais x( )

36. Here are some more words. Read them before your instructor does.

    louer x( )
    doué   x( )
    voué   x( )
    nouez x( )
    jouer x( )

1.23

24   INTRODUCTION TO FRENCH PHONOLOGY

37. Here are more words for you to read. Remember that final consonants are not pronounced.

   mais x( )   laid x( )   lait x( )   fait x( )

38. Read the following sentence.

   Il est midi.   x( )

39. Look at the French again. What does it mean in English.

   Il est midi.

   Student's answer: It's noon.

40. Here is that sentence again. Read the underlined word.

   Il est midi.   x( )

41. Are there other words that you have learned in chapter one which contain that same vowel sound?

   Student's answer: yes

42. Does the following word contain that vowel sound? Listen.

   Je ( )

   Student's answer: No

43. Say the underlined parts of the following words.

   allez, déjeuner, vais, est   x( )

44. Look at the following letters or combination of letters. Is it correct to say that they all share the same pronunciation?

   é, ez, er, ais, est

   Student's answer: Yes

45. Read the following sentences.

   Il est midi.   x( )
   Il est fini.   x( )
   Il est vidé.   x( )
   Il est doublé.   x( )
   Il est miné.   x( )
   Il est soudé.   x( )

1.24

INTRODUCTION TO FRENCH PHONOLOGY

6.

French syllable division.

46. Read the following sentence, then say how many syllables it contains.

    Il est midi. x( )

    Student's answer: <u>4</u>

47. Here is the sentence again. Say the first syllable.

    Il est midi.

    Student's answer: <u>i</u>

48. What is the second syllable?

    Student's answer: <u>lest</u>

49. Here is the sentence again. Would you say that the first syllable is a word? Look and listen.

    Il est midi. ( )

    Student's answer: <u>No</u>

50. Say the first syllable.

    x( )

51. Look at the sentence again. Is the second word a complete syllable or only part of a syllable?

    Il est midi.

    Student's answer: <u>Part of a syllable</u>

52. Look and listen to the following sentence then look at the way that the syllables are divided. Is it right or wrong?

    Il est midi. ( )   i lest mi di

    Student's answer: <u>Right</u>

53. Read the following words.

    a. déminer x( ) cinéma x( ) décidé x( )
    b. animé   x( ) défilé x( ) décédé x( ) valider x( )

54. Read the following sentences.

    a. Il est fini.   x( )
    b. Il a fini.   x( )
    c. Il est midi. x( )
    d. Il a décidé. x( )
    e. Il a déjeuné. x( )

55. Read the following sentences and make a short pause between syllables.

    a. Il est midi. x( )
    b. Il est fini. x( )
    c. Il a fini.   x( )
    d. Il a décidé. x( )
    e. Il a déjeuné. x( )

56. Again make a short pause between syllables while reading these words.

    a. déminer x( ) décider x( ) cinéma x( )
    b. défilé x( ) animer x( )

7.

Vowels: e, eu

57. Read the following sentence.

    Je vais déjeuner. x( )

58. Say the first syllable.

    x( )

59. What is the first word of that sentence?

    x( )

60. What is the last word of that sentence?

    x( )

INTRODUCTION TO FRENCH PHONOLOGY

61. Listen to that word. How many syllables are there?

    ( )

    Student's answer: 3

62. Say the second syllable of that word.

    x( )

63. Now say the sentence again.

    x( )

64. For many French speakers there is no difference in pronunciation in the underlined vowels. Look and listen.

    Je vais déjeuner. ( ) ( )

65. However, many other French speakers have a slight difference in pronunciation in the vowels "eu" and "e". Look and listen.

    Je/jeux ( )

66. These differences in pronunciation which are related to the writing system present no problem with regard to meaning. Listen to the following pairs.

    de/deux ( )
    je/jeux ( )
    ce/ceux ( )

67. For the sake of pedagogical simplicity we will not make any difference in pronunciation between "e" and "eu" throughout this chapter. Look, listen and imitate.

    neveu ( )x   peu ( )x   le feu ( )x   le deux ( )x

68. In the future accept either of the two pronunciations. Some French speakers use one; some, the other. Listen to the vowel differences in 1, 2 and 3.

    1. Je sais   1. Je sais ( )
    2. Le nez   2. Le nez ( )
    3. Neveu   3. Neveu   ( )

1.27

INTRODUCTION TO FRENCH PHONOLOGY

69. Read the following French words before your instructor does.

    je x( ) se x( ) de x( ) le x( ) me x( ) ne x( )

70. Read these.

    jeux x( ) feu x( ) veut x( ) deux x( ) eux x( )

71. Read the following.

    a. jeux x( ) je x( )
    b. deux x( ) de x( )

72. Now read these.

    a. le nez x( ) le dé x( ) je sais x( )
    b. le feu x( ) je veux x( ) le bas x( )
    c. le nid x( ) le fou x( ) le sous x( )

73. Here are more sentences to read.

    a. Je la sais. x( ) Je la veux. x( )
       Je la finis. x( )
    b. Je vais déjeuner. x( ) Je veux déjeuner. x( )
    c. Je vais la doubler. x( ) Je veux la doubler. x( )
    d. Je veux le doubler. x( ) Ne le doublez pas. x( )

74. Here are questions for you to read. Read them before your instructor does.

    a. Le voulez-vous? x( ) La voulez-vous? x( )
    b. Le savez-vous? x( ) La savez-vous? x( )
    c. Devez-vous déjeuner à midi? x( )
    d. Voulez-vous déjeuner à midi? x( )
    e. Allez-vous déjeuner à midi? x( )
    f. Avez-vous déjeuné à midi? x( )
    g. Aimez-vous déjeuner à midi? x( )

Report to your classroom

INTRODUCTION TO FRENCH PHONOLOGY

8.

Preparation for class.

Drill 1
Say in French

1.	Noon	1.	midi
2.	I	2.	Je
3.	I'm going	3.	Je vais
4.	I go	4.	Je vais
5.	Where	5.	Où
6.	To lunch	6.	déjeuner
7.	To have lunch	7.	déjeuner
8.	It is	8.	Il est
9.	It	9.	Il
10.	Is	10.	Est
11.	You	11.	Vous
12.	Are you going?	12.	Allez-vous?
13.	Do you go?	13.	Allez-vous?
14.	Yes	14.	Oui

Drill 2

Say in French

1. It's noon. I'm going for lunch.
2. For lunch? Where?
3. Where are you going to lunch?
4. It's noon?
5. Where do you go for lunch?
6. I'm going to lunch.
7. Are you going to lunch?
8. Are you going to have lunch? It's noon.
9. Where are you going to lunch? It's noon.
10. Yes. I'm going to lunch.

1. Il est midi. Je vais déjeuner.
2. Déjeuner? Où?
3. Où allez-vous déjeuner?
4. Il est midi?
5. Où allez-vous déjeuner?
6. Je vais déjeuner.
7. Allez-vous déjeuner?
8. Allez-vous déjeuner? Il est midi.
9. Où allez-vous déjeuner? Il est midi.
10. Oui. Je vais déjeuner.

9.

Reading exercises.*

Lecture.

1. Read.

    1. bout; doux; loup; goût
    2. sous; vous; nous; fou
    3. joue; loue; mou

2. Read.

    1. nid; mi; dit; lit
    2. mie; si; midi; fini

3. Read.

    1. ms; bas; va; na; la; sa
    2. ananas; Alabama; Alaska

4. Read.

    1. ami; oubli; amis; soucis
    2. soumis; minou; fini; amas

5. Read.

    1. blé; vider; ciné, décidé, vidé
    2. saler; décidé, bouder; salé

6. Read.

    1. Allez-vous?
    2. Finissez-vous?
    3. Boudez-vous?
    4. dessinez-vous?
    5. Savez-vous?

7. Read.

    1   le; me; se; de; ne

8. Read.

    1. jeu; veut; eux; deux
    2. le deux; le jeu; le feu
    3. nous deux; vous deux; boueux

*Do not translate or ask for translations of words or sentences contained in the reading exercises.

INTRODUCTION TO FRENCH PHONOLOGY

9. Read.

    1. déjeuner; déjeunez; déjeuné
    2. décider; décidez; décidé
    3. déminer; déminez; déminé

10. Read.

    1. Il est midi.
    2. Il est fini.
    3. Il est salé.
    4. Il est soudé.
    5. Il est décidé.

11. Read.

    1. Je vais déjeuner.
    2. Je vais décider.
    3. Je vais le souder.
    4. Je vais le vider.

12. Read.

    1. Où allez-vous?
    2. Où allez-vous déjeuner?
    3. Où voulez-vous déjeuner?
    4. Où allez-vous la laisser?

    5. Allez-vous déjeuner?
    6. Allez-vous le souder?
    7. Allez-vous le laisser?
    8. Voulez-vous déjeuner?

Chapter One, end of Part Two.

INTRODUCTION TO FRENCH PHONOLOGY

Chapter One, Part Three

Tests

Part three is a short section consisting of three tests. Be sure your tape recorder is turned off since you won't need it for Test 1.

Test 1

The following sentences have been divided into syllables. The syllables are numbered to the right of each sentence. In the space provided over each number, write the corresponding syllable.

Example: Il est fini.   1. $\frac{i}{1}$ $\frac{l'est}{2}$ $\frac{fi}{3}$ $\frac{ni}{4}$

2. Où allez-vous?   2. ___ ___ ___ ___
                        1   2   3   4

3. Voulez-vous passer?   3. ___ ___ ___ ___ ___
                           1   2   3   4   5

4. Il a fini les travaux.   4. ___ ___ ___ ___ ___ ___ ___
                               1   2   3   4   5   6   7

5. Il est déjà midi passé.   5. ___ ___ ___ ___ ___ ___ ___ ___
                                1   2   3   4   5   6   7   8

6. Je vais les trouver.   6. ___ ___ ___ ___ ___
                             1   2   3   4   5

7. Je sais où il est.   7. ___ ___ ___ ___ ___
                           1   2   3   4   5

Start your tape recorder for test 2.

1.32

INTRODUCTION TO FRENCH PHONOLOGY

Test 2

In the space provided, write the number of syllables for each of the following sentences.

Example:

    Listen. Ne les tapez pas. ( )   You write <u>5</u>

1. ( )   1. _____
2. ( )   2. _____
3. ( )   3. _____
4. ( )   4. _____
5. ( )   5. _____
6. ( )   6. _____
7. ( )   7. _____
8. ( )   8. _____

Test 3

Listen then write the following words or sentences.

    Listen   Write

1. ( )   1. _____
2. ( )   2. _____
3. ( )   3. _____
4. ( )   4. _____
5. ( )   5. _____
6. ( )   6. _____
7. ( )   7. _____
8. ( )   8. _____

END OF CHAPTER ONE

Chapter Two

PART 1

Dialogue. (Laboratory)

PART 2

1. Question Forms.   (Laboratory)
   Rising intonation with non-inversion.
   Rising intonation with inversion.

2. Statement/question. (Laboratory)

3. Pronunciation of vowels: o, au, eau, ô. (Laboratory)

4. Contrast of vowels oral/nasal: o, au, eau, on, om. (Lab.)

5. Liaison with "s."   (Laboratory)
   Pronounced/not pronounced.

6. Contrast of vowels oral/nasal: a/an, en, em, am. (Lab.)

7. Contrast between nasal vowels: on, om/an, en, em, am.
   (Lab.)

8. Vowel "e" first part.   (Laboratory)

9. Preparation for Class (Homework)

10. Reading exercises.   (Classroom)

PART 3

Tests.   (Classroom and laboratory)

Dialogue

A. Où avez-vous déjeuné? — Where did you have lunch?

B. Au café à côté. — At the café next door.

A. Vous y allez souvent? — Do you go there often?

B. Non, de temps en temps seulement. — No, once in a while only.

INTRODUCTION TO FRENCH PHONOLOGY

Part One

1. Listen to the following conversation in French.

    A: (?)
    B: ( )
    A: (?)
    B: ( )

2. Listen to the rhythm of each sentence.

    A: (?)
    B: ( )
    A: (?)
    B: ( )

3. The first sentence is a question. Listen.

    ( ) ( ) ( )

4. Listen again to the question. How many syllables are there?

    ( ) ( )

(7)

5. Listen to the last word and imitate.

    ( )x   ( )x   ( )x

6. Listen again to the question.

    ( ) ( )

7. Listen to the question and imitate.

    ( )x   ( )x   ( )x

8. Listen again and imitate.

    ( )x   ( )x   ( )x

9. This is the answer to the question you have just imitated. Listen..

    ( ) ( )

INTRODUCTION TO FRENCH PHONOLOGY

10. Listen again.

    ( ) ( )

11. Listen to the last word of that sentence.

    ( ) ( )

12. We'll add another word in front. Listen.

    ( ) ( ) ( )

13. There are three distinct syllables in these two words.

    ( ) ( ) ( )

14. Listen to syllables one, two and three.

    (- - -)   (- - -)   (- - -)

15. One of the vowels is new to you. Is it in syllable one, two or three?

    (- - -)   (- - -)
    1 2 3   1 2 3

(2)

16. Here are the two words again. They are pronounced at normal speed. Listen.

    ( ) ( )

17. This is the wrong pronunciation. Listen.

    ( ) ( )

18. Listen to the (R) right, then the wrong (W) pronunciation of these words.

    (R)/(W)   (R)/(W)

19. Which one is right? No. 1 or No. 2?

    (1) (2)   (1) (2)

(2)

2.4

INTRODUCTION TO FRENCH PHONOLOGY

20. Listen to the last three and imitate correctly.

    ( ) ( ) ( )x ( )x ( )x

21. Listen to the (R)/(W) contrast.

    (R)/(W)   (R)/(W)   (R)/(W)

22. Which syllable was wrong? One, two or three? Listen again.

    (- - -)   (- - -)
     1 2 3   1 2 3

(2)

23. Listen to this (R)/(W) contrast again.

    (R)/(W)   (R)/(W)

24. Is the pronunciation of these words right? Listen.

    ( ) ( )

(yes)

25. Is it right this time? Listen.

    ( ) ( )

(yes)

26. Which ones are <u>wrong</u>? Listen.

    (1) (2) (3)

(all)

27. Listen again. Which ones are <u>wrong</u>?

    (1) (2) (3)

(1 & 2)

28. Pick out the right ones.

    (1) (2) (3) (4) (5)

(3 & 4)

29. Listen to this (R)/(W) contrast.

    (R)/(W)(W)   (R)/(W)(W)

30. Here is the right pronunciation. Listen and imitate.

    ( )X ( )X ( )X

2.5

INTRODUCTION TO FRENCH PHONOLOGY

31. Here are two more words. Listen.

    ( )   ( )

32. Listen again to these two words.

    ( )   ( )

33. Now listen and imitate.

    ( )x   ( )x   ( )x

34. Imitate again.

    ( )x   ( )x   ( )x

35. Be careful not to say this. Listen.

    ( )   ( )

36. This is the correct pronunciation.

    ( )   ( )

37. Which of the following three is <u>correct</u>?

    (1)   (2)   (3)

(2)

38. Listen and imitate the correct pronunciation.

    ( )x   ( )x   ( )x

39. Listen to this sentence.

    ( )   ( )   ( )

40. How many syllables do you hear? Listen.

    ( )   ( )

(6)

41. Listen to the syllable division of this sentence.

    (- - - - - -)

42. Is the vowel in the last syllable the same as the one in the third? Listen.

  (- - - - - -)
  1 2 <u>3</u> 4 5 <u>6</u>

  (- - - - - -)
  1 2 <u>3</u> 4 5 <u>6</u>

(yes)

43. One syllable contains a vowel similar to the vowel in syllable no. 1. Which one is it?

  (- - - - - -)
  <u>1</u> 2 3 4 5 6

  (- - - - - -)
  <u>1</u> 2 3 4 5 6

(5)

44. Listen and imitate.

  ( )x   ( )x   ( )x

45. Imitate again at more normal speed.

  ( )x   ( )x   ( )x

46. Listen to another pronunciation.

  ( )   ( )

47. Listen to the right (R) then the wrong (W) pronunciation.

  (R)/(W)   (R)/(W)

48. Which one is the right pronunciation, number one or two?

  (1)   (2)   (1)   (2)

(1)

49. Listen again to the sentence and imitate.

  ( )x   ( )x   ( )x

50. Here is the way it is written. Look at the writing and listen.

  Au café à côté.   ( )   ( )

2.7

INTRODUCTION TO FRENCH PHONOLOGY

51. Look at the writing again, listen and imitate.

    Au café à côté.   ( )x ( )x

52. Listen to the following exchange while looking at the meaning.

    A: Where did you have lunch? (Fr)
    B: At the café next door. (Fr)

    Listen again to no. 52.

53. Listen again to the exchange.

    A: (?)
    B: ( )

    Listen again to no. 53.

54. Answer the question before your instructor answers for you.

    Instructor: (Q)
    You   :   ____A____ ( )

55. Answer the question again.

    Instructor: (Q)
    You   :   ____A____ ( )

56. This time, you ask the question. Then listen to the answer (A).

    (Begin)
    You   :   _____?
    Instructor: (A)

57. Ask the question again.

    (Begin)
    You   :   _____?
    Instructor: (A)

58. This is a new word. Listen.

    ( ) ( )

2.8

59. It's in a question. Listen.

    ( ) ( )

60. The vowel in the last syllable is new. Listen.

    ( ) ( )

61. Listen to the last syllable.

    ( ) ( )

62. It's a nasal vowel. Listen again.

    ( ) ( )

63. The following syllable doesn't have a nasal vowel. Listen.

    ( ) ( )

64. Listen to the nasal (1) and non-nasal (2) syllables.

    (1)/(2)   (1)/(2)

65. Listen again to the contrast: nasal and non-nasal vowels.

    (1)/(2)   (1)/(2)

66. Which is the nasal syllable, No. 1 or No. 2?

    (1)/(2)   (1)/(2)

(1)

67. Listen to the following syllable and imitate.

    ( )x ( )x ( )x ( )x

68. Listen now to the full word.

    ( ) ( )

69. Listen to the word again and imitate.

    ( )x ( )x ( )x

70. Imitate again.

    ( )x ( )x ( )x

INTRODUCTION TO FRENCH PHONOLOGY

71. We'll add another word in front of the word that you have repeated. Listen.

    ( ) ( ) ( )

72. Was the added word a familiar one or a new one?

    ( ) ( )

(fam)

73. Listen again and imitate.

    ( )x ( )x ( )x

74. Imitate again.

    ( )x ( )x ( )x

75. Here is the question with two more words added in front. Listen.

    ( ) ( )

76. Listen again to the sentence.

    ( ) ( )

77. Listen and imitate.

    ( )x ( )x ( )x

78. Listen carefully to the rhythm of the question and imitate.

    ( )x ( )x ( )x

79. Here is the sentence in writing. Look and listen.

    Vous y allez souvent?   ( ) ( )

80. Look at the writing again, listen and imitate.

    Vous y allez souvent?   ( )x ( )x

81. Listen to the syllable division of those four words.

    ( ) ( ) ( )

2.10

44   INTRODUCTION TO FRENCH PHONOLOGY

    82. How many syllables do you hear?

            ( )   ( )
(6)

    83. Here is the English meaning. Listen and imitate.

            You go there often?   ( )x   ( )x

    84. Listen to the sentence again and imitate.

            ( )x   ( )x   ( )x

    85. This is a new word. Listen.

            ( )   ( )   ( )

    86. The vowel in that word is nasal. Listen.

            ( )   ( )   ( )

    87. Here is the word "often" in French. Notice the nasal vowel in the last syllable.

            ( )   ( )

    88. Both of the following words have nasal vowels. Are the nasal vowels same or different?

            ( )/( )
(D)

    89. Listen to these sounds. Are they (S) same or (D) different?

            ( )/( )
(D)

    90. Listen again. Is it (s) or (D) this time?

            ( )/( )
(S)

    91. Listen and imitate.

            ( )x   ( )x   ( )x

    92. Again.

            ( )x   ( )x   ( )x

2.11

INTRODUCTION TO FRENCH PHONOLOGY

93. Which word ends in a vowel sound? No. 1 or No. 2?
    Listen.

    (1)/(2)

(2)

94. Listen and imitate the word ending with a nasal vowel.

    ( )x   ( )x   ( )x

95. Listen to these three new words.

    ( )   ( )   ( )

96. Are the vowels nasal? Listen.

    ( )   ( )

(yes)

97. Are all three vowels the same?

    ( )   ( )

(yes)

98. Listen again. This time the vowels will not be nasalized.

    ( )   ( )   ( )

99. When the vowels of those three words are not nasalized, we obtain a non-French utterance. Listen.

    ( )   ( )

100. With nasal vowels, the result is French. Listen.

    ( )   ( )

101. Listen to the contrast French (1)/non French (2).

    (1)/(2)   (1)/(2)

102. Which utterance is French? No. 1 or No. 2?

    (1)/(2)   (1)/(2)

(2)

103. Listen and repeat the following French words.

    ( )x   ( )x   ( )x

2.12

104. Listen and repeat again. Be careful not to produce an "n" following each vowel.

   ( )x   ( )x   ( )x

105. These are the same words but the pronunciation is wrong. Listen.

   ( )   ( )

106. Listen to the (R) right /(W) wrong contrast.

   (R)/(W)   (R)/(W)

107. Which is the right pronunciation? No. 1 or No. 2?

   (1)/(2)   (1)/(2)

(1)

108. Here is the right pronunciation again. Listen then imitate.

   ( )   ( )   ( )x   ( )x   ( )x

109. We'll add another word in front. Listen.

   ( )   ( )

110. The word we've added is a one syllable word. Listen.

   ( )   ( )

111. Here is the word we've added. Listen.

   ( )   ( )   ( )

112. Here it is in front of the others. Listen. Then imitate.

   ( )   ( )   ( )x   ( )x

113. How many syllables do you hear. Listen.

   ( )   ( )

(4)

114. Listen to the (W) wrong pronunciation of the first syllable.

   ( )   ( )

2.13

INTRODUCTION TO FRENCH PHONOLOGY

115. Listen to the right (R) pronunciation.

    ( ) ( )

116. Listen to the (R) right/ (W) wrong contrast.

    (R)/(W)   (R)/(W)

117. Which is right? No. 1 or No. 2?

(1)

    (1)/(2)   (1)/(2)

118. Is this right?

(yes)

    ( )

119. Listen and imitate.

    ( )x   ( )x   ( )x

120. Imitate again the correct pronunciation and rhythm.

    ( )x   ( )x   ( )x

121. Here is a new word. Listen.

    ( ) ( ) ( )

122. It has two syllables. Listen.

    ( ) ( )

123. The last syllable contains a nasal vowel which is well known to you. Listen.

    ( ) ( )

124. Listen again and notice the vowel in the <u>first</u> syllable.

    ( ) ( )

125. Here is the same word with the vowel in the first syllable pronounced wrong.

    ( ) ( )

2.14

126. Listen to the (R) right /(W) wrong contrast.

    (R)/(W)   (R)/(W)

127. Which is the right one? No. 1 or No. 2?

    (1)/(2)   (1)/(2)

(1)

128. Listen to the French word and imitate.

    ( )x ( )x ( )x

129. Here again are four words that you have repeated. Listen.

    ( ) ( )

130. Listen and imitate.

    ( )x ( )x ( )x

131. We'll add one more word at the end. Listen.

    ( ) ( ) ( )

132. Listen and imitate.

    ( )x ( )x ( )x

133. Imitate again.

    ( )x ( )x ( )x

134. How many syllables are there? Listen.

    ( ) ( )

(6)

1. Are the nasal vowels (S) same or (D) different?

    ( ) ( )

(S)

136. Which syllables do not contain a nasal vowel?

    (- - - - - -) (- - - - - -)
     1 2 3 4 5 6   1 2 3 4 5 6

(1) (5)

2.15

INTRODUCTION TO FRENCH PHONOLOGY

137. Here are the six syllables again with a small pause between them. Listen and imitate.

   (- - - - - -)x   (- - - - - -)x

138. Imitate again.

   (- - - - - -)x   (- - - - - -)x

139. Listen and imitate at a more normal speed.

   ( )x   ( )x   ( )x

140. Once more.

   ( )x   ( )x   ( )x

141. You've heard this word before. Listen.

   ( )   ( )   ( )   ( )

142. This word begins the sentence. Listen.

   ( )   ( )   ( )

143. Does the first syllable contain a nasal vowel? Listen.

   ( )   ( )

(yes)

144. Is the first nasal vowel (S) the same as or (D) different from the other nasal vowels? Listen.

   ( )   ( )

(D)

145. Listen to the sentence and imitate.

   ( )x   ( )x   ( )x

146. Look at the English meaning and then listen to the French.

   No, once in a while only.   ( )   ( )

2.16

147. And this is how it's written in French. Look and
     listen.

     Non, de temps en temps seulement. ( ) ( )

148. Look at the writing again. Listen and imitate.

     Non, de temps en temps seulement. ( )x ( )x ( )x

149. Listen to this exchange.

     A: (?)
     B: ( )
     A: (?)
     B: ( )

150. Look at the writing and listen.

     A: Où avez-vous déjeuné? ( )
     B: Au café à côté. ( )
     A: Vous y allez souvent? ( )
     B: Non, de temps en temps seulement. ( )

151. Listen and imitate.

     A: ( )x
     B: ( )x
     A: ( )x
     B: ( )x

152. Again.

     A: ( )x
     B: ( )x
     A: ( )x
     B: ( )x

153. Look at the writing again and listen.

     A: Où avez-vous déjeuné? ( )
     B: Au café à côté. ( )
     A: Vous y allez souvent? ( )
     B: Non, de temps en temps seulement. ( )

INTRODUCTION TO FRENCH PHONOLOGY

154. Listen and imitate.

    A: (?)x
    B: ( )x
    A: (?)x
    B: ( )x

155. Participate in the conversation. Answer the question.

    Instructor: (Q)
    You   : _____
    Instructor: (Q)
    You   : _____

156. Once more.

    Instructor: (Q)
    You   : _____
    Instructor: (Q)
    You   : _____

157: This time, you ask the questions.

    (Begin)
    You   : _____?
    Instructor: (A)
    You   : _____?
    Instructor: (A)

158. Again.

    (Begin)
    You   : _____?
    Instructor: (A)
    You   : _____?
    Instructor: (A)

159. Practice frames No. 149 to No. 158 several times.

    End of Chapter Two, Part One.

    Report to your classroom.

INTRODUCTION TO FRENCH PHONOLOGY

Part Two.

1.

Question Forms.
Rising intonation with statement word order.
Rising intonation with inversion.

1. Read the following question.

    Où avez-vous déjeuné?   x( )

2. How many syllables are there? Listen.

    ( )

    Student's answer: __7__

3. Read the following sentence again.

    Où avez-vous déjeuné?   x( )

4. Listen again to that sentence.
   What does it mean in English?

    ( )

    Student's answer: Where did you have lunch?

5. Here is another sentence. Listen.

    ( )

6. Listen again.

    ( )

7. Now, listen and imitate.

    ( )x   ( )x   ( )x

8. What does it mean in English?

    Student's answer: Did you have lunch?

9. Now, say it in French.

    x( )

INTRODUCTION TO FRENCH PHONOLOGY

10. Say it in French again.

    x( )

11. This is also a question. Listen.

    Vous avez déjeuné? ( )

12. Listen again to the question and imitate.

    ( )x

13. Look at questions A & B and listen.

    A. Vous avez déjeuné? ( )
    B. Avez-vous déjeuné? ( )

14. Listen again to A & B. Do they have the same meaning?

    A. ( )
    B. ( )

    Student's answer: <u>Yes</u>

15. You know two ways of asking questions. Here is one. Look and listen.

    Avez-vous déjeuné? ( )

16. Here it is again. Listen.

    ( )

17. What is the other way?

    x( )

18. Read the following sentences.

    a. Vous allez déjeuner?   x( )
    b. Vous avez déjeuné?   x( )
    c. Vous allez au café?   x( )

19. Is there another way of asking questions a, b, c above?

    Student's answer: <u>Yes</u>

2.20

INTRODUCTION TO FRENCH PHONOLOGY

20. Your instructor will ask question. Ask the same questions in a different way.

    Instructor: You:

    a. Vous allez déjeuner?   ( )   a. _____?
    b. Vous avez déjeuné?   ( )   b. _____?
    c. Vous allez au café?   ( )   c. _____?

                           2.

                    Statement/question

21. Listen to this sentence.

    ( )   ( )

22. Listen to the same sentence. Then read.

    ( ) Vous avez déjeuné. x( )

23. Is that sentence a question? Listen again.

    ( )

    Student's answer: No

24. Here is that statement again. Listen and imitate.

    ( )x ( )x

25. This time, listen to the statement, then change it to a question without changing the word order.

    Instructor: ( )   You: _____?

26. Say sentence A (question) and sentence B (statement)

    A. Vous avez déjeuné? x( )
    B. Vous avez déjeuné. x( )

27. Without changing the word order, make questions from the following statements.

    a. Vous avez déjeuné.   You: _____? ( )
    b. Au café à côté.   You: _____? ( )
    c. Vous y allez.   You: _____? ( )
    d. Il est midi.   You: _____? ( )
    e. Je vais déjeuner.   You: _____? ( )
    f. Non.   You: _____? ( )

                         2.21

INTRODUCTION TO FRENCH PHONOLOGY

28. Read the following sentences before your instructor does.

    Il a fini?   x( )
    Vous avez fini?   x( )
    Il a cédé?   x( )
    Vous avez cédé?   x( )

29. Read these.

    Il a fini.   x( )
    Vous avez fini.   x( )
    Il a cédé.   x( )
    Vous avez cédé.   x( )

30. Read the following statement.

    Vous avez déjeuné. x( )

31. Look at the sentence, do not change the word order and make a question.

    Vous avez déjeuné. x( )

32. This time, change the word order and make a question.

    Vous avez déjeuné. x( )

3.

Pronunciation of vowels: o, au, eau, ô

33. How do you say the following sentence?

    Au café à côté.   x( )

34. Say the last word of that sentence.

    x( )

35. Say the first syllable of that word.

    x( )

36. Look at the sentence again and say it.

    Au café à côté.   x( )

37. Now say the first word.

    x( )

2.22

INTRODUCTION TO FRENCH PHONOLOGY

38. Read the following.

    au x( )   co x( )

39. Listen to these words again. Do the vowels sound alike?

    ( )

    Student's answer: <u>Yes</u>

40. Read the following words.

    au x( ), aux x( ), faux x( ), saut x( )

41. The following combination of vowels is pronounced exactly like the ones you have just read. Look and listen.

    eau ( )

42. "au" and "eau" sound exactly alike. Read the following words.

    eau x( ), saut x( ) veau x( ), beau x( ), faux x( ).

43. Now read these.

    nouveau x( ), niveau x( )

44. The vowels in the following words sound the same. Listen.

    lot ( ), veau ( ), saut ( ), sot ( ), dos ( ).

45. Read.

    sabot x( ), tacot x( ), labo x( ), galop x( ).

46. Read.

    cadeau x( ), sabot x( ), auto x( ), allo x( ),
    galop x( ), labo x( ).

47. Would you say that "o, os, ot, op" sound exactly like "au, eau, aut, aux"?

    Student's answer: <u>Yes</u>

48. Look at this word and listen.

    tôt ( )

INTRODUCTION TO FRENCH PHONOLOGY

49. Now look at this one and listen.

    mot ( )

50. Here are the two words. Look and listen. Do you hear the same vowel?

    tôt ( ), mot ( )

    Student's answer: <u>Yes</u>

51. Listen to the "o" and "ô" in these two words.

    cote ( ), côte ( )

    Listen again. Do they sound alike?

    cote ( ), côte ( )

    Student's answer: <u>No</u>

52. For the time being, we will work with words in which "o" and "ô" are the same as in:

    tôt ( ), mot ( ), côté ( )

53. Read the following words: They have the same vowel sound.

    beau x( ), veau x( ), dos x( ), sot x( ),
    tôt x( ), taux ( ).

54. Look at the following. Would you say that they all sound alike?

    ô, o, ot, op, au, eau, aut, aux

    Student's answer: <u>Yes</u>

55. Say the following words.

    mot x( ), tôt x( ), nigaud x( ), sauté x( ),
    côté x( ).

2.24

4.

Contrast of vowels oral/nasal: o, au, eau/on, om

56. You probably remember this word, look at it and listen.

    non ( )

    Listen again. ( )

57. Is the final "n" pronounced?

    Student's answer: <u>No</u>

58. Here are two words. Say them before your instructor does.

    mot x( )   mon x( )

59. Listen again. Was the final "t" and "n" pronounced?

    ( )   ( )

    Student's answer: <u>No</u>

60. Did the final "t" of the word "mot" have any influence on the preceding vowel "o"? Look and listen.

    mot ( )

    Student's answer: <u>No</u>

61. How about the final "n" of the word "non". Did it influence the preceding vowel? Look and and listen.

    mon ( )

    Student's answer: <u>Yes</u>

62. How would you say these?

    mon x( )   son x( )   don x( )

63. How would you say these?

    mot x( )   sot x( )   dos x( )

64. Read the following words.

    a. mot   x( )   mon   x( )
    b. sot   x( )   son   x( )
    c. saut x( )   sont x( )

2.25

INTRODUCTION TO FRENCH PHONOLOGY

65. Here are other words. Read them.

> long x( ), bon x( ), non x( ), ton x( ),
> jonc x( ), don x( ).

66. Contrast nasal and non-nasal vowels. Read.

> a. lot/long x( )
> b. beau/bon x( )
> c. sot/son x( )
> d. mot/mont x( )
> e. dos/don x( )

67. Now contrast the following.

> mon x( ), non x( ), taux x( ), long x( ),
> saut x( ), jonc x( ), beau x( ).

68. Here are some more French words. Which ones contain a nasal vowel?

> 1. long 2. sot 3. morne 4. beau
> 5. pont 6. dos 7. sont   8. seau
> 9. sont

> Student's answer: <u>1, 5, 7, 9</u>

5.

Liaison with "s" - Pronounced/not pronounced

69. Read the following sentence.

> Vous y allez souvent? x( )

70. How many syllables are there? Listen.

> ( )

> Student's answer: <u>6</u>

71. Say the first syllable.

> x( )

72. Say the second.

> x( )

2.26

60   INTRODUCTION TO FRENCH PHONOLOGY

73. Does the consonant sound like "s" or like "z"?

    Student's answer: <u>z</u>

74. Read the following sentences.

    a. Vous allez déjeuner.   x( )
    b. Vous avez déjeuné.   x( )
    c. Vous y allez.   x( )
    d. Vous avez fini.   x( )

75. Look at the following statement. Which letter begins the second syllable?

    Vous écoutez.

    Student's answer: <u>s</u>

76. Does that consonant sound like "z" or "s"?

    Student's answer: <u>z</u>

77. Here is that statement again. Say it. Be sure that you are using a "z" sound.

    Vous écoutez. x( )

78. In the following statement, should the "s" be pronounced?

    Vous pouvez.

    Student's answer: <u>No</u>

79. In the following sentences, which underlined "s" should be pronounced as a "z"? Number 1 or 2?

    1. Vou<u>s</u> avez déjeuné.
    2. Vou<u>s</u> voulez déjeuner.

    Student's answer: <u>1</u>

80. Read the following sentences.

    a. Vous déjeunez au café.   x( )
    b. Nous déjeunons.   x( )
    c. Nous allons déjeuner.   x( )
    d. Nous avons déjeuné.   x( )

2.27

INTRODUCTION TO FRENCH PHONOLOGY   61

6.

Contrast of vowels oral/nasal: a/an, en, em, am

81. Here is an English sentence. Say it in French.

    Do you go there often?

    x( )

82. Say the last syllable.

    x( )

83. Listen to that syllable. Is the vowel nasal or non-nasal?

    ( )

    Student's answer: <u>Nasal</u>

84. Read the following words. They all have the same nasal sound.

    a. vent x( ), dans x( ), dent x( ), temps x( )
    b. en   x( ), an   x( ), sang x( ), blanc x( )

85. Read these.

    a. Sent   x( ), sans x( )
    b. en   x( ), an   x( )
    c. temps x( ), tant x( )
    d. dent   x( ), dans x( )

86. Contrast the vowels in the following words, oral/nasal.

    a. la/lent   x( )
    b. bas/banc x( )
    c. cas/camp x( )
    d. sa/sang   x( )
    e. tas/temps x( )

87. Read the following sentence.

    Non, de temps en temps seulement. x( )

88. What does it mean in English?

    Student's answer: <u>No, once in a while only.</u>

2.28

INTRODUCTION TO FRENCH PHONOLOGY

89. Now, say it in French.

    x( )

90. How many syllables are there? Listen.

    ( )

    Student's answer: 7

91. How do you pronounce this one?

    temps en temps x( )

92. This phrase contains three vowels. Listen.

    ( )

93. Are those vowels different from one another? Listen.

    ( )

    Student's answer: No

94. How many consonants do you hear? Listen.

    ( )

    Student's answer: 3

95. How many different consonants are there? Listen.

    ( )

    Student's answer: 2

96. Listen again. What are those consonants?

    ( )

    Student's answer: t z t

97. Say the following in French.

    from time to time x( )

98. Read this.

    de temps en temps x( )

2.29

INTRODUCTION TO FRENCH PHONOLOGY

99. Look at the sentence and say the 2nd syllable.

   de temps en temps.

   x( )

100. Look again at the sentence, then say the 2nd word.

   de temps en temps

   x( )

101. Now, say the third word.

   de temps en temps

   x( )

102. Here is the sentence again. What is the third syllable sound?

   de temps en temps

   x( )

                    7.

Contrast between nasal/vowels: on, om/an, en, em, am

103. How do you translate the following English word to French?

   no   x( )

104. Look at the word and say it.

   non   x( )

105. Is the vowel sound nasal?

   Student's answer: Yes

106. How about this word. Listen. Does it have a nasal vowel?

   temps   ( )

   Student's answer: Yes

2.30

INTRODUCTION TO FRENCH PHONOLOGY

107. Listen to the nasal vowels in these two words. Are the vowels the same?

    temps/ton ( )

    Student's answer: No

108. Read the following words before your instructor does.

    non x( ), son x( ), bon x( ), long x( )

109. Now, read these.

    vent x( ), dans x( ), sang x( ), banc x( )

110. How do you say these words?

    a. vent/vont   x( )
    b. dans/dont   x( )
    c. vont/vent   x( )
    d. son/sans   x( )
    e. dent/dont   x( )
    f. long/lent   x( )

111. Here are some more words. How do you say them?

    a. amont   x( )
    b. amant   x( )
    c. auto   x( )
    d. autant   x( )
    e. Gaston   x( )
    f. manteau   x( )
    g. pendant   x( )

8.

Vowel "e"

112. Read the following sentence before your instructor does.

    Non, de temps en temps seulement. x( )

113. Say the last word of the sentence.

    x( )

114. What's the first syllable? Listen to the word.

    ( )

    Student's answer: Seul

INTRODUCTION TO FRENCH PHONOLOGY

115. Here is the word. Say it.

    seulement x( )

116. We'll underline one of the vowels. Is that vowel pronounced? Look and listen.

    seul<u>e</u>ment ( )

    Student's answer: <u>No</u>

117. Many times, the written vowel "e" is not pronounced.

    We'll have more discussion and practice about the vowel "e" in later chapters.

Report to your classroom.

9.

Homework

Drill 1

Say in French

1.	At noon	1.	A midi
2.	At the café	2.	Au café
3.	Next door	3.	A côté
4.	You	4.	Vous
5.	I	5.	Je
6.	No	6.	Non
7.	Only	7.	Seulement
8.	Often	8.	Souvent
9.	Once in awhile	9.	De temps en temps

Drill 2

Say in English

1. Est-il midi?
2. Vous allez au café?
3. Vous y allez?
4. Avez-vous déjeuné?
5. Allez-vous à côté?
6. Vous avez déjeuné?
7. Allez-vous souvent au café?
8. Où allez-vous déjeuner?
9. Allez-vous au café de temps en temps?
10. Je vais déjeuner à côté.
11. Je vais au café.
12. Vous allez à côté?
13. De temps en temps, je vais au café.
14. Je vais à côté seulement.
15. Je vais au café à côté.

1. Is it noon?
2. You're going to the café?
3. You're going (there)?
4. Did you have lunch?
5. Are you going next door?
6. Did you have lunch?
7. Do you often go to the café?
8. Where are you going to lunch?
9. Do you go to the café once in a while?
10. I'm going to have lunch next door.
11. I'm going to the café.
12. Are you going next door?
13. Once in a while I go to the café.
14. I'm only going next door.
15. I'm going to the café next door.

2.33

INTRODUCTION TO FRENCH PHONOLOGY

Drill 3

Say in French

1.	Once in a while I go next door.	1.	De temps en temps je vais à côté.
2.	Do you go there often?	2.	Vous y allez souvent?
3.	Have you had lunch?	3.	Avez-vous déjeuné?
4.	Where do you go for lunch?	4.	Où allez-vous déjeuné?
5.	Did you have lunch?	5.	Avez-vous déjeuné?
6.	Yes, Next door.	6.	Oui. A côté.
7.	Where do you go?	7.	Où allez-vous?
8.	You're going next door?	8.	Vous allez à côté?
9.	Do you often go next door?	9.	Allez-vous souvent à côté?
10.	I'm going to the café. Are you going?	10.	Je vais au café. Vous y allez?
11.	Is it noon?	11.	Il est midi?
12.	I'm going to have lunch.	12.	Je vais déjeuner.
13.	Is it next door?	13.	Il est à côté?
14.	Do you often go next door?	14.	Allez-vous souvent à côté?

Drill 4

	Questions		Possible answers
1.	Vous allez déjeuner?	1.	Non. Je vais à côté.
			Non. Je vais au café.
			Oui. Je vais déjeuner.
			Oui. Vous allez déjeuner?
2.	Vous allez à côté?	2.	Oui. Je vais à côté.
			Non. Je vais au café.
			Oui. Je vais déjeuner.
			Non. Je vais déjeuner.
3.	Il est midi?	3.	Non.
			Oui, il est midi.
			Oui. Vous avez déjeuné?
			Oui. Je vais déjeuner.
			Oui. Vous allez déjeuner?
			Oui. Où allez-vous déjeuner?

2.34

4.	Où allez-vous?	4.	Je vais déjeuner. Je vais à côté. Je vais au café. Au café à côté.
5.	Vous y allez souvent?	5.	Oui, souvent. Non. De temps en temps seulement.
6.	Où avez-vous déjeuné?	6.	A côté. Au café. Au café à côté. A côté, au café.

Drill 5

	Teacher		You - Possible questions
1.	Je vais au café.	1.	Vous y allez souvent? Il est midi? Vous allez déjeuner? Où? A côté? Vous avez déjeuné?
2.	Je vais déjeuner.	2.	Vous allez à côté? Vous allez au café? Vous allez au café à côté? Où? Au café à côté? Il est midi?
3.	Il est midi.	3.	Vous allez déjeuner? Où allez-vous déjeuner? Il est midi? Je vais déjeuner. Je vais déjeuner. Vous y allez? Vous allez djeuner à côté?

2.35

INTRODUCTION TO FRENCH PHONOLOGY

10.

Reading Exercises

Lecture.

1. Read.

    1. Au café?
    2. A côté?
    3. Vous y allez?
    4. Midi?
    5. Souvent?

2. Read.

    1. Au cinéma?
    2. Nous déjeunons?
    3. Vous dansez?
    4. Vous en voulez?

3. Read.

    1. Vous avez déjeuné?
    2. Vous avez fini?
    3. Vous avez dansé?
    4. Vous avez son nom?

4. Read.

    1. Nous en vendons
    2. Nous en voulons.
    3. Nous allons déjeuner.
    4. Nous avons déjeuné.

5. Read.

    1. On va déjeuner.
    2. On va danser.
    3. On va à côté.
    4. On va au café.
    5. On va décider.

6. Read.

    1. Il est blessé.
    2. Il est jaloux.
    3. Il est soudé.
    4. Il est tombé.
    5. Il est cassé.

7. Read.

    1. beau, dos, vos, lot, mot
    2. flot, veau, faux, nos, saut

8. Read.

    1. nouveau, badaud, nigaud
    2. couteau, cadeau, manteau

9. Read.

    1. Où sont vos cadeaux?
    2. Il a laissé son manteau.
    3. Vous y allez souvent?
    4. Vous en voulez beaucoup?

10. Read.

    1. Nous avons déjeuné à midi.
    2. De temps en temps nous allons danser.
    3. Il ne veut pas danser.
    4. Il ne sait pas où vous allez.
    5. Nous vous attendons au café.

11. Read.

    1. Vous dansez?
    2. Vous entendez?
    3. Vous écoutez?
    4. Vous savez?
    5. Nous y allons?
    6. Nous allons à côté?
    7. Vous avez son nom?
    8. Nous avons fini?
    9. Vous voulez son nom?
    10. Vous en voulez?
    11. Vous la voulez?

    Do not translate or ask for the translations of words or sentences contained in the reading exercises.

    Chapter Two, end of Part Two.

    Go to the lab for Tests 1 to 6.

INTRODUCTION TO FRENCH PHONOLOGY

Chapter Two, Part Three.

Test 1

Look at the sentences on the left, then write the syllables in the space provided.

(Example) Je vais déjeuné. $\underline{\text{je}}_1$ $\underline{\text{vais}}_2$ $\underline{\text{dé}}_3$ $\underline{\text{jeu}}_4$ $\underline{\text{ner}}_5$ ___

1. Il a déjà déjeuné.   ___ ___ ___ ___ ___ ___ ___
2. Nous y avons déjeuné.   ___ ___ ___ ___ ___ ___ ___
3. Il est souvent au café.   ___ ___ ___ ___ ___ ___ ___
4. Avez-vous téléphoné?   ___ ___ ___ ___ ___ ___ ___
5. Vous y avez déjeuné?   ___ ___ ___ ___ ___ ___ ___

Start tape recorder.

Test 2

Listen to the vowel sounds in the following words. Determine whether they are same (S) or different (D) and check the appropriate answer column.

(Example)   Answer column

                                              S   D

Listen ( )/( )   ✓   ___

The vowels were same, so column S
was checked.

1. ( )/( )   1. ___ ___
2. ( )/( )   2. ___ ___
3. ( )/( )   3. ___ ___
4. ( )/( )   4. ___ ___
5. ( )/( )   5. ___ ___

2.38

INTRODUCTION TO FRENCH PHONOLOGY

			S	D
6.	( )/( )	6.	___	___
7.	( )/( )	7.	___	___
8.	( )/( )	8.	___	___
9.	( )/( )	9.	___	___
10.	( )/( )	10.	___	___

Test 3

Here are more vowels. Determine whether they are same (S) or different (D).

(Example)   Answer Column

			S	D
Listen:	( )/( )		___	___
1.	( )/( )	1.	___	___
2.	( )/( )	2.	___	___
3.	( )/( )	3.	___	___
4.	( )/( )	4.	___	___
5.	( )/( )	5.	___	___
6.	( )/( )	6.	___	___
7.	( )/( )	7.	___	___
8.	( )/( )	8.	___	___

INTRODUCTION TO FRENCH PHONOLOGY

Test 4

Write the number of syllables for each of the following sentences in the space provided. Listen.

(Example)

    Oui, de temps en temps. ( ) You write: 5

1. ( )		1. ____
2. ( )		2. ____
3. ( )		3. ____
4. ( )		4. ____
5. ( )		5. ____
6. ( )		6. ____
7. ( )		7. ____
8. ( )		8. ____
9. ( )		9. ____
10. ( )		10. ____

2.40

Test 5

Listen to the following French words. Write them down as you hear them.

1. ( )   1. _____
2. ( )   2. _____
3. ( )   3. _____
4. ( )   4. _____
5. ( )   5. _____
6. ( )   6. _____
7. ( )   7. _____
8. ( )   8. _____

Test 6

Listen to the following French sentences. Write them down as you hear each one. (Stop tape recorder after each number.)

1. ( )   1. _____
2. ( )   2. _____
3. ( )   3. _____
4. ( )   4. _____
5. ( )   5. _____
6. ( )   6. _____
7. ( )   7. _____
8. ( )   8. _____
9. ( )   9. _____
10. ( )   10. _____

END OF CHAPTER TWO.

INTRODUCTION TO FRENCH PHONOLOGY

Chapter Three.

PART 1

Dialogue. (Laboratory)

PART 2

1. Intonation (questions)
   Question words/no question words. (Laboratory)

2. Vowel "e" (silent). (Laboratory)

3. Final consonant "r." (Laboratory)

4. Pronunciation of "qu." (Laboratory)

5. Pronunciation of "u." (Laboratory)

6. Review. (Laboratory)

7. Preparation for Class (Homework)

8. Reading exercises. (Classroom)

PART 3

Tests. (Classroom end laboratory)

Chapter Three

Dialogue

A. Quand partez-vous?   -When do you leave?

B. Je pars samedi.   -I'm leaving Saturday.

A. A quelle heure?   -At what time?

B. A une heure.   -At one o'clock.

INTRODUCTION TO FRENCH PHONOLOGY

Part One

1. Listen to the following conversation in French.

   A: Quand partez-vous?
   B: Je pars samedi.
   A: A quelle heure?
   B: A une heure.

2. Listen again.

   A: (?)
   B: ( )
   A: (?)
   B: ( )

3. Listen to the rhythm of each sentence.

   A ( ) B ( ) A ( ) B ( )

4. The first sentence is a question. Listen.

   ( ) ( )

5. Listen to the rhythm of that question.

   ( ) ( )

6. How many syllables are there. Listen.

   ( ) ( )

(4)

7. Listen to the last two words of the question.

   ( ) ( )

8. Listen again.

   ( ) ( )

9. Listen to the syllable division of these two words.

   ( ) ( )

3.3

10. Here is the first syllable. Listen

( ) ( ) ( )

11. Listen again. Notice the final consonant.

( ) ( ) ( )

12. We shall not pronounce the final consonant. Listen.

( ) ( ) ( )

13. The syllable now ends in a vowel. Listen.

( ) ( ) ( )

14. Listen to this contrast.

( )/( ) ( )/( )

15. One syllable ends in a vowel, the other in a consonant.

( )/( ) ( )/( )

16. Which one ends in a consonant? The first or the second one?

(1) (2) (1) (2)

(2)

17. Which one ends in a vowel?

(1) (2) (1) (2)

(2)

18. Listen to these words. Do they sound (S) same or (D) different?

( ) ( ) ( ) ( )

(D)

19. How about these? Are they (S) same or (D) different?

( ) ( ) ( ) ( )

(D)

3.4

INTRODUCTION TO FRENCH PHONOLOGY

    20. Here is another pair of French words. Do they sound (S) or (D)?

        ( ) ( )

(S)

    21. Here are some other different words. Listen.

        ( ) ( ) ( ) ( )

    22. Here they are again. Listen carefully.

        ( ) ( ) ( ) ( )

    23. Would you say that all four words have the same consonant at the end?

        ( ) ( ) ( ) ( )

(yes)

    24. Here is that final consonant again with other French words.

        ( ) ( ) ( ) ( )

    25. Does this final consonant sound exist in English?

        ( ) ( ) ( ) ( )

(no)

    26. Listen to the following English words.

        ( ) ( )

    27. Listen to the same word in French.

        ( ) ( )

    28. Does this French word end in a consonant?

        ( ) ( )

(yes)

    29. How about this French word?

        ( ) ( )

(no)

3.5

30. Listen (1) first to the English, then to the (2) French word.

    (1)(2)   (1)(2)

31. Listen to the contrast again.

    (1)(2)   (1)(2)

32. Which one is the French word?

    (1)(2)   (1)(2)

(1)

33. The writing of the French word you heard could be something like this.

    pahkh ( )   pahkh ( )

34. Now look at the "writing", listen and imitate.

    pahkh ( )x   pahkh ( )x   pahkh ( )x

35. Imitate again.

    ( )x ( )x ( )x ( )x

36. Notice the pronunciation of the "p". Listen.

    ( ) ( ) ( )

37. This pronunciation of the letter "p" is wrong. Listen.

    ( ) ( ) ( )

38. Listen to the contrast R/W.

    (R)/(W)   (R)/(W)

39. Which one is right? One or two?

    (1)/(2)   (1)/(2)

(1)

40. Imitate again the correct pronunciation.

    ( )x ( )x ( )x

3.6

INTRODUCTION TO FRENCH PHONOLOGY

41. Listen to the following question.

    ( ) ( )

42. How many syllables do you hear?

    ( ) ( )

(4)

43. Listen to the syllable division.

    ( ) ( )

44. The question is pronounced at slower than normal speed. Listen and imitate.

    ( )x ( )x

45. Imitate the question at normal speed.

    ( )x ( )x ( )x

46. Now, look at the writing and listen.

    Quand partez-vous? ( ) ( )

47. Look at the writing again. Listen and imitate.

    Quand partez-vous? ( )x ( )x

48. Here is the English meaning. Listen and imitate the French.

    When are you leaving? (French)x (French)x

49. Listen again to the question and imitate.

    ( )x ( )x ( )x

50. Here is the answer to the question. Listen.

    ( ) ( )

51. Listen to the (Q) question followed by the (A) answer.

    (Q)(A)   (Q)(A)

52. Ask the question and listen to the answer.

> (begin) You: _____?
> Instructor: (A)

53. Again.

> (begin) You: _____?
> Instructor: (A)

54. Listen to the answer. How many syllables are there?

> ( ) ( )

(4)

55. Listen again. Do you hear French "r"?

> ( ) ( )

(yes)

56. Which syllable ends in a French "r"?

> (- - - -) (- - - -)
> 1 2 3 4   1 2 3 4

(2)

57. Listen to the last word of the sentence.

> ( ) ( ) ( )

58. Listen again and imitate.

> ( )x ( )x ( )x

59. The word you have imitated means Saturday. Here is the writing in French. Look and listen.

> samedi ( ) ( )

60. Look, listen and imitate.

> samedi ( )x ( )x ( )x

61. Here is the full sentence again. Listen.

> ( ) ( )

62. Listen and imitate.

> ( )x ( )x ( )x

3.8

INTRODUCTION TO FRENCH PHONOLOGY

63. Look at the meaning in English and listen to the French.

    I'm leaving Saturday. (Fr) (Fr)

64. Here is the writing in French. Look and listen.

    Je pars samedi. ( ) ( )

65. Read, listen and imitate.

    Je pars samedi. ( )x ( )x ( )x

66. Here again is the question to the preceding sentence. Listen.

    ( ) ( )

67. And here is the answer.

    ( ) ( )

68. Listen and imitate the (Q) question and then the (A) answer.

    (Q)x (A)x

69. Again.

    (Q)x (A)x

70. Answer your instructor.

    Instructor: (Q)
    You: _____?

71. Once more.

    Instructor: (Q)
    You: _____?

72. Ask the question.

    (begin) You: _____?
             Instructor: (A)

3.9

73. Once more.

       (begin) You: _____?
                  Instructor: (A)

74. This is another question. Listen.

    ( ) ( )

75. How many syllables are there. Listen.

    ( ) ( )

(3)

76. Does the last syllable end in a (V) vowel or a (C) consonant?

    ( ) ( )

(C)

77. Would you say that the last consonant is a French "r"?

    ( ) ( )

(yes)

78. Listen to the last syllable.

    ( ) ( ) ( )

79. Listen to a wrong pronunciation of the vowel and final consonant.

    ( ) ( )

80. Here is the correct pronunciation. Listen.

    ( ) ( )

81. Listen to the (R) right/(W) wrong contrast.

    (R)/(W)   (R)/(W)

82. Is this right?

    ( ) ( )

(yes)

83. Which is the right one?

    (1)/(2)   (1)/(2)

(1)

INTRODUCTION TO FRENCH PHONOLOGY

84. Is number (1) one right?

   (1)/(2) (1)/(2)

(yes)

85. Which of the four is right?

   (1) (2) (3) (4)

(3)

86. Listen and imitate.

   ( )x ( )x ( )x

87. Again.

   ( )x ( )x ( )x

88. Listen to the full sentence.

   ( ) ( )

89. Listen and imitate.

   ( )x ( )x ( )x

90. Imitate the question again.

   ( )x ( )x ( )x

91. Look at the meaning and listen to the question in French.

   At what time? (Fr) (Fr)

92. Here is the question written in French. Look and listen.

   A quelle heure? ( ) ( )

93. Look, listen and imitate.

   A quelle heure? ( )x ( )x ( )x

94. Imitate again while reading.

   A quelle heure? ( )x ( )x ( )x

3.11

95. Imitate the question again.

    ( )x ( )x ( )x

96. Listen to the answer to the question.

    ( ) ( )

97. How many syllables are there? Listen.

    ( ) ( )

(3)

98. The second syllable is new. Listen.

    ( ) ( ) ( )

99. This sound does not exist in English. Listen.

    ( ) ( ) ( )

100. Here is a wrong pronunciation of that vowel.

    ( ) ( )

101. Here is another wrong pronunciation of that sound.

    ( ) ( )

102. This pronunciation is also wrong.

    ( ) ( )

103. And this is the correct pronunciation.

    ( ) ( ) ( )

104. Listen to this (R) right/(W) wrong contrast.

    (R)/(W)   (R)/(W)

105. Here is another R/W contrast.

    (R)/(W)   (R)/(W)

106. This is the correct sound. Listen.

    ( ) ( ) ( )

3.12

INTRODUCTION TO FRENCH PHONOLOGY

107. One of the following is <u>correct</u>. Which is it?

      (1) (2) (3) (4) (5)

(5)

108. Of the following sounds, only one is <u>wrong</u>. Which one is it?

      (1) (2) (3) (4) (5)

(1)

109. Listen again to the correct pronunciation of the vowel.

      ( ) ( ) ( ) ( )

110. Listen and imitate. Be sure that the tip of your tongue is pressed tightly against the lower part of your bottom teeth.

      ( )x ( )x ( )x

111. Imitate again. Be sure to round your lips tightly as if you were going to whistle.

      ( )x ( )x ( )x

112. Round your lips as if you were ready to whistle, keep the tip of your tongue against the lower part of your bottom teeth and imitate.

      ( )x ( )x ( )x

113. Here is the three-syllable sentence again. Listen.

      ( ) ( ) ( )

114. Listen to the last two syllables.

      ( ) ( ) ( )

115. Listen again. Does the last syllable end in a (V) vowel or in a (C) consonant?

      ( ) ( ) ( )

(C)

116. Does this consonant sound exist in English?

      ( ) ( )

(no)

3.13

88 INTRODUCTION TO FRENCH PHONOLOGY

117. Are you familiar with this final consonant sound?

( ) ( )

(yes)

118. Listen and imitate.

( )x ( )x ( )x

119. Before you imitate, be sure to round your lips tightly as if you were about to whistle. Listen.

( ) ( ) ( )

120. Now imitate.

( )x ( )x ( )x

121. Once more.

( )x ( )x ( )x

122. Listen to the complete sentence.

( ) ( ) ( )

123. How many syllables do you hear?

( ) ( ) ( )

(3)

124. This pronunciation is wrong. Listen.

( ) ( ) ( )

125. This pronunciation is right. Listen.

( ) ( ) ( )

126. Listen to the (R)/(W) contrast.

(R)/(W)   (R)/(W)

127. Which is the correct pronunciation? One or two?

(1)/(2)   (1)/(2)

(1)

3.14

INTRODUCTION TO FRENCH PHONOLOGY

128. Here is another wrong pronunciation. Listen.

   ( ) ( ) ( )

129. Listen to the (R)/(W) contrast.

   (R)/(W)   (R)/(W)

130. One of the following phrases is right. Which one is it?

(2)
   (1) (2) (3) (4)

131. Listen again. Is what you hear (R) right or (W) wrong?

(W)
   ( ) ( )

132. How about this time? Is it (R) or (W)?

(W)
   ( ) ( )

133. Which one is right? One, two or three?

(1)
   (1) (2) (3)

134. Listen and imitate.

   ( )x ( )x ( )x

135. Imitate again.

   ( )x ( )x ( )x

136. Look at the meaning in English and listen to the French utterance.

   At one o'clock. (Fr) (Fr)

137. Here is the writing in French. Look, listen and imitate.

   A une heure. ( )x ( )x ( )x

138. Imitate again while reading.

   A une heure. ( )x ( )x ( )x

3.15

139. Listen to the following exchange. You will hear it twice.

    A: (?)
    B: ( )

140. Listen and imitate.

    A: (?)x
    B: ( )x

141. Again.

    A: (?)x
    B: ( )x

142. Answer your instructor.

    Instructor: (Q)
    You: _____

143. Once more.

    Instructor: (Q)
    You: _____

144. This time you ask the question.

    (begin) You: _____?
    Instructor: (A)

145. Again.

    (begin) You: _____?
    Instructor (A)

146. The following exchange has four sentences. Listen.

    A: (?)
    B: ( )
    A: (?)
    B: ( )

147. Look at the writing and listen.

    A: Quand partez-vous? ( )
    B: Je pars samedi.   ( )
    A: A quelle heure?   ( )
    B: A une heure.   ( )

INTRODUCTION TO FRENCH PHONOLOGY

148. Listen and imitate.

    A: (?)x
    B: ( )x
    A: (?)x
    B: ( )x

149. Look at the writing again and listen.

    A: Quand partez-vous? ( )
    B: Je pars samedi.   ( )
    A: A quelle heure?   ( )
    B: A une heure.   ( )

150. Listen and imitate.

    A: (?)x
    B: ( )x
    A: (?)x
    B: ( )x

    Repeat No. 150.

151. Participate in this conversation. Answer your instructor.

    Instructor: (Q)
    You:_____
    Instructor: (Q)
    You:_____

    Repeat No. 151.

152. You ask the questions.

    (begin) You:_____?
              Instructor: (A)
              You:_____?
              Instructor: (A)

    Repeat No. 152.

153. Practice frames No. 147 to No. 152, several times.

    End of Chapter Three, Part One.

    Report to your classroom.

INTRODUCTION TO FRENCH PHONOLOGY

Part Two.

1.

Intonation
<u>Intonation (questions)</u>
<u>Question words/no question words.</u>

1. Read the following sentence before your instructor does.

    Quand partez-vous?   x( )

2. Say this in French.

    When are you leaving?   x( )

3. Now say this in French.

    When do you leave?   x( )

4. Is there a difference in French between "when are you leaving?" and "when do you leave?"

    Student's answer: <u>No</u>

5. Say in French.

    Where are you going?   x( )
    Where do you go?   x( )

6. Now, say these in French.

    When do you leave?   x( )
    At what time are you leaving?   x( )
    Where are you going?   x( )
    At what time do you leave?   x( )
    When are you going to the café?   x( )

7. Here are two French questions: (A) & (B). Listen and look.

    A. Quand partez-vous? ( )
    B. Partez-vous? ( )

8. Listen again to A and B. Which one has a rising intonation on the last syllable?

    A. Quand partez-vous? ( )
    B. Partez-vous? ( )

    Student's answer: <u>B</u>

3.18

INTRODUCTION TO FRENCH PHONOLOGY

9. Look and listen to sentences A and B. Notice that A begins with a question word.

    A. Quand partez-vous? ( )
    B. Partez-vous? ( )

10. Is the last syllable of sentence B on the same level as the last syllable of sentence A? Listen again.

    A. ( )
    B. ( )

    Student's answer: <u>No</u>

11. Since the last syllable of sentences A and B are on different levels, which one is higher? Listen again to A and B, then answer.

    A. ( )
    B. ( )

    Student's answer: <u>B</u>

12. Is it correct to assume that the last syllable of an interrogative sentence which does not begin with a question word is higher than the other syllables in that same sentence?

    Student's answer: <u>Yes</u>

13. Look at the following sentences. Would you say that all the underlined syllables should be pronounced on the same level?

    a. Il est mi<u>di</u>?
    b. A quelle <u>h</u>eure partez-<u>vous</u>?
    c. Quand partez-<u>vous</u>?
    d. Vous y allez <u>souvent</u>?

    Student's answer: <u>No</u>

14. Read the following sentences before your instructor does.

    Quand partez-vous? x( )
    Quand déjeunez-vous? x( )
    Où déjeunez-vous? x( )
    Où allez-vous? x( )

3.19

INTRODUCTION TO FRENCH PHONOLOGY

15. Now, read these before your instructor does.

    Avez-vous déjeuné? x( )
    Allez-vous à côté? x( )
    Vous déjeunez à une heure? x( )
    Il est midi? x( )
    Vous partez? x( )
    Vous partez samedi? x( )

16. Here are more sentences. Read them before your instructor does.

    Avez-vous déjeuné? x( )
    Quand avez-vous déjeuné? x( )
    Vous déjeunez à une heure? x( )
    A quelle heure déjeunez-vous? x( )
    Vous partez? x( )
    Quand partez-vous? x( )
    Vous partez samedi? x( )
    Où allez-vous? x( )

2.

Vowel "e". (silent)

17. Look at the following sentence and listen.

    Je pars samedi. ( )

18. Listen to the sentence again. What does it mean in English?

    ( )

    Student's answer: I'm leaving Saturday.

19. Say it in French before your instructor does.

    x( )

20. Look at the sentence divided into syllables and say them.

    je/pars/sam/di x( )

21. Notice that when two consonants follow each other and are pronounced, the first consonant ends a syllable and the second consonant begins the next syllable. Look and listen.

    je-parś-samędi. ( )
    par -tez ( )
    seuĺ-ment ( )

3.20

INTRODUCTION TO FRENCH PHONOLOGY

22. Make a short pause between syllables while saying the following words before your instructor does.

    armé x( ), fermer x( ), calmer x( ), estimer x( ), escalader x( )

23. Listen to the following word and imitate.

    samedi ( )x

24. Notice that the vowel "e" is not pronounced.

    sam̸edi ( )   ( )

25. Here is another word where the vowel "e" is not pronounced.

    seul̸ement ( ) ( )

26. Here are new French words. Say them before your instructor does.

    sain̸ement x( ), douc̸ement x( ), lent̸ement x( )

27. In the following words, the vowel "e" is pronounced. Look and listen.

    ferm_e_ment ( ), calm_e_ment x( ), parl_e_ment x( )

28. Look at these three words and say them before your instructor does.

    fermement x( ), calmement x( ), parlement x( )

29. In the following words, some "e's" are pronounced, some are not. Listen and imitate.

    samedi ( )x, calmement ( )x, lentement ( )x, parlement ( )x

30. There are many cases governing the disappearance or retention of the vowel "e" in pronunciation. We are concerned here with words with more than two syllable which all have "e" in the middle syllable. Look at the following words and listen.

    parv_e_nir ( ), lest_e_ment ( )

3.21

INTRODUCTION TO FRENCH PHONOLOGY

31. Here are these two words again. Look and listen. Are the underlined "e's" in words 1 and 2 pronounced?

    1. parv<u>e</u>nir ( )   2. lest<u>e</u>ment ( )

    Student's answer: <u>Yes</u>

32. Notice that if we cross out the underlined "e" in words 1 and 2, we obtain 3 speech consonants in succession.

    1. parv∅nir   2. tendrement
       12 3   12 3

33. Thus, to avoid having 3 speech consonants in a row, the vowel "e" must be pronounced. Look and listen.

    doubl<u>e</u>ment ( ), pars<u>e</u>mer ( ), vast<u>e</u>ment ( )

34. Look at this word. By crossing out the "e", how many consonants follow each other?

    sam∅di

    Student's answer: <u>2</u>

35. Since there are no more than 2 speech consonants in a row, is it necessary to pronounce the "e" underlined?

    sam∅di

    Student's answer: <u>No</u>

36. Say the following words. Do not pronounce the "e".

    samedi x( ), saleté x( ), sauveteur x( )

37. Pronounce the "e" in the following words.

    ferm<u>e</u>té x( ), vers<u>e</u>ment x( ), exact<u>e</u>ment x( )

38. Look at words 1 and 2. How many speech syllables do they have?

    1. lourdement
    2. doucement

    Student's answer: 1. <u>3</u>

                      2. <u>2</u>

3.22

INTRODUCTION TO FRENCH PHONOLOGY

39. Here are more French words. Before saying them, determine whether or not the "e" should be pronounced.

    légalement x( ), faiblement x( ), avancement x( )
    parvenir x( ), martelé x( )

40. Look at the following one-syllable words, listen and imitate.

    le ( )x, de ( )x, ne ( )x, me ( )x, se ( )x

41. Look at these words again and listen. Notice that the final "e" is pronounced in one-syllable words consisting of a consonant and the vowel "e".

    le ( ), de ( ), ne ( ), me ( ), se ( )

42. Now say these words.

    je x( ), ce x( ), te x( )

43. Look at these one-syllable words and listen.

    date ( ), vide ( ), coupe ( )

44. Listen again to these words. Is the final "e" pronounced?

    date ( ), vide ( ), coupe ( )

    Student's answer: No

45. The final vowel "e" is not pronounced in words of one syllable or more ending in a consonant plus "e". Look and listen.

    a. gare ( ), place ( ), lime ( )
    b. cabane ( ), malade ( ), moustique ( )

46. In fact, the letter "e" is not pronounced in French or in English in words ending in a consonant plus "e". Look and listen.

French	English
a. place ( )	place ( )
b. course ( )	course ( )
c. machine ( )	machine ( )

47. Say the following French words.

    je x( ), vide x( ), me x( ), vite x( ), bourse x( )

3.23

48. Now say these.

> parvenir x( ), saleté x( ), le x( ), vaste x( )
> seulement x( ), doublement x( ), samedi x( ),
> deviné x( )

3.

Final consonant "r"

49. You know this sentence. Look at it and say the second word.

> je pars samedi. x( )

50. Does the French "r" sound like the American "r"?

> Student's answer: <u>No</u>

51. Practice with the following words. Say them before your instructor does.

> par x( ), partir x( ), parc x( ), pour x( ),
> servir x( ), marteau x( ), tire x( ), mare x( ),
> fourneau x( )

52. Now, say these before your instructor does.

> a. par, par ici x( )
> b. pour, pour ici x( )
> c. par, par ans x( )
> d. finir, finir en beauté x( )

53. Read the following.

> a. parvenir x( ) devenir x( ) dire x( )
> b. faire x( ) plaire x( ) appartenir x( )

54. Look and listen.

> a. pour, pour elle ( )
> b. Je pars, je pars à midi ( )
> c. Voulez-vous partir? Voulez-vous partir à midi? ( )
> d. On va nous servir. On va nous servir à côté. ( )

55. Look, then say the following words or sentences before your instructor does.

> a. la mer; la mer est bleue x( )
> b. la cour; la cour est finie x( )

INTRODUCTION TO FRENCH PHONOLOGY

56. The consonant "r" in final position, unlike other final consonants, is always pronounced except when preceded by the vowel "e" in words consisting of more than one syllable. Look and listen.

    a. déjeuner ( )   déjeuné ( )
    b. vider   ( )   vidé   ( )
    c. aller   ( )   allé   ( )
    d. parler ( )   parlé   ( )

57. There is an exception to that rule. Here are words ending in "er" where the "r" is pronounced. None of these words are verbs and their quantity is limited to about twenty. Look and listen.

    Esther ( ) revolver ( ) pull-over ( ) éther ( )
    starter ( ) tender ( ) amer ( ) hiver ( )
    inter ( ) Jupiter ( ) cancer ( )

58. Look at the following words. Would you pronounce the final "r"?

    fer, mer, par, pour, tir

    Student's answer: Yes

59. In the following words numbered one to six, some final "r's" are pronounced, some are not. Which ones are pronounced?

    1. saler   2. salir   3. aimer
    4. couler   5. couleur 6. tenir

    Student's answer: 2, 5, 6

60. Look at the following words and say them before your instructor does.

    a. mer   x( ) air   x( ) aider x( )
    b. berner x( ) passer x( ) fer   x( )

4.

Pronunciation of "qu".

61. Look at the following sentence and say it before your instructor does.

    A quelle heure? x( )

3.25

INTRODUCTION TO FRENCH PHONOLOGY

62. Here is the second word of that sentence meaning "what". Listen.

    quelle ( )

63. Notice that the combination "qu" is pronounced "k". Look and Listen.

    quelle ( ), que ( ), qui ( )

64. Say the following words before your instructor does.

    quand x( ), quelle x( ), qui x( ), que x( )

65. Here are some more words, say them before your instructor does. Remember that syllables are pronounced with an even rythm.

    a. qualité   x( )   quantité   x( )   quitter   x( )
    b. quantité x( )   quitter   x( )   qualité   x( )

5.

Pronunciation of "u"

66. Say the following sentence before your instructor does.

    à une heure   x( )

67. Listen to that sentence again. What does it mean in English?

    ( )

    Student's answer: <u>at one o'clock</u>

68. Look at the following word and listen.

    une ( ) ( )

69. Here is another word containing the vowel "u". Look and listen.

    unis ( )

70. Look, listen and imitate the following words.

    unis ( )x, dune ( )x, nu ( )x, fume ( )x

INTRODUCTION TO FRENCH PHONOLOGY

71. Say the following words before your instructor does.

    a. lu x( )   su x( )   du x( )   nu x( )   bu x( )
    b. sur x( ) dur x( ) mur x( ) pur x( )

72. Now, say these before your instructor does.

    a. si, su   x( )
    b. dit, du   x( )
    c. nid, nu   x( )
    d. lit, lu   x( )
    e. dire, dur x( )

73. Here is another set of words. Say them before your instructor does.

    a. si, se, su   x( )
    b. mi, me, mu   x( )
    c. dit, de, du x( )
    d. nid, ne, nu x( )

74. Say these before your instructor does.

    a. sous, su   x( )
    b. doux, du   x( )
    c. vous, vu   x( )
    d. nous, nu   x( )
    e. bout, bu   x( )

75. Look at the following sentence, then say it before your instructor does.

    Il a voulu partir. x( )

76. Look at the sentence again. How many syllables are there?

    Il a voulu partir.

    Student's answer: <u>6</u>

77. Here is the sentence again. Look, listen, then say the first syllable.

    Il a voulu partir. ( )x

    Student's answer: <u>i</u>

3.27

102   INTRODUCTION TO FRENCH PHONOLOGY

78. Look at the sentence again, then say it separating all syllables.

   Il a voulu partir.

   Student's answer: ___ ___ ___ ___ ___ ___ ( )
                      1   2   3   4   5   6

79. Here are more sentences. Say them before your instructor does.

   a. Il a dû partir. x( )
   b. Il a tout su. x( )
   c. Il veut déjeuner à une heure. x( )
   d. Que veut-il? x( )
   e. Il a plu. x( )

                        6.

                      Review.

80. Here is a review. Look at the words or sentences and say them before your instructor does.

   a. nez x( ) ais x( ) dé x( ) les x( ) fait x( )
      aller x( ) passé x( ) passez x( ) évadé x( )

   b. lit x( ) dos x( ) mot x( ) nous x( )
      goût x( ) jeux x( ) peu x( ) peut x( )
      de x( ) deux x( )

   c. deux x( ) dé x( ) de x( ) des x( ) peut x( )
      pai x( ) me x( ) mais x( ) mes x( ) se x( )
      sai x( ) ses x( )

   d. midi x( ) dit x( ) mis x( ) qui x( ),
      nid x( ) jeux x( ) je x( ) jus x( )
      joue x( ) joué x( )

   e. non x( ) mon x( ) tond x( ) font x( )
      plomb x( ) bon x( ) jonc x( ) dont x( )
      don x( )

   f. plan x( ) banc x( ) temps x( ) sang x( )
      dent x( ) lent x( ) camp x( ) sans x( )
      dans x( )

   g. blanc x( ) blond x( ) plan x( ) plomb x( )
      sang x( ) son x( ) banc x( ) bond x( )
      lent x( ) long x( )

                      3.28

INTRODUCTION TO FRENCH PHONOLOGY

h. longtemps x( )   souvent x( )   seulement x( )
    partons x( )   jouons x( )   avant x( )
    amplement x( )   calmement x( )

i. Vous y allez souvent? x( )
    Nous allons déjeuner? x( )
    Vous avez des amis? x( )
    Vous les avez montés x( )
    Vous partez samedi? x( )

j. A quelle heure y allez-vous? x( )
    Où avez-vous déjeuné? x( )
    A quelle heure avez-vous déjeuné? x( )
    Quand partez-vous pour Palerme? x( )
    A quelle heure allez-vous au café? x( )

k. De temps en temps seulement x( )
    Je vais déjeuner à midi. x( )
    Il est au café à côté. x( )
    Je ne sais pas où elle est. x( )
    Je ne peux pas les finir. x( )
    Il a voulu y aller. x( )
    On va déjeuner à côté. x( )
    Nous avons tout su. x( )

Report to your classroom

3.29

7.

Homework

Drill 1

Dites en français

1.	I'm leaving	1.	Je pars
2.	One	2.	Une
3.	One o'clock	3.	Une heure
4.	When	4.	Quand
5.	Saturday	5.	Samedi
6.	Where	6.	Où
7.	Next door	7.	A côté
8.	At noon	8.	A midi

Drill 2

1.	Je pars. Vous partez?	1.	I'm leaving. Are you leaving?
2.	Vous partez à midi?	2.	Are you leaving at noon?
3.	Est-il une heure?	3.	Is it one o'clock?
4.	Il est une heure?	4.	It's one o'clock?
5.	A quelle heure partez-vous?	5.	What time are you leaving?
6.	Quelle heure est-il?	6.	What time is it?
7.	Il est une heure.	7.	It's one o'clock.
8.	De temps en temps je vais à côté.	8.	Once in awhile I go next door.
9.	Quand y allez-vous?	9.	When are you going (there)?
10.	Y allez-vous samedi?	10.	Are you going (there) Saturday?
11.	Je vais à côté.	11.	I'm going next door.
12.	Vous y allez à midi?	12.	You're going (there) at noon?
13.	Allez-vous déjeuner à une heure?	13.	Do you go to lunch at one o'clock?
14.	Je pars à une heure.	14.	I'm leaving at one.
15.	Vous partez samedi?	15.	Are you leaving on Saturday?

Drill 3

Dites en français

1.	What time do you leave?	1.	A quelle heure partez-vous?
2.	I leave at noon.	2.	Je pars à midi.
3.	I'm going to San Francisco.	3.	Je vais à San Francisco.
4.	You go there often?	4.	Vous y allez souvent?
5.	No. Once in awhile only.	5.	Non. De temps en temps seulement.
6.	When are you going there?	6.	Quand y allez-vous?

INTRODUCTION TO FRENCH PHONOLOGY

7.	What time do you go there?	7.	A quelle heure y allez-vous?
8.	What time did you have lunch?	8.	A quelle heure avez-vous déjeuné?
9.	You're leaving?	9.	Vous partez?
10.	No. I'm going to lunch.	10.	Non. Je vais déjeuner.
11.	Is it one o'clock?	11.	Il est une heure?
12.	It's one o'clock.	12.	Il est une heure.
13.	Where are you going?	13.	Où allez-vous?
14.	You're going next door?	14.	Vous allez à côté?
15.	Did you have lunch next door?	15.	Avez-vous déjeuné à côté?
16.	I'm leaving.	16.	Je pars.
17.	I'm leaving at one.	17.	Je pars à une heure.

Drill 4

Questions	Possible answers

1. Vous partez?

1. Non. Je vais à côté.
   Oui, je pars.
   Non. Je vais déjeuner.

2. A quelle heure partez-vous?

2. (Je pars) à une heure.
   (Je pars) à midi.

3. Il est midi?

3. Non. Il est une heure.
   Oui. Vous allez déjeuner?
   Oui, il est midi.
   Oui. Vous avez déjeuné?
   Oui. Je vais déjeuner.

4. Quand partez-vous?

4. Je pars samedi.

5. Quelle heure est-il?

5. Il est une heure.
   Il est midi.

6. Où allez-vous?

6. Je vais à côté.
   Je vais déjeuner.
   Je vais au café.
   Au café à côté.

7. Je pars à une heure?

7. Oui, vous partez à une heure.
   Non. Vous partez à midi.

3.31

Drill 5

Teacher	Possible answers
1. Je vais à Chicago.	1. Quand partez-vous? Vous y allez souvent? Quand y allez-vous? Y allez-vous samedi? Vous partez samedi?
2. Je vais déjeuner au café.	2. Vous y allez à midi? Vous y allez souvent? A quelle heure y allez-vous? Vous y allez à une heure? A quelle heure? A une heure? A midi?

Drill 6

Teacher	You
1. Je pars samedi.	Listen.

Questions	You
Je pars samedi?	Oui, vous partez samedi.
Je pars dimanche?	Non. Vous partez samedi.
Vous partez samedi?	Non. Vous partez samedi.
Je pars?	Oui, vous partez.
Quand?	(Vous partez) samedi.

Teacher	You
2. Vous partez samedi?	Listen.

Questions	You
Quand partez-vous?	Je pars samedi.
Vous partez mardi?	Non. Je pars samedi.
Je pars samedi?	Non. Je pars samedi.
Je pars?	Non. Je pars.
Vous partez?	Oui. Je pars.
Quand?	(Je pars) samedi.

3.32

Teacher	You
3. Vous partez samedi à midi.	Listen.
Questions	You
Quand partez-vous?	Je pars samedi.
A quelle heure?	(Je pars) à midi.
A une heure?	Non. A midi.
A midi? Samedi?	Oui, à midi, samedi.
Samedi à une heure?	Non. Samedi à midi.
Samedi à deux heures?	Non. Samedi à midi.
Vous partez à midi?	Oui, (je pars) à midi.
Je pars?	Non. Je pars.
A quelle heure partez-vous?	Je pars à midi.
Quand?	Samedi.

8.

Reading exercises.

Lecture.

1. Read.

    1. armement; doublement; appartement
    2. calmement; gouvernement; ouvertement

2. Read.

    1. amicalement; matelas; doucement
    2. sûreté; avancement; bourrelet; samedi

3. Read.

    1. fermeture; saleté; département; matelot
    2. justement; parsemer; côtelé; canneton

4. Read.

    1. pire; pur
    2. cire; sur
    3. dire; dur
    4. mire; mur

5. Read.

    1. pour; sourd; court; lourd; four
    2. par; car; tard; lard; dart; mare
    3. sur; lire; cure; mûre; mur; tir; tire

3.33

6. Read.

    1. du, dur
    2. fou; four
    3. pas; part
    4. dit; dire
    5. sourd; sous
    6. lire; lit

7. Read.

    1. Vous partez?
    2. Nous partons?
    3. Vous y pensez?
    4. Vous y allez?
    5. Nous y allons?
    6. Vous en voulez?

8. Read.

    1. Quand partez-vous?
    2. Où allez-vous?
    3. De qui parlez-vous?
    4. Par où passez-vous?
    5. A quelle heure?
    6. A quelle heure partez-vous?
    7. Où allons-nous?
    8. Que voulez-vous?

9. Read.

    1. Que pensez-vous?
    2. Y pensez-vous?
    3. Est-il toujours ici? (never link "S" of <u>toujours</u>)
    4. Où est-il?
    5. Est-il midi?
    6. Il est midi?
    7. Où voulez-vous déjeuner?
    8. Allez-vous déjeuner à une heure?
    9. A quelle heure déjeunons-nous?
    10. Vous déjeunez à midi?
    11. A quelle heure allez-vous à la gare?
    12. Tu vas déjeuner à côté?
    13. Que voulez-vous nous dire?
    14. Il ne va pas partir à midi?

10. Read.

1. Voulez-vous parler lentement?
2. Le café est fermé.
3. Il ferme à une heure?
4. Voulez-vous du café?
5. Je pars à une heure?
6. Il ne veut pas partir.
7. Vous allez passer par le Danemark?
8. Il me faut deux minutes.

Chapter Three, end of Part Two.

Go to lab for Tests 1 to 10.

INTRODUCTION TO FRENCH PHONOLOGY

Chapter Three, Part Three

Tests

Test 1

Write the syllables of the following sentences in the space provided.

Example:

Où avez-vous déjeuné? $\underline{Où}_1 \quad \underline{a}_2 \quad \underline{vez}_3 \quad \underline{vous}_4 \quad \underline{dé}_5 \quad \underline{jeu}_6 \quad \underline{né?}_7$

1. Nous devons les finir.   1. $\underline{}_1 \underline{}_2 \underline{}_3 \underline{}_4 \underline{}_5 \underline{}_6$

2. Il va au café à une heure.   2. $\underline{}_1 \underline{}_2 \underline{}_3 \underline{}_4 \underline{}_5 \underline{}_6 \underline{}_7 \underline{}_8$

3. A quelle heure y allez-vous?   3. $\underline{}_1 \underline{}_2 \underline{}_3 \underline{}_4 \underline{}_5 \underline{}_6 \underline{}_7$?

4. Venez par ici.   4. $\underline{}_1 \underline{}_2 \underline{}_3 \underline{}_4 \underline{}_5$

5. Que voulez-vous nous dire?   5. $\underline{}_1 \underline{}_2 \underline{}_3 \underline{}_4 \underline{}_5 \underline{}_6$?

6. Il a dû partir à midi.   6. $\underline{}_1 \underline{}_2 \underline{}_3 \underline{}_4 \underline{}_5 \underline{}_6 \underline{}_7 \underline{}_8$

INTRODUCTION TO FRENCH PHONOLOGY

Test 2

Write the syllables of the following sentences in the space provided. When a final "s" is pronounced like a "z", write a "z" instead of the "s".

Example: De temps en temps.   <u>De</u> <u>temp</u> <u>zen</u> <u>temps</u>.
                                                          1   2   3   4

1. Vous avez déjeuné?   1. __ __ __ __ __ __
                                                      1 2 3 4 5 6

2. Vous voulez partir?   2. __ __ __ __ __
                                                      1 2 3 4 5

3. Je les ai vus.   3. __ __ __ __
                                                      1 2 3 4

4. Nous vous avons servi.   4. __ __ __ __ __ __
                                                      1 2 3 4 5 6

5. Vous devez les finir.   5. __ __ __ __ __ __
                                                      1 2 3 4 5 6

6. Quand les avez vous   6. __ __ __ __ __ __ __
    finis?   1 2 3 4 5 6 7

7. Nous partons pour   7. __ __ __ __ __ __ __
    le Japon.   1 2 3 4 5 6 7

8. Nous allons les aider.   8. __ __ __ __ __ __
                                                      1 2 3 4 5 6

3.37

INTRODUCTION TO FRENCH PHONOLOGY

Test 3

Rewrite the following words and put a slash (/) through the vowel "e" when not pronounced.

Example:

   une   You write: un/

1. de
2. calme
3. verte
4. le
5. aime
6. belle
7. te
8. Je
9. ne
10. quelle
11. que
12. se
13. laisse
14. me

INTRODUCTION TO FRENCH PHONOLOGY

Test 4

Rewrite the following sentences and put a slash (/) through the "e" when not pronounced.

Example:

    Je pars à une heure.   You write: Je pars à un/e/ heur/e/.

1. Quelle heure est-il?
2. Elle déjeune à midi.
3. Il aime aller au café.
4. On pense que vous les avez.
5. Je pense arriver vers une heure.
6. De quelle auto parlez-vous?
7. Elle écoute le discours.
8. Alice prépare le déjeuner.

Test 5

Count the syllables of the following words.

Example: soudé   You write: 2

          soude   1

1. salé   1. _____
2. sale   2. _____
3. passe   3. _____
4. passé   4. _____
5. vidé   5. _____
6. goûté   6. _____
7. vide   7. _____
8. goûte   8. _____
9. foulé   9. _____
10. nagé   10. _____
11. nage   11. _____
12. foule   12. _____

3.40

INTRODUCTION TO FRENCH PHONOLOGY

Test 6

Rewrite the following words and put a slash through the final consonnant when not pronounced.

Example:

    banc   You write: ban¢

1. sous
2. bar
3. mare
4. joug
5. vert
6. fond
7. mur
8. verte
9. loup
10. long
11. tape
12. foule
13. pars
14. tard
15. tarde
16. bout
17. jonc
18. sourd

3.41

INTRODUCTION TO FRENCH PHONOLOGY

Test 7

Some French vowels have a nasal quality. In the French writing system these vowels are immediately followed by "n" or "m."

Example: non, nom

This written "n" or "m" must be in syllable final position. As, for instance when another consonant follows. (See Chapter 3, frames 17 - 26.)

Examples of nasals: ban<u>d</u>it, en<u>v</u>ie, em<u>p</u>orter.

Examples of non-nasals: annulé, amnistie, amour.

	nasal	non-nasal

Example: <u>en</u>tier

1. <u>a</u>mis
2. <u>a</u>ninés
3. ann<u>o</u>nce
4. d<u>on</u>
5. bl<u>an</u>che
6. bl<u>am</u>e
7. <u>am</u>poule
8. <u>am</u>is
9. <u>amu</u>sant
10. <u>en</u>fant
11. <u>é</u>numéré
12. pard<u>on</u>
13. pl<u>om</u>b
14. s<u>a</u>nitaire
15. s<u>an</u>té

Start tape recorder.

3.42

INTRODUCTION TO FRENCH PHONOLOGY

Test 8

Count the syllables.

Example:

    Ne partez pas jeudi. ( )   You write: ____6____

1. ( )   1. _____
2. ( )   2. _____
3. ( )   3. _____
4. ( )   4. _____
5. ( )   5. _____
6. ( )   6. _____
7. ( )   7. _____
8. ( )   8. _____
9. ( )   9. _____
10. ( )   10. _____

Test 9

Write the following French words.

1. ( ) 1. _____
2. ( ) 2. _____
3. ( ) 3. _____
4. ( ) 4. _____
5. ( ) 5. _____
6. ( ) 6. _____
7. ( ) 7. _____
8. ( ) 8. _____
9. ( ) 9. _____
10. ( ) 10. _____

Test 10

Write in French.

1. ( ) 1. _____
2. ( ) 2. _____
3. ( ) 3. _____
4. ( ) 4. _____
5. ( ) 5. _____
6. ( ) 6. _____
7. ( ) 7. _____
8. ( ) 8. _____
9. ( ) 9. _____
10. ( ) 10. _____

END OF CHAPTER THREE.

INTRODUCTION TO FRENCH PHONOLOGY

Chapter Four

PART 1

    Dialogue. (Laboratory)

PART 2

    1. Contrast: oui/ui (Laboratory)

    2. Apostrophe. (Laboratory)

    3. Mute "h." (Laboratory)

    4. Pronunciation of final "x" (Liaison z). (Laboratory)

    5. Pronunciation of final consonants: c, f, l, r.

    6. Review. (Laboratory)

    7. Preparation for class. (Homework)

    8. Reading exercises. (Classroom)

PART 3

    Tests. (Classroom and laboratory)

Chapter Four

Dialogue

A.	Je suis en retard?	-	Am I late?
B.	De quelques minutes, c'est tout.	-	A few minutes, that's all.
A.	Quelle heure est-il?	-	What time is it?
B.	Il est dix heures cinq.	-	It is five past ten.

INTRODUCTION TO FRENCH PHONOLOGY

Part One

1. Listen to the following conversation in French.

   A: (?)
   B: ( )
   A: (?)
   B: ( )

2. Listen again.

   A: (?)
   B: ( )
   A: (?)
   B: ( )

3. Now listen to the first sentence in the conversation.

   ( ) ( )

4. It's a question.   Listen.

   ( ) ( )

5. Listen to the four syllables in the question.

   ( ) ( )

6. Here is the sentence again at normal speed.

   ( ) ( )

7. How many nasal vowels do you hear? One or two?

   ( ) ( )

(1)

8. How many French "r" sounds do you hear? One? Two?

   ( ) ( )

(2)

9. Listen and imitate.

   ( )x ( )x ( )x

10. Listen and imitate again.

    ( )x ( )x ( )x

4.3

11. This is the same sentence without the nasalization of syllable 3.

   ( ) ( )

12. The first sentence is (R) right; the second, (W) wrong. Listen.

   (R)/(W)   (R)/(W)

13. Listen to the contrast again. Which is the right sentence? One or two?

   (1) (2) (1) (2)

(2)

14. Is this right?

   ( ) ( )

(yes)

15. How about this? Is it right?

   ( ) ( )

(yes)

16. Listen and imitate the question.

   ( )x ( )x ( )x

17. Imitate again. Be sure to produce the French "r" at the end of syllables three and four.

   ( )x ( )x ( )x

18. Here is how the question is written. Look and listen.

   Je suis en retard? ( ) ( )

19. And here is the meaning in English. Look and listen.

   Am I late? (French) (French)

20. Look at the French sentence again, listen and imitate.

   Je suis en retard? ( )x ( )x ( )x

INTRODUCTION TO FRENCH PHONOLOGY

21. Notice the underlined letter in the last word.
     Is it pronounced?

   Je suis en retar<u>d</u>?   ( )   ( )

(no)

22. Look, listen and imitate.

   Je suis en retard?   ( )x   ( )x   ( )x

23. Here is the answer to that question. Listen.

   ( )   ( )

24. Listen again to that long sentence.

   ( )   ( )

25. Here is a word from that sentence. Listen.

   ( )   ( )   ( )

26. Here it is again. Notice the vowels.

   ( )   ( )   ( )

27. Are the vowels (S) same or (D) different?

   ( )   ( )   ( )

(D)

28. Listen to word (A) and word (B). Are they the same?

   (A)   (B)   (A)   (B)

(no)

29. Here is the right word.

   ( )   ( )

30. Is this right?

   ( )   ( )

(no)

31. How about this?

   ( )   ( )

(yes)

4.5

32. Listen carefully and imitate.

    ( )x ( )x ( )x

33. Imitate again. Notice the rhythm.

    ( )x ( )x ( )x

34. This pronunciation is wrong. Listen.

    ( ) ( )

35. Here is another wrong pronunciation.

    ( ) ( )

36. Here again is the right pronunciation.

    ( ) ( ) ( )

37. Listen to (A) right, then to (B) and (C) wrong.

    (A) (B) (C)

38. Which of the following words is right?

    (1) (2) (3) (4)

(3)

39. Listen again to the right pronunciation.

    ( ) ( ) ( )

40. Listen to the right pronunciation and imitate.

    ( )x ( )x ( )x

41. Imitate again. Be sure to follow the rhythm.

    ( )x ( )x ( )x

42. There is no difference in writing this word in English or in French. Look and listen.

    minute ( ) ( )

43. Look at the written word again and imitate.

    minute ( )x ( )x ( )x

INTRODUCTION TO FRENCH PHONOLOGY 125

    44. We'll add two more words in front of minute. Listen.

        ( ) ( ) ( )

    45. Listen to this pronunciation. Is it (R) right or (W) wrong?

(R)   ( ) ( ) ( )

    46. How about this pronunciation? (R) or (W)?

(W)   ( ) ( ) ( )

    47. Here is the right pronunciation. Listen.

        ( ) ( ) ( )

    48. You'll hear one right pronunciation followed by two wrong. Listen.

        (R) (W) (W)

    49. Which one is right? One, two or three?

(2)   (1) (2) (3)

    50. Listen to the right pronunciation and imitate.

        ( )x ( )x ( )x

    51. Listen to the sentence again. Is the rhythm correct?

(yes)   ( ) ( )

    52. Listen to this rhythm. Is it (R) or (W)?

(W)   ( ) ( ) ( )

    53. Which one do you think is right? One, two or three?

(3)   (1) (2) (3)

4.7

54. Listen again to the sentence and imitate.

   ( )x ( )x ( )x

55. Imitate again. Be sure to follow the rhythm.

   ( )x ( )x ( )x

56. Look at the meaning of the sentence and listen to the French.

   a few minutes ( ) ( )

57. Now, look at the writing in French. Then listen and imitate.

   de quelques minutes ( )x ( )x ( )x

58. Look again at the writing. Notice the underlined letters. Are they pronounced?

   de quelque<u>s</u> minute<u>s</u> ( )x ( )x ( )x

(no)

59. Look, listen and imitate. Notice the rhythm of the sentence.

   de quelques minutes ( )x ( )x ( )x

60. Listen to these three words.

   ( ) ( ) ( )

61. Listen again to these three words. How many syllables do you hear?

   ( ) ( )

(2)

62. You know this sentence. Listen.

   ( ) ( )

63. We'll make the sentence longer by adding two more syllables at the end. Listen.

   ( ) ( ) ( )

4.8

INTRODUCTION TO FRENCH PHONOLOGY

64. How many syllables are there now?

    ( ) ( )

(7)

65. Is there a small pause between two of the syllables?

    ( ) ( )

(yes)

66. Here is the sentence again. Listen and imitate.

    ( )x ( )x ( )x

67. Here is what the sentence means. Look and listen.

    a few minutes, that's all ( ) ( )

68. Imitate again. Be sure to follow the rhythm.

    ( )x ( )x ( )x

69. Look at the writing in French. Listen and imitate.

    de quelques minutes, c'est tout. ( )x ( )x ( )x

70. Notice that the underlined letters are not pronounced.

    de quelques minutes, c'es_t_ tou_t_. ( ) ( )

71. There are four letters which are not pronounced. Here they are underlined. Look and Listen.

    de quelque_s_ minute_s_, c'es_t_ tou_t_. ( ) ( )

72. Look again at the writing. Listen and imitate.

    de quelques minutes, c'est tout. ( )x ( )x ( )x

73. The underlined syllable has two words: ce + est = c'est
    Look and listen.

    de quelques minutes, <u>c'est</u> tout. ( ) ( )

74. Imitate the rhythm and pronunciation again.

    ( )x ( )x

4.9

128 INTRODUCTION TO FRENCH PHONOLOGY

75. Listen to this exchange and look at the meaning.

    A: ( ) Am I late?
    B: ( ) A few minutes, that's all.

76. Listen again.

    A: (?)
    B: ( )

77. Answer your instructor.

    Instructor: (Q)
    You: _____

78. Again.

    Instructor: (Q)
    You: _____

79. Ask the question this time and listen to the answer.

    (begin)
    You: _____?
    Instructor: (A)

80. Again.

    (begin)
    You: _____?
    Instructor: (A)

81. Listen to this question.

    ( ) ( )

82. Listen again. How many syllables do you hear?

    ( ) ( ) ( )

(4)

83. Listen to the syllable division of that question.

    ( ) ( )

84. Does each syllable begin with a consonant?

    ( ) ( )

(yes)

4.10

INTRODUCTION TO FRENCH PHONOLOGY

85. The question is said at normal speed. Listen.

    ( )   ( )   ( )

86. Listen to this. Is it (R) right or (W) wrong?

    ( )   ( )

(W)

87. How about this? Is it right or wrong?

    ( )   ( )

(W)

88. Which of the following three sentences is right?

    (1)   (2)   (3)

(1)

89. Here is the right pronunciation. Listen.

    ( )   ( )

90. Listen again to the right pronunciation and imitate.

    ( )x   ( )x   ( )x

91. Imitate again. Be sure to begin each syllable with a consonant.

    ( )x   ( )x   ( )x

92. Rhythm is also very important. In the following sentence, the rhythm is wrong. Listen.

    ( )   ( )

93. This rhythm is also wrong. Listen.

    ( )   ( )

94. The pronunciation is right, the syllables are well divided, but the rhythm is wrong. Listen.

    (W)   (W)

4.11

130   **INTRODUCTION TO FRENCH PHONOLOGY**

(3)

95. One of the following three sentences is right. Which one is it?

        (1)   (2)   (3)

96. Here is the right pronunciation, rhythm and syllable division.

        ( )   ( )

97. Listen and imitate.

        ( )x   ( )x   ( )x

98. Look at the meaning and imitate.

        What time is it?   ( )x   ( )x   ( )x

99. This is the writing in French. Look and listen.

        Quelle heure est-il?   ( )   ( )

100. Look at the writing again. Listen and imitate.

        Quelle heure est-il?   ( )x   ( )x   ( )x

101. This is the wrong syllable division. Listen.

        ( )   ( )

102. This is the right syllable division since French syllables usually begin with a consonant.

        ( )   ( )

103. Listen to the (R) right/ (W) wrong syllable division.

        (R)/(W)   (R)/(W)

104. Imitate the full question again.

        ( )x   ( )x   ( )x

105. Here is the answer to that question. Listen.

        ( )   ( )   ( )

4.12

INTRODUCTION TO FRENCH PHONOLOGY

106. Count the syllables. How many are there?

( ) ( ) ( )

(5)

107. Listen to the syllable division of that sentence.

( ) ( )

108. Do all syllables begin with a consonant? Listen.

( ) ( )

(no)

109. Which syllable does not begin with a consonant?

(- - - - -)   (- - - - -)
1 2 3 4 5   1 2 3 4 5

(1)

110. Here is the sentence at normal speed again. Listen.

( ) ( )

111. Listen carefully. Does the first syllable end in a consonant?

( ) ( )

(no)

112. How about syllables four and five? Do they end in a consonant?

(- - - - -)   (- - - - -)
1 2 3 4 5   1 2 3 4 5

(yes)

113. Listen to the last syllable of the sentence.

( ) ( ) ( )

114. The last syllable is a word. It means: "five". Listen again.

five ( ) ( )

115. Now listen to this word.

( ) ( ) ( )

4.13

INTRODUCTION TO FRENCH PHONOLOGY

    116. Compare the word "five" and the other word. Are they they pronounced the same way?

        ( )/( )   ( )/( )   ( )/( )

(no)

    117. Which one is five? Number one or number two?

        (1)/(2)   (1)/(2)

(1)

    118. Listen again to the contrast. Which one has a nasal vowel?

        (1)/(2)   (1)/(2)

(1)

    119. The nasal vowel in this word is new. Listen.

        ( )   ( )   ( )

    120. Here are two nasal vowels that you know. Listen.

        (1)/(2)   (1)/(2)

    121. Listen again to the new vowel.

        ( )   ( )   ( )

    122. The vowels you know are marked (1) and (2); the new one is marked (3). Listen.

        (1)/(2)/(3)   (1)/(2)/(3)

    123. Listen again. Does (3) represent the new nasal vowel?

        (1)/(2)/(3)   (1)/(2)/(3)

(yes)

    124. How about this time? Does three still represent the new vowel?

        (1)/(2)/(3)   (1)/(2)/(3)

(no)

    125. Which one is the new vowel?

        (1)/(2)/(3)   (1)/(2)/(3)

(1)

INTRODUCTION TO FRENCH PHONOLOGY

126. Listen and imitate this nasal vowel.

   ( )x   ( )x   ( )x

127. This vowel is easy to say if you smile just before and while you say it.

   ( )x   ( )x   ( )x

128. Listen again to the word "five" and imitate.

   ( )x   ( )x   ( )x

129. We'll add two more words. Listen.

   ( )   ( )   ( )

130. Look at the meaning and listen.

   five past ten   ( )   ( )

131. This is the way it is written in French. Look and listen.

   dix heures cinq   ( )   ( )

132. Now listen and imitate these familiar sounds.

   ( )x   ( )x   ( )x

133. Listen and imitate again.

   ( )x   ( )x   ( )x

134. Is this (R) right or (W) wrong? Listen.

   ( )   ( )

(W)

135. How about this?

   ( )   ( )

(W)

136. Which of the following is right?

   (1)   (2)   (3)

(1)

4.15

INTRODUCTION TO FRENCH PHONOLOGY

137. Are these right?

        ( ) ( )

(no)

138. Which of these is right?

        (1) (2) (3)

(2)

139. Listen and imitate the correct pronunciation.

        ( )x ( )x ( )x

140. Let's add two more words in front of the three.

        ( ) ( ) ( )

141. Look at the writing in French and listen.

        Il est dix heures cinq. ( ) ( )

142. Look at the meaning and listen.

        It's five past ten. ( ) ( )

143. Now, listen and imitate.

        ( )x ( )x

144. Listen to the following exchange.

        A: (?)
        B: ( )

145. Answer your instructor.

        Instructor: (Q)
        You:_____

146. Again.

        Instructor: (Q)
        You:_____

INTRODUCTION TO FRENCH PHONOLOGY

147. This time you ask the question. Then listen to the answer.

> (begin)
> You:_____?
> Instructor: (A)

148. Again.

> (begin)
> You:_____?
> Instructor: (A)

149. The following exchange has four sentences. Listen

> A: (?)
> B: ( )
> A: (?)
> B: ( )

150. Look at the writing and listen.

> A: Je suis en retard? ( )
> B: De quelques minutes, c'est tout. ( )
> A: Quelle heure est-il? ( )
> B: Il est dix heures cinq. ( )

151. Look at the writing in English and listen.

> A: Am I late? (French)
> B: A few minutes, that's all. (French)
> A: What time is it? (French)
> B: It's five past ten. (French)

152. Listen to your instructors and imitate.

> A: (?)x
> B: ( )x
> A: (?)x
> B: ( )x

153. Imitate again.

> A: (?)x
> B: ( )x
> A: (?)x
> B: ( )x

154. Answer your instructor.

>Instructor: (Q)
>You: _____
>Instructor: (Q)
>You: _____

155. Again.

>Instructor: (Q)
>You: _____
>Instructor: (Q)
>You: _____

156. Ask the questions. Your instructor will answer you.

>(begin)
>You: _____?
>Instructor: (A)
>You: _____?
>Instructor: (A)

157. Again.

>(begin)
>You: _____?
>Instructor: (A)
>You: _____?
>Instructor: (A)

158. Practice frames 150 to 157 several times.

End of Chapter Four, Part One.

Report to your classroom.

INTRODUCTION TO FRENCH PHONOLOGY

Part Two

1.

Constrast: oui/ui

1. Read the following sentence before your instructor does.

    Je suis en retard? x( )

2. Here is the sentence again. Say the second word.

    Je suis en retard? x( )

3. Now say these words.

    puis x( ), nuit x( ), buis x( ), cuit x( )

4. Here are more words for you to say.

    fuir x( ), cuir x( ), nuire x( )

5. Listen to some of the words you said. How many syllables do they have?

    lui ( ), puis ( ), nuit ( )

    Student's answer: <u>1</u>

6. Listen to words 1 and 2. How do they sound? Do they have the same sound?

    (1)/(2)

    Student's answer: <u>no</u>

7. Listen again. One of the words means "yes". Is it 1 or 2?

    (1)/(2)

    Student's answer: <u>1</u>

8. Are the following words same or different? Listen.

    (1)/(2)

    Student's answer: <u>D</u>

4.19

138   INTRODUCTION TO FRENCH PHONOLOGY

9. Here are the last two words you have heard. Look at them, and then say them before your instructor does.

   Louis x( ), lui x( )

10. How do you say the following? Say it before your instructor does.

    oui x( ), Louis x( ), enfouit x( )

11. Here are some more words. Say them before your instructor does.

    a. enfuit x( ), enfouit x( )
    b. lui   x( ), Louis   x( )

12. Look at the following words and say them before your instructor does.

    a. lu   x( )/ lui   x( )
    b. nu   x( )/ nuit x( )
    c. pu   x( )/ puit x( )
    d. fut x( )/ fuit x( )
    e. ou   x( )/ oui   x( )
    f. loup x( )/ Louis x( )

13. Say the following words.

    a. suite x( ), suivante x( ), cambouis x( )
    b. enduire x( ), séduire x( )

14. Now read these before your instructor does.

    a. Je le lis x( )
    b. Je le lui lis. x( )
    c. Je le lui ai lu. x( )
    d. Je le lis. x( )
    e. Louis le lit. x( )
    f. Louis le lui lit. x( )
    g. Louis le lui a lu. x( )

                      2.

                  Apostrophe

15. Look at the following words and say what they mean in English.

    C'est tout.

    Student's answer: That's all.

                                         4.20

INTRODUCTION TO FRENCH PHONOLOGY

16. Look at these words again. How many words are there?

    C'est tout.

    Student's answer: <u>3</u>

17. Usually an apostrophe (') replaces the final vowel "e" when the following word begins with a vowel.

    Example: ce + est = c'est
              ne + a   = n'a
              je + ai = j'ai

    Say the following words before your instructor does.

    c'est x( ), m'avez x( ), j'ai x( ), l'ami x( )

18. The final "e" of the following words (ten of them) is replaced by an apostrophe (') when followed by a word beginning with a vowel. Look and listen.

    le, me, se, te, que, ne, je, ce, de, jusque* ( )

    *There are other words in French involving the word "que" or ending with that word. The rule applies with all those words.

19. The vowel of the word "la" is also replaced by an apostrophe when followed by a word beginning with a vowel.

    Example: la + amie = l'amie
              la + auto = l'auto
              la + eau = l'eau

20. Are the following sentences written correctly?

    le ami est ici.
    la auto est à côté.

    Student's answer: <u>No</u>

21. Which of the following sentences are incorrectly written?

    1. Ce est tout.
    2. C'est tout.
    3. Quel ami?
    4. Jusqu'à midi.
    5. Il ne est pas midi.

    Student's answer: <u>1, 5</u>

4.21

INTRODUCTION TO FRENCH PHONOLOGY

                     3.

                 Mute "h"

22. Look at the following English sentence. How do you say it in French?

      It's five past ten. x( )

23. Here is another English sentence. Say it in French.

      Ten o'clock. x( )

24. Read the following.

      Il est dix heures. x( )

25. Look at the following sentence and listen. Notice the pronunciation of the underlined words.

      Il est <u>dix heures</u>. ( ) ( )

26. Look at the sentence again and listen.

      Il est dix heures. ( ) ( )

      Did you hear an "x"? an "h"?

      Student's answer: <u>No</u>

27. There are two kinds of initial "h" in French. Here we are dealing with the <u>mute "h"</u> meaning that the "h" is not pronounced. Look and listen to these French words.

      leur, l'heure ( )   or, hors ( )

28. Say the following French words.

   a. hôtel x( ), l'hôtel x( ), heure x( ) l'heure x( )
   b. hiver x( ), l'hiver x( ), hôpital x( ), l'hôpital x( )

                     4.

          Pronunciation of final "x"

29. Look and listen again to this French sentence.

      Il est dix heures cinq. ( )

INTRODUCTION TO FRENCH PHONOLOGY

30. In the sentence above, is the "x" in the word "dix" pronounced as "x" or "z"? Listen.

    Il est dix heures cinq. ( )

    Student's answer: _z_

31. When "x" is the final consonant of a word and is in a linking position, it is always pronounced "z". Look and listen.

    Il est dix heures. ( )
    Il est six heures. ( )
    Il est deux heures. ( )
    Il a six ans. ( )

32. The final "s" is also pronounced "z" in linking position. Look and listen.

    Vous y allez souvent? ( )
    Vous allez au café? ( )
    Vous avez déjeuné? ( )
    De temps en temps. ( )

33. Look at the following sentences and say them before your instructor does.

    J'ai deux enfants.   x( )
    Mes amis.   x( )
    De temps en temps.   x( )
    Vous avez fini.   x( )
    Deux heures cinq.   x( )

    5.

    Pronunciation of final consonants.

34. Il was stated in lesson one that in general final consonants were not pronounced. Look and listen.

    bout ( ), doux ( ), temps ( ), loup ( )

35. There are final consonants that must be pronounced. But the number of words in which final consonants are pronounced is limited. Here are a few words. Look and listen.

    seul ( ), cinq ( ), talc ( ), donc ( ), fatal ( )
    canif ( )

4.23

INTRODUCTION TO FRENCH PHONOLOGY

36. Here are, underlined, the consonants that may be pronounced in final position. Imitate your instructor.

    cinq   ( )x
    talc   ( )x
    parc   ( )x
    naval   ( )x
    canal   ( )x
    massif ( )x
    tour   ( )x
    tir   ( )x

37. Notice that the consonants most likely to be pronounced are: c, l, f, and r. Say the following words.

    sel x( ), sec x( ), vif x( ), car x( )

6.

Review

38. Here is a review. Look at the words or sentences and say them before your instructor does.

    a. nuit x( ), oui x( ), séduite x( ), déduit x( ),
        Louis x( ), fouine x( )

    b. j'ai fini x( ), l'ami x( ) de l'eau x( ),
        de l'air x( ), jusqu'à midi x( ), je t'ai vu x( ),
        vous m'avez parlé x( )

    c. j'habite ici x( ), j'espère x( ), c'est l'heure x( )
        les habits x( ), dix heures x( ), deux autos x( )

    d. camp x( ), tond x( ), parc x( ), sac x( ) sel x( )
        amer x( ), partez x( ), passons x( )

    e. La lune x( ), la lune luit x( ), la lune luit la
        nuit x( )
        Nous passons par le parc. x( )
        Nous avons terminé à deux heures. x( )
        Quand avez-vous déjeuné?
        Avez-vous terminé? x( )
        Vous avez déjeuné? x( )
        Quelle heure est-il? x( )
        Il est midi cinq. x( )
        Vous ne savez pas. x( )
        Que savez-vous? x( )
        Vous le voulez? x( )
        Vous partez tout de suite. x( )

        Report to your classroom.

4.24

INTRODUCTION TO FRENCH PHONOLOGY

7.

Homework

Drill 1

Dites en français

1. Ten o'clock
2. Five o'clock
3. It is
4. I am
5. Five
6. That's all
7. I go
8. Late
9. What time
10. All

1. Dix heures
2. Cinq heures
3. Il est
4. Je suis
5. Cinq
6. C'est tout
7. Je vais
8. En retard
9. Quelle heure
10. Tout

Drill 2

Dites en anglais

1. A quelle heure allez-vous déjeuner?
2. De quelques minutes, c'est tout.
3. En retard de cinq minutes?
4. Il est une heure dix.
5. Je suis en retard de cinq minutes.
6. Je suis américain.
7. Vous partez samedi à midi?
8. Il est midi cinq.
9. Je suis en retard de quelques minutes.
10. Je suis souvent en retard.
11. De temps en temps je vais déjeuner à une heure.
12. Je suis en retard de dix minutes.

1. What time are you going to lunch?
2. A few minutes that's all.
3. Five minutes late?
4. It's ten past one.
5. I'm five minutes late.
6. I'm American.
7. You're leaving Saturday at noon?
8. It's five past twelve (noon).
9. I'm a few minutes late.
10. I'm often late.
11. Once in a while I go to lunch at one.
12. I'm ten minutes late.

4.25

Drill 3

Dites en français

1. You're leaving?
2. I'm going next door.
3. I'm five minutes late.
4. What time do you leave?
5. I leave at five past ten.
6. You're going to the café?
7. You're going (there) at ten?
8. Is it ten o'clock?
9. Once in awhile I'm late.
10. At what time are you leaving Saturday?
11. I'm a few minutes late.
12. Where are you going at one?
13. I'm next door.
14. I'm going to have lunch next door.
15. I'm leaving on Saturday.
16. I'm often late.

1. Vous partez?
2. Je vais à côté.
3. Je suis en retard de cinq minutes.
4. A quelle heure partez-vous?
5. Je pars à dix heures cinq.
6. Vous allez au café?
7. Vous y allez à dix heures?
8. Est-il dix heures?
9. De temps en temps je suis en retard.
10. A quelle heure partez-vous samedi?
11. Je suis en retard de quelques minutes.
12. Où allez-vous à une heure?
13. Je suis à côté.
14. Je vais déjeuner à côté.
15. Je pars samedi.
16. Je suis souvent en retard.

Drill 4

Questions

1. Je suis en retard?

2. Quelle heure est-il?

Possible answers

1. Oui.
   Non.
   (Oui). De quelques minutes, c'est tout.
   De cinq minutes, c'est tout.

2. Il est une heure dix.
   Il est midi dix.
   Il est cinq heures cinq.
   Il est midi cinq.
   Il est dix heures.
   Il est midi.
   Il est une heure.
   Il est cinq heures.
   Il est une heure cinq.
   Il est cinq heures dix.
   Il est dix heures cinq.
   Il est dix heures dix.

Drill 5

Je pars à midi.
Je pars à dix heures.
Je pars à une heure.
Je pars à midi.
Je pars à cinq heures.
Je pars à midi dix.
Je pars à une heure cinq.
Je pars à cinq heures cinq.

Drill 6

1. Je vais au café.
2. Vous allez au café.
3. Vous allez à côté.
4. Je suis à côté.
5. Je suis à New York.
6. Je vais à New York.
7. Je vais au café.

Drill 7

Expansion drill

	Teacher		Student
1.	Je vais au café.	1.	Je vais au café.
2.	déjeuner	2.	Je vais déjeuner au café.
3.	souvent	3.	Je vais souvent déjeuner au café.
4.	à côté	4.	Je vais souvent déjeuner au café à côté.

Drill 8

Expansion drill

1.	Vous y allez?	1.	Vous y allez?
2.	samedi	2.	Vous y allez samedi?
3.	à une heure	3.	Vous y allez samedi à une heure?
4.	dix	4.	Vous y allez samedi à une heure dix?

4.27

Drill 9

Teacher	Student
1. déjeuner	1. Déjeuner
2. allez-vous	2. Allez-vous déjeuner?
3. au café	3. Allez-vous déjeuner au café?
4. a quelle heure	4. A quelle heure allez-vous déjeuner au café?
5. à côté	5. A quelle heure allez-vous déjeuner au café à côté?

Drill 10

1. samedi	1. samedi
2. je pars	2. Je pars samedi.
3. à dix heures	3. Je pars samedi à dix heures.
4. cinq	4. Je pars samedi à dix heures cinq.

INTRODUCTION TO FRENCH PHONOLOGY

8.
Reading exercises
Lecture

1. Read.

    1. suite; cuite; luire; fuir
    2. lui; puis; nuit; buis

2. Read.

    1. Louis; oui; fouine; enfouir
    2. enfuir; traduire; enfouir; cambouis

3. Read.

    1. Je lui parle.
    2. Je vais déjeuner avec Louis.
    3. Je vais déjeuner avec lui.
    4. Parlez-nous de lui.
    5. Nous partons mardi dans la nuit.
    6. Je n'ai pas lu la suite.

4. Read.

    1. l'ami; l'auto; l'étang; l'idée; l'urne; l'oubli

5. Read.

    1. Ce n'est pas lui.
    2. C'est mon café.
    3. J'ai perdu.
    4. C'est l'ami de Louis.
    5. Il part pour l'Italie.
    6. C'est pour qu'il entende.

6. Read.

    1. Nous y allons à une heure.
    2. Il est toujours à l'heure.
    3. Nous partons le neuf mai.
    4. Ils ont peur de lui.
    5. C'est pour le gouvernement.
    6. Je n'ai pas écouté la suite.

7. Read.

    1. Le lui avez-vous dit?
    2. Non, je ne le lui ai pas dit.
    3. Louis vous a vu?

4.29

4. Non, il ne m'a pas vu.
5. Avez-vous vu Louis?
6. Oui, nous l'avons vu.
7. Où l'avez-vous lu?
8. Nous l'avons lu dans le journal.
9. Que lui avez-vous dit?
10. Nous lui avons dit qu'il pouvait partir.

8. Read.

   1. Vous partez à dix heures?
   2. Non, je pars à deux heures.
   3. Ce sont de beaux enfants.
   4. Nous y allons à six heures.
   5. Vous avez quelques minutes?
   6. Où sont les nouveaux outils?

9. Read.

   1. J'habite à Nice.
   2. Où habitez-vous?
   3. Aimez-vous l'hiver?
   4. L'hôtel est fermé.
   5. C'est l'ami de Louis.
   6. Les hôtels sont fermés.

10. Read.

    1. le lac; les lacs
    2. le fil; les fils
    3. détour; départ
    4. le vert; la verte
    5. l'aqueduc; le talc,
    6. le canif; le massif

11. Dictation.

    1. De temps en temps je suis en retard.
    2. Je pars à une heure cinq.
    3. C'est à dix heures.
    4. C'est au café.
    5. A quelle heure partez-vous?
    6. Où allez-vous samedi?
    7. Vous avez déjeuné?
    8. Quand y allez-vous?

Chapter 4, end of Part Two.

Go to lab for Test 1 to 7.

INTRODUCTION TO FRENCH PHONOLOGY

Chapter Four, Part Three

Tests

Test 1

Copy the following words. Underline those which contain a nasal vowel.

1. bonté
2. bandit
3. vanité
4. tendu
5. unité
6. pensé
7. famine
8. embarqué

1. _____
2. _____
3. _____
4. _____
5. _____
6. _____
7. _____
8. _____

Test 2

Look at the following words and write only those whose final consonant is pronounced.

1. lac
2. doux
3. l'amas
4. nul
5. nid
6. neuf
7. vent
8. laid
9. plomb
10. fer

you write:
1. _____
2. _____
3. _____
4. _____
5. _____
6. _____
7. _____
8. _____
9. _____
10. _____

4.31

INTRODUCTION TO FRENCH PHONOLOGY

Test 3

Look at the following words and listen. The pronunciation may be right or wrong. Check the appropriate column.

			Right	Wrong
1.	pluie ( )	1.	_____	_____
2.	Saint-Louis ( )	2.	_____	_____
3.	oui ( )	3.	_____	_____
4.	buisson ( )	4.	_____	_____
5.	du buis ( )	5.	_____	_____
6.	cambouis ( )	6.	_____	_____
7.	la suite ( )	7.	_____	_____
8.	l'enduit ( )	8.	_____	_____

Test 4

Write the vowel sounds that you hear.

1. ( )   You write: 1._____
2. ( )   2._____
3. ( )   3._____
4. ( )   4._____
5. ( )   5._____
6. ( )   6._____
7. ( )   7._____
8. ( )   8._____

INTRODUCTION TO FRENCH PHONOLOGY

Test 5

The following words are said in pairs. Listen and determine whether they are same (S) or (D) different. Check the appropriate column.

			Same	Different
1.	( )	1.	___	___
2.	( )	2.	___	___
3.	( )	3.	___	___
4.	( )	4.	___	___
5.	( )	5.	___	___
6.	( )	6.	___	___
7.	( )	7.	___	___
8.	( )	8.	___	___

Test 6

Listen to these words. Are they (S) same or (D) different? Check the appropriate column.

			Same	Different
1.	( )	1.	___	___
2.	( )	2.	___	___
3.	( )	3.	___	___
4.	( )	4.	___	___
5.	( )	5.	___	___
6.	( )	6.	___	___
7.	( )	7.	___	___

Test 7

Listen, then write the French sentences you hear.

1. ( )   You write: 1. _____
2. ( )   2. _____
3. ( )   3. _____
4. ( )   4. _____
5. ( )   5. _____
6. ( )   6. _____
7. ( )   7. _____
8. ( )   8. _____
9. ( )   9. _____
10. ( )   10. _____

END OF CHAPTER 4

INTRODUCTION TO FRENCH PHONOLOGY

Chapter Five

PART 1

Dialogue. (Laboratory)

PART 2

1. Question forms with: Est-ce que ... (Laboratory)

2. Pronunciation of "r" between vowels. (Laboratory)
   Pronunciation of "r" after consonant. (Laboratory)

3. Nasal vowel "un." (Laboratory)
   Contrast: un/an/on/in

4. Il y a. (Laboratory)

5. "en" and "un" preceding vowel beginning words.

6. Pronunciation of "oi." (Laboratory)

7. "dix" in final position. (Laboratory)

8. Review. (Laboratory)

9. Preparation for Class. (Homework)

10. Reading exercises. (Classroom)

PART 3

Tests. (Classroom and laboratory)

Chapter Five

Dialogue

A.	Est-ce qu'il y a un train pour Paris le matin?	-	Is there a train for Paris in the morning?
B.	Oui, mais vous l'avez manqué.	-	Yes, but you've missed it.
A.	Est-ce qu'il y en a l'après-midi?	-	Are there any in the afternoon?
B.	Non, pas l'après-midi. Dans la soirée seulement.	-	No, not in the afternoon. In the evening only.
A.	A quelle heure est le premier?	-	At what time is the first one?
B.	A dix-huit heures dix.	-	At 6:10 pm.

INTRODUCTION TO FRENCH PHONOLOGY 155

1. Listen to the conversation in French.

    A: (?)
    B: ( )
    A: (?)
    B: ( )
    A: (?)
    B: ( )

2. Listen to the intonation and rhythm of the sentences.

    A: (?)
    B: ( )
    A: (?)
    B: ( )
    A: (?)
    B: ( )

3. This is the first sentence of the conversation. Listen.

    ( ) ( ) ( )

4. Here are the last two words of the sentence. Listen.

    ( ) ( )

5. These two words have three syllables. Notice the last one.

    ( ) ( )

6. Does the last syllable contain a nasal vowel? Listen again.

    ( ) ( )

(known)

7. Is that nasal vowel new, or known to you? Listen again.

    ( ) ( )

(new)

8. Here are two nasal sounds. Would you say that they sound alike?

    ( )/( )

(no)

5.3

156   INTRODUCTION TO FRENCH PHONOLOGY

9. Listen again to the last two words of the sentence and imitate.

   ( )x ( )x ( )x

10. This pronunciation is wrong. Listen.

    ( ) ( )

11. This is the (W) wrong/(R) right pronunciation. Listen.

    (W)/(R)   (W)/(R)

12. Listen again. Which is the right one? No. 1 or No. 2?

    (1)/(2)   (1)/(2)

(1)

13. Listen again to the correct pronunciation and imitate.

    ( )x ( )x ( )x

14. Imitate again while looking at the meaning.

    In the morning? ( )x ( )x

15. Here again is the first sentence of the conversation. Listen.

    ( ) ( )

16. Listen to the last four words of that sentence.

    ( ) ( ) ( )

17. Listen to the name of the French capital.

    ( ) ( ) ( )

18. There are two syllables in that word. Listen.

    ( ) ( )

19. The second syllable begins with an "r" but it doesn't sound like the one you have learned. Listen again to the syllable division of that word.

    (Pa ris) (Pa ris)

5.4

INTRODUCTION TO FRENCH PHONOLOGY

20. This is the wrong pronunciation of that word. Listen

    ( ) ( ) ( )

21. Now this is the right pronunciation.

    ( ) ( ) ( )

22. Listen to the (R)/(W) contrast.

    (R)/(W)   (R)/(W)

23. Which one is right? Number one or two?

    (1)/(2)   (1)/(2)

(2)

24. Listen to the right pronunciation again and imitate.

    ( )x ( )x ( )x

25. We'll isolate the "r" of Paris. Listen.

    Pa(r)is, Pa(r)is, Pa(r)is

26. This is another kind of "r". The final "r". Listen.

    Pa(r), Pa(r), Pa(r)

27. Listen to this contrast. The "r" in pa(r) and the "r" in Pa(r)is.

    (Pa(r)/Pa(r)is   Pa(r)/Pa(r)is

28. The right pronunciation of the "r" in Paris, is as follows. Listen.

    ( ) ( ) ( )

29. Which is the "r" used in the word Paris?

    (1)/(2)   (1)/(2)   (1)/(2)

(2)

30. Listen now to the name of the French capital.

    ( ) ( )

31. Now, listen and imitate.

    ( )x ( )x ( )x

32. Imitate again.

   ( )x   ( )x   ( )x

33. Listen again to the complete sentence.

   ( )   ( )

34. Listen and imitate the last four words.

   ( )x   ( )x   ( )x

35. Here is the meaning of those words. Imitate the French.

   For Paris in the morning?   (Fr)x   (Fr)x

36. Look at the last part of the sentence and imitate.

   Pour Paris le matin?   ( )x   ( )x

37. Now, listen to the first part of the sentence.

   ( )   ( )   ( )

38. Look at the meaning in English and listen to the French.

   Is there a train?   (Fr)   (Fr)

39. Look and listen again.

   Is there a train?   (Fr)   (Fr)

40. This is the complete sentence. Look and listen.

   Is there a train for Paris in the morning?
   (Fr)   (Fr)

41. Listen to the whole sentence.

   ( )   ( )

42. Listen again to the first part of the sentence.

   ( )   ( )

43. Listen again. How many syllables are there?

   ( )   ( )

(5)

INTRODUCTION TO FRENCH PHONOLOGY 159

44. Listen and imitate.

( )x   ( )x   ( )x

45. Listen to the last 2 words.

( )   ( )

46. How many nasal vowels are there? Listen.

(2)
( )   ( )

47. One of those nasal vowels is new. Which one is it?

(- -)   (- -)
 1 2   1 2

(1)

48. Listen to the new nasal vowel.

( )   ( )   ( )

49. That nasal vowel is a French word. Here is the meaning. Look at the meaning and listen.

a, an, one.   (Fr)   (Fr)   (Fr)

50. This is a word you have learned. Listen to the vowel in that word.

heure   ( )   ( )   ( )

51. Listen to that word again without the final consonant.

( )   ( )   ( )

52. The vowel you hear is not a nasal vowel. Listen again.

( )   ( )   ( )

53. This time the vowel is nasalized. Listen.

( )   ( )   ( )

54. Listen to the contrast - nasal/non nasal.

( )/( )   ( )/( )

5.7

(1)

55. Which one is nasal? Number one or number two?

    (1)/(2)   (1)/(2)   (1)/(2)

56. Here is that nasal vowel. Look, listen and imitate.

    un ( )x ( )x ( )x

57. Imitate again.

    ( )x ( )x ( )x

58. Listen to the nasal (1)/non nasal (2) vowels and imitate.

    (1)/(2)x   (1)/(2)x   (1)/(2)x

59. Listen again to the complete sentence.

    ( ) ( )

60. We'll divide the sentence in two parts. Listen to the first part and imitate.

    ( )x ( )x ( )x

61. Listen to the second part of the sentence and imitate.

    ( )x ( )x ( )x

62. After listening and imitating the first part of the sentence, listen and imitate the second part.

    (1st part)x (2nd part)x (1st part)x (2nd part)x

63. This is the complete sentence. Listen and imitate.

    ( )x ( )x ( )x

64. The sentence is quite long. How many syllables are there? Listen.

    ( ) ( )

(10)

65. The sentence looks like this. Look, listen and imitate.

    Est-ce qu'il y a un train pour Paris le matin?
    ( )x ( )x ( )x

INTRODUCTION TO FRENCH PHONOLOGY

66. Here is the meaning again. Look, listen and imitate.

    Is there a train for Paris in the morning?

    (Fr)x   (Fr)x   (Fr)x

67. Listen to the answer to that sentence.

    ( )   ( )   ( )

68. Listen again. Are the vowels familiar to you?

    ( )   ( )   ( )

(yes)

69. Here is part of the sentence. Listen and imitate.

    ( )x   ( )x   ( )x

70. And now the full sentence. Listen and imitate.

    ( )x   ( )x   ( )x

71. Listen carefully to the rhythm of the sentence and imitate.

    ( )x   ( )x

72. Look at the sentence in French and imitate again.

    Oui, mais vous l'avez manqué.   ( )x   ( )x

73. Imitate again. Notice the rhythm and pronunciation.

    ( )x   ( )x

74. Listen to the following exchange and look at the meaning.

    A: ( )   Is there a train for Paris in the morning?
    B: ( )   Yes, but you've missed it.

75. Listen again.

    A: (?)   B: ( )
    A: (?)   B: ( )

5.9

76. Answer your instructor.

    Instructor: (Q)
    You: _____

77. Again.

    Instructor: (Q)
    You: _____

78. Ask the question this time, then listen to the answer.

    (begin)
    You: _____?
    Instructor: (A)

79. Again.

    (begin)
    You: _____?
    Instructor: (A)

80. Here is another question. Listen.

    ( ) ( ) ( )

81. Listen to the question again. How many syllables are there?

    ( ) ( ) ( )

(8)

82. Listen to the last part of the sentence and imitate.

    ( )x ( )x ( )x

83. Now, imitate the first part.

    ( )x ( )x ( )x

84. Listen and imitate the first part then the second part of the question.

    (1st part)x (2nd part)x (1st part)x (2nd part)x

85. Here is the sentence in full. Listen and imitate.

    ( )x ( )x ( )x

INTRODUCTION TO FRENCH PHONOLOGY

86. Listen very carefully to the rhythm and imitate again.

    ( )x ( )x ( )x

87. This time, look at the sentence and imitate again.

    Est-ce qu'il y en a l'après-midi? ( )x ( )x

88. Look at the meaning in English and imitate the French.

    Are there any in the afternoon? (Fr)x (Fr)x

89. Listen to the preceding question again and then, the answer to that question.

    (Q) (A) (Q) (A) (Q) (A)

90. Here is the answer only. Listen.

    ( ) ( )

91. There are two parts in that answer. Listen to the first part only.

    ( ) ( ) ( )

92. This time, listen and imitate.

    ( )x ( )x ( )x

93. This rhythm is wrong. Listen.

    ( ) ( ) ( )

94. This time the rhythm is right but the pronunciation is wrong. Listen.

    ( ) ( ) ( )

95. And this time, both the rhythm and pronunciation are wrong. Listen.

    ( ) ( ) ( )

96. This is the correct rhythm and pronunciation. Listen and imitate.

    ( )x ( )x ( )x

5.11

97. One is wrong; one is right. Which is right?

    (1)/(2)   (1)/(2)

(1)

98. Is this (R) or (W)? Listen.

    ( ) ( )

(W)

99. Which one is right? 1, 2 or 3?

    (1) (2) (3)

(3)

100. This is the right pronunciation. Be sure to imitate the rhythm and pronunciation.

    ( )x ( )x

101. Listen to the second part of the sentence.

    ( ) ( )

102. This time, listen and imitate.

    ( )x ( )x ( )x

103. Here are both parts of the sentence again. Look at the writing and listen.

    Non, pas l'après-midi. Dans la soirée seulement.
    ( ) ( )

104. Listen and imitate the first part, then the second part of the sentence.

    (1st)x (2nd)x (1st)x (2nd)x

105. The sentence is now complete. Listen and imitate.

    ( )x ( )x ( )x

106. Listen to the following exchange and look at the meaning.

    A: (?) Are there any in the afternoon?
    B: ( ) No, not in the afternoon. In the evening only.

INTRODUCTION TO FRENCH PHONOLOGY

107. Listen again.

    A: (?) B: ( )
    A: (?) B: ( )

108. Now, answer your instructor.

    Instructor: (Q)
    You: _____

109. Again.

    Instructor: (Q)
    You: _____

110. Ask the question this time and listen to the answer.

    (begin)
    You: _____?
    Instructor: (A)

111. Again.

    (begin)
    You: _____?
    Instructor: (A)

112. Listen to this four-sentence exchange.

    A: (?) B: ( ) A: (?) B: ( )
    A: (?) B: ( ) A: (?) B: ( )

113. Look at the writing, listen and imitate.

    -Est-ce qu'il y a un train pour Paris le matin? ( )x
    -Oui, mais vous l'avez manqué. ( )x
    -Est-ce qu'il y en a l'après-midi? ( )x
    -Non, pas l'après-midi. Dans la soirée seulement. ( )x

114. Imitate again.

    A: (?)x B: ( )x A: (?)x B: ( )x

115. Participate in the conversation. Answer your instructor.

    Instructor: (Q)
    You: _____
    Instructor: (Q)
    You: _____

116. Participate again.

> Instructor: (Q)
> You: _____
> Instructor: (Q)
> You: _____

117. This time, you ask the questions your instructor will answer you.

> (begin)
> You: _____
> Instructor: (A)
> You: _____
> Instructor: (A)

118. Again.

> (begin)
> You: _____
> Instructor: (A)
> You: _____
> Instructor: (A)

119. Here is another question. Listen.

> ( ) ( ) ( )

120. Listen to the last two words of that question.

> ( ) ( ) ( )

121. Listen to the syllable division of these two words.

> ( ) ( )

122. Listen again. Does the second syllable end in a (V) vowel or a (C) consonnant?

> ( ) ( )

(V)

123. Is this (R) or (W)?

> ( ) ( )

(W)

124. This pronunciation is wrong. Listen.

> ( ) ( )

INTRODUCTION TO FRENCH PHONOLOGY

125. Which one is right? No. 1 or No. 2?

       (1)/(2)   (1)/(2)

(1)

126. Imitate the correct pronunciation.

    ( )x ( )x ( )x

127. We'll add the rest of the sentence in front. Listen.

    ( ) ( )

128. Listen and imitate.

    ( )x ( )x ( )x

129. Look at the writing and imitate.

    A quelle heure est le premier? ( )x ( )x

130. Imitate again.

    ( )x ( )x

131. Here is the answer to that question. Listen.

    ( ) ( )

132. How many syllables do you hear? Listen.

    ( ) ( )

(5)

133. Are there any French "r" sounds in that sentence?

    ( ) ( )

(yes)

134. If there is a French "r", does it begin a syllable?

    ( ) ( )

(no)

135. Listen again to that sentence. Which syllable ends with an "r"?

        (- - - - -) (- - - - -)
         1 2 3 4 5   1 2 3 4 5

(4)

5.15

INTRODUCTION TO FRENCH PHONOLOGY

136. Here is the sentence again. Listen and imitate.

    ( )x ( )x ( )x

137. Look at the French sentence. Be sure to divide the syllables properly.

    A dix huit heures dix. ( )x ( )x

138. Look at the syllable division of that sentence and imitate.

    <u>à</u>/<u>di</u>/<u>xhui</u>/<u>theures</u>/<u>dix</u>   ( )x ( )x
     1   2   3   4   5

139. Listen to the last two sentences of the dialogue.

    A: (?)   B: ( )

140. This time, listen to the question-answer exchange and look at the meaning.

    A: (?)   At what time is the first one?
    B: ( )   At 6:10 P.M.

141. Now look at the French. Listen and imitate.

    A: Aquelle heure est le premier? ( )x
    B: A dix huit heures dix. ( )x

142. Imitate again.

    A: (?)x B: ( )x
    A: (?)x B: ( )x

143. Let's listen to the whole conversation.

    A: (?)   B: ( )
    A: (?)   B: ( )
    A: (?)   B: ( )

144. Listen to the conversation again.

    A: (?)   B: ( )
    A: (?)   B: ( )
    A: (?)   B: ( )

INTRODUCTION TO FRENCH PHONOLOGY

145. This time look at the meaning and listen to the French.

   A: Is there a train for Paris in the morning? (Fr)
   B: Yes, but you've missed it. (Fr)
   A: Are there any in the afternoon? (Fr)
   B: No, not in the afternoon. In the evening only. (Fr)
   A: At what time is the first one? (Fr)
   B: At 6:10 PM. (Fr)

146. Listen to the conversation and imitate each sentences.

   A: (?)x   B: ( )x   A: (?)x   B: ( )x   A: (?)x   B: ( )x

147. Answer your instructor.

   Instructor: (Q)
   You:_____
   Instructor: (Q)
   You:_____
   Instructor: (Q)
   You:_____

148. Again.

   Instructor: (Q)
   You:_____
   Instructor: (Q)
   You:_____
   Instructor: (Q)
   You:_____

149. Listen to the conversation again.

   A: (?)   B: ( )   A: (?)   B: ( )   A: (?)   B: ( )

150. Now ask the questions. Your instructor will answer you.

   (begin)
   You:_____?
   Instructor: (A)
   You:_____?
   Instructor: (A)
   You:_____?
   Instructor: (A)

151. Again.

>(begin)
>You: _____?
>Instructor: (A)
>You: _____?
>Instructor: (A)
>You: _____?
>Instructor: (A)

152. Practice frames 140 to 152 several times.

End of Chapter Five, Part One.

Report to your classroom.

INTRODUCTION TO FRENCH PHONOLOGY

Part Two

1.

Question forms with: Est-ce que...

1. Look at the following French sentence. What does it mean in English?

    Est-ce qu'il y a un train pour Paris le matin?

    Student's answer: <u>Is there a train for Paris in the morning?</u>

2. Now look at this one. What does it mean in English?

    Est-ce que vous avez déjeuné?

    Student's answer: <u>Did you have lunch?</u>

3. Both of the preceding questions begin with the same words. Say these words before your instructor does.

    x( )

4. Actually those three words "est-ce que" are a signal. A signal that a question is being asked. Look at the following sentences, then say them before your instructor does.

    Est-ce qu'il est midi? x( )
    Est-ce que vous allez à Paris? x( )
    Est-ce que c'est tout? x( )

5. Listen to questions beginning with "est-ce que". Does the intonation rise on the last syllable of each sentence?

    Est-ce que vous partez? ( )
    Est-ce qu'il est dix heures? ( )
    Est-ce que c'est à côté? ( )

    Student's answer: <u>Yes</u>

6. Listen again. With the exception of the "est-ce-que" formula, is there an inversion subject-verb?

    Est-ce que vous partez? ( )
    Est-ce qu'il est dix heures? ( )
    Est-ce que c'est à côté? ( )

    Student's answer: <u>No</u>

5.19

INTRODUCTION TO FRENCH PHONOLOGY

7. In order to make a question, you may add "est-ce que" in front of any statement. Be sure also to pronounce the last syllable of the sentence with a rise in intonation. Listen.

   a. Vous partez?   ( )   Est-ce que vous partez?   ( )
   b. Je pars?   ( )   Est-ce que je pars?   ( )
   c. Je vais au café? ( )   Est-ce que je vais au café? ( )

8. Your instructor will form a question. Form the same question using "est-ce que".

   Instructor: a. (Q) You: _____?
                b. (Q) You: _____?
                c. (Q) You: _____?

9. You have learned three ways of forming a question in French. Say the following sentences before your instructor does. Be sure to pronounce the last syllable with a rise in intonation.

   a. Est-ce qu'il y a un train pour Paris? x( )
   b. Il y a un train pour Paris?   x( )
   c. Y a-t-il un train pour Paris?   x( )

10. There are three ways of asking questions and it doesn't matter which one you prefer or choose. There is an exception however, and that is when you're talking about yourself and you are using the subject pronoun "I" (am I, do I go, etc...). In this particular case, the inversion verb-subject cannot be applied. Look at the following sentences and listen.

    a. Je pars samedi? ( )
       Est-ce que je pars samedi? ( )
    b. Je vais déjeuner?
       Est-ce que je vais déjeuner? ( )
    c. Je suis en retard? ( )
       Est-ce que je suis en retard? ( )

11. Transform the following statements into questions by making an inversion only. When the inversion is not possible, use "est-ce que".

    a. Je pars souvent.   x( )
    b. Vous partez samedi. x( )
    c. Il est cinq heures. x( )
    d. Vous allez à Paris. x( )
    e. Je vais à Paris.   x( )

5.20

INTRODUCTION TO FRENCH PHONOLOGY

12. How many ways are there to transform the following statement into a question.

    Il y a un train pour Paris.

    Student's answer: <u>3</u>

13. Look at the following question. Is it right or wrong?

    Pars-je à une heure?

    Student's answer: <u>W</u>

14. Listen to this sentence. Is it a question or a statement?

    ( )

    Student's answer: <u>Q</u>

15. Listen to the following phrases. One of them is not a question. Which one is it?

    a. ( )   c. ( )
    b. ( )   d. ( )

    Student's answer: <u>C</u>

2.

<u>Pronunciation of "r" between vowels.</u>
<u>Pronunciation of "r" after consonant.</u>

16. Here are French words containing the French consonant "r". Look, listen and imitate.

    a. mars   ( )x, marqué ( )x, Margot ( )x, Marie   ( )x
    b. part   ( )x, partez ( )x, pardon ( )x, Paris   ( )x

17. Here are more French words containing the consonant "r". Look, listen and imitate.

    a. terre   ( )x, terrain ( )x, train ( )x
    b. fer   ( )x, ferré   ( )x, frais ( )x

18. Look at the following words. Then say them before your instructor does.

    a. part x( ), partir x( ), partirez x( )
    b. sert x( ), servir x( ), servirez x( )

5.21

INTRODUCTION TO FRENCH PHONOLOGY

19. Look at the following sentences, listen and imitate.

    a. Il part. ( )x   Il part à dix heures. ( )x
       Il part à dix heures. ( )x

    b. Je sers. ( )x   Je sers à boire. ( )x
       Je sers à boire. ( )x

    c. La mer. ( )x   La mer est belle. ( )x
       La mer est belle. ( )x

20. Now say the following before your instructor does.

    pour x( )   pour eux x( )
    par   x( )   par ici   x( )

21. Here are more words. Say them before your instructor does.

    peur, peureux   x( )
    mer, mairie   x( )
    par, parent   x( )
    sourd, souris   x( )

22. Look at the following words and listen.

    par ans   ( )   parent   ( )
    vers eux ( )   verreux   ( )

23. Look at the following words then say them before your instructor does.

    par ans x( )   pour eux x( )   viré   x( )
    Paris   x( )   maré   x( )   bureau x( )

24. Look, listen and imitate.

    écrou ( )   écrit ( )   écran ( )

25. Look, listen and imitate.

    écrou ( )x   écrit ( )x   écran ( )x

26. Listen to these two words. Are they (S) same or (D) different?

    ( )/( )

    Student's answer: <u>D</u>

5.22

INTRODUCTION TO FRENCH PHONOLOGY

27. Which one has a French "r"? The first one or the second one?

    (1)/(2)

    Student's answer: <u>1</u>

28. Does the following word have an "r"?

    ( )

    Student's answer: <u>Yes</u>

29. Only one of the following words has a French "r". Which one is it?

    (1) (2) (3) (4)

    Student's answer: <u>2</u>

30. Look at the following words, listen and imitate.

    écran ( )x, abri ( )x, éprouve ( )x, aigri ( )x

31. Listen and imitate.

    ( )x   ( )x   ( )x

32. Look at the following words. Then say them before your instructor does.

    a. écrivez x( )   le gris x( )   le cris x( )
    b. le brin x( )   c'est vrai x( )   c'est frais x( )
    c. entrer x( )   tendrement x( )   vous comprendrez x( )

33. The following words also contain a French "r". Look and listen.

    marbré ( )   primeur ( )   rendre ( )   directeur ( )
    briser ( )   retrouver ( )   prendre ( )   partir ( )

34. Now look, listen and imitate.

    vernir ( )x   brunir ( )x   briser ( )x   reprendre ( )x
    espérer ( )x   trouver ( )x   respirer ( )x   pardon ( )x

35. This time, say the following words before your instructor does.

    perforer x( )   partir x( )   préparer x( )   écrire x( )
    pervers x( )   abrité x( )   maigreur x( )   mercredi x( )

5.23

INTRODUCTION TO FRENCH PHONOLOGY

3.

Nasal vowel "un"
Contrast: un/an/on/in

36. Do the following words sound alike? Listen.

    ( )   ( )   ( )

    Student's answer: <u>No</u>

37. Are the vowels in those three words nasal or oral. Listen again.

    ( )   ( )   ( )

    Student's answer: <u>Nasal</u>

38. The French word meaning "one" contains a new nasal vowel. Listen.

    ( )   ( )

39. Now, listen to the vowel contrast (N) nasal/ (O) oral.

    (N)/(O)   (N)/(O)

40. Listen again. Which is nasal?

    (1)/(2)   (1)/(2)

    Student's answer: <u>1</u>

41. Look at the following words and listen.

    un ( ), brun ( ), parfum ( )

42. Now say the following words before your instructor does.

    un repos x( )   un retard x( )   un peu   x( )
    un mot   x( )   un bout   x( )   un saut x( )

43. Look at these words and listen.

    brin ( ), brun ( )

44. Some French speakers do not make a distinction in pronouncing these words. Listen again.

    1. brin   ( )   2. brun   ( )
    1. un père ( )   2. impair ( )

5.24

INTRODUCTION TO FRENCH PHONOLOGY

45. Furthermore the words containing the nasal vowel sound "un" are limited to such a small number that you may memorize all of them. Here are the important ones. Look, listen and imitate.

French		English
chacun	( )x	each one
parfum	( )x	perfume
emprunt	( )x	loan
défunt	( )x	defunct
à jeun	( )x	on an empty stomach
brun	( )x	brunette
quelqu'un	( )x	someone

46. We left out the word "un". This is the most important one due to its high frequency. Look, listen and imitate.

    un tas ( )x   un livre ( )x   un sous ( )x
    un mur ( )x   un tour   ( )x   un feu   ( )x

47. In order to simplify your learning of French, we will not expect you to use four nasal vowels. Look at the following words, listen and imitate.

    un pont ( )x   un pain ( )x   chacun ( )x   parfum ( )x
    quelqu'un ( )x   un brun ( )x   un père ( )x   impair ( )x

48. So here are three words with the important nasal vowels. Listen and imitate.

    ( )x   ( )x   ( )x

49. Again.

    ( )x   ( )x   ( )x

50. You will hear two different nasal vowel. Supply the third one before your instructor does.

    a. (1) (2) 3x (3)
    b. (1) (2) 3x (3)
    c. (1) (2) 3x (3)
    d. (1) (2) 3x (3)

51. Again. This time we'll use another set of words.

    a. (1) (2) 3x (3)
    b. (1) (2) 3x (3)
    c. (1) (2) 3x (3)
    d. (1) (2) 3x (3)

52. Now say the following words before your instructor does.

   bonbon x( ), tampon x( ), pinson x( ), enfant x( )
   passant x( ), malin x( ), américain x( ), éteint x( )

                    4.

                  Il y a.

53. Here is an English sentence. Say it in French.

   Is there a train for Paris? x( )

54. Now say this in French.

   There's a train. x( )

55. Look at the following French words, then say the English equivalent.

   Il y a.

   Student's answer: <u>There is</u>

56. "Il y a" also means "there are" in English. Look and listen.

   There are a few cafés. Il y a quelques cafés. ( )

57. Here are a few French sentences. Say them in English.

   a. Il y a cinq cafés.
   b. Il y a un café.
   c. Il y a quelques trains.

   Student's answer: a. <u>There are five cafés.</u>
                      b. <u>There is one café.</u>
                      c. <u>There are a few trains.</u>

58. Look at the following sentences and translate them into French.

   There is a train in the afternoon. x( )
   There is one train in the evening. x( )
   There are a few cafés.   x( )

59. Here is a French sentence. Say it in English.

   Est-ce qu'il y en a l'après-midi?

   Student's answer: <u>Are there any in the afternoon?</u>

                  5.26

INTRODUCTION TO FRENCH PHONOLOGY

60. Here is the sentence again. Notice the underlined word meaning "any" or "some". Then say the sentence.

    Est-ce qu'il y en a l'aprè-midi? x( )

61. Look at this English sentence. Then listen to the French.

    There are some in the afternoon. ( )

62. Now say the following sentences in French.

    a. There are some in the morning. x( )
    b. There are some in the afternoon. x( )
    c. There are some in the evening. x( )

63. Here are more sentences. Say them in French.

    a. There are a few trains in the morning. x( )
    b. There are some in the morning. x( )
    c. There are a few trains in the afternoon. x( )
    d. There are some in the afternoon. x( )

                            5.

"en" and "un" preceding words beginning with a vowel

64. Look at the following question and listen. Notice how the underlined word "en" links with the following word.

    Est-ce qu'il y en a l'après-midi? ( )

65. The "n" of the French word "en" must begin the word following it when that word begins with a vowel.

    Example: en auto = en/nau/to

    Look at the following and listen.

    en été   ( )
    en auto   ( )

66. The same rule applies to the word "un". Look and listen.

    un été   ( )
    un effort ( )

67. Here are more examples. Look at them, then listen.

    a. un café   ( )   un ami   ( )
    b. en vérité ( )   en ami   ( )
    c. en effet ( )   un effet ( )

5.27

180 INTRODUCTION TO FRENCH PHONOLOGY

68. Now look at the following words, then say them.

   a. un aimant   x( )
   b. un nouveau   x( )
   c. un été   x( )
   d. un enfant   x( )
   e. en anglais   x( )
   f. en face   x( )
   g. en Amérique   x( )
   h. en tout   x( )

69. Here is a sentence. Listen to the syllable division.

   Il en a ( )

70. Listen again. Then say the first syllable.

   Il en a ( )

   Student's answer: i

71. Listen again. What's the second syllable?

   Il en a ( )

   Student's answer: l'en

72. What is the third syllable? Listen.

   Il en a ( )

   Student's answer: na

73. Here are sentences for you to say.

   a. Vous en avez.   x( )
   b. Ils en ont.   x( )
   c. Vous vous en allez. x( )
   d. Nous en avons.   x( )
   e. Il en parle.   x( )

74. Say the following questions in French. Begin your questions with "est-ce que".

   a. Are there any in the afternoon?   x( )
   b. Are there any next door?   x( )
   c. Is there a café next door?   x( )
   d. Is there a train in the evening?   x( )

5.28

INTRODUCTION TO FRENCH PHONOLOGY

75. Answer the following questions affirmatively. First listen to the example.

    Questions: ( )
    Answer: ( )

    Now listen. Then answer.

	Questions	You answer:
a.	(Q)	_____ ( )
b.	(Q)	_____ ( )
c.	(Q)	_____ ( )
d.	(Q)	_____ ( )
e.	(Q)	_____ ( )

76. Here are more questions; answer them negatively. Listen to this example first.

    Question: ( )
    Answer: ( )

    Now, listen to the question. Then answer.

	Questions	You answer:
a.	(Q)	_____ ( )
b.	(Q)	_____ ( )
c.	(Q)	_____ ( )
d.	(Q)	_____ ( )

                    6.

            Pronunciation of "oi"

77. Look at the following French words, then say them before your instructor does.

    la soirée x( )

78. Look at these words and say them.

    poire x( ), foire x( ), noir x( )
    noix x( ), doit x( ), moi x( ), loi x( )

79. Say these other combinations before your instructor does.

    a. nuit x( ), oui x( ), mois x( )
    b. Louis x( ), puit x( ), fois x( )
    c. bout x( ), feux x( ), faut x( )
    d. mais x( ), toit x( ), peux x( )

5.29

INTRODUCTION TO FRENCH PHONOLOGY

7.

"dix" in final position

80. Look at the following sentence and listen. Notice the pronunciation of the last word.

    A dix huit heures <u>dix</u>. ( )

81. Was the "x" of the last word pronounced as "x", "z" or "s"? Listen again.

    A dix huit heures <u>dix</u>. ( )

    Student's answer: <u>S</u>

82. When the word "dix" is the only word you're saying or the last one of any utterance, you must pronounce the "x" as "s." Look, listen and imitate.

    dix ( )x, dix ( )x

83. The same rule should be applied to this word. Look at it. Then say it.

    six x( ), six x( )

84. Now, say these before your instructor does.

    Il est <u>dix</u> heures. x( )

85. There was no "x" sound at the end of "dix," but a "z." Right or wrong? Listen again.

    Il est dix heures. ( )

    Student's answer: <u>Right</u>

86. Say the following sentences before your instructor does.

    a. Il est dix heures.   x( )
    b. Vous en avez dix.   x( )
    c. Il est midi six.   x( )
    d. Il est six heures.   x( )
    e. Il est dix heures dix. x( )

5.30

INTRODUCTION TO FRENCH PHONOLOGY

8.

Review

87. Here is a review. Look at the following words or sentences and say them before your instructor does.

    a.   Vous allez à Paris? x( )
         Est-ce que vous avez déjeuné? x( )
         Avez-vous une minute? x( )

    b.   Où allez-vous? x( )
         A quelle heure partez-vous? x( )
         Où est-ce que vous avez déjeuné? x( )

    c.   Il y a un train à six heures. x( )
         Le train arrive à dix heures. x( )
         Je pars samedi à deux heures dix. x( )

    d.   Je pars samedi. x( )
         J'arrive mercredi. x( )
         Je veux leur parler. x( )

    e.   Un aviron. x( )
         Un navire. x( )
         Un pont. x( )
         Un train. x( )

    f.   Il y en a un. x( )
         Il y en a dix. x( )
         Il y en a deux. x( )
         Il y en a six. x( )
         Il y en a cinq. x( )

    g.   Je pars en auto. x( )
         Il pleut en hiver. x( )
         J'en ai trois. x( )
         Il en veut dix. x( )
         Il en a six. x( )

Report to your classroom.

9.

Preparation for class

Drill 1

Dites en français

1.	The morning	1.	Le matin
2.	In the morning	2.	Le matin
3.	For the morning	3.	Pour le matin
4.	For you	4.	Pour vous
5.	For one o'clock	5.	Pour une heure
6.	A train	6.	Un train
7.	The afternoon	7.	L'après-midi
8.	In the afternoon	8.	L'après-midi
9.	In the evening	9.	Dans la soirée
10.	The evening	10.	La soirée
11.	The morning	11.	Le matin
12.	You missed it	12.	Vous l'avez manqué
13.	There is	13.	Il y a
14.	The first one	14.	Le premier
15.	Not the afternoon	15.	Pas l'après-midi
16.	Not Saturday	16.	Pas samedi
17.	The first	17.	Le premier
18.	The first one	18.	Le premier
19.	Eight o'clock	19.	Huit heures
20.	Eighteen	20.	Dix-huit
21.	Ten	21.	Dix
22.	At 6:00 PM	22.	A dix-huit heures.
23.	Eight	23.	Huit

Drill 2

Dites en anglais

1. A quelle heure part le premier train.
2. Il part le matin à cinq heures dix.
3. Il y a quelques trains le matin.
4. L'après-midi il y a un train seulement.
5. Pas dans l'après-midi.

1. What time does the first train leave?
2. It leaves in the morning at ten past five. (It leaves at ten after five AM)
3. There are a few trains in the morning.
4. In the afternoon there is one train only.
5. Not in the afternoon.

INTRODUCTION TO FRENCH PHONOLOGY

6.	Pas l'après-midi.	6.	Not (in) the afternoon.
7.	Je pars pour Paris.	7.	I'm leaving for Paris.
8.	Où est le café?	8.	Where is the café?
9.	Je pars.	9.	I'm leaving.
10.	Le train part à dix heures.	10.	The train leaves at 10.
11.	Vous avez manqué le train.	11.	You missed the train.
12.	L'après-midi, non.	12.	(in) The afternoon, no.
13.	Je pars dans la soirée.	13.	I leave in the evening.
14.	Samedi seulement.	14.	Saturday only.
15.	Pas samedi.	15.	Not Saturday.
16.	Le premier train.	16.	The first train.
17.	A côté.	17.	Next door.
18.	Le café est à côté.	18.	The café is next door.

Drill 3

Dites en français

1.	In the evening I go to the café.	1.	Dans la soirée je vais au café.
2.	In the afternoon I'm at the café.	2.	L'après-midi je suis au café.
3.	The café is next door.	3.	Le café est à côté.
4.	There is a train for Paris.	4.	Il y a un train pour Paris.
5.	Did you miss it?	5.	Vous l'avez manqué? L'avez-vous manqué? Est-ce que vous l'avez manqué?
6.	I often go to Paris.	6.	Je vais souvent à Paris.
7.	I'm going to Paris. Are you going?	7.	Je vais à Paris. Vous y allez?
8.	I'm leaving in the morning.	8.	Je pars le matin.
9.	Are you leaving in the evening?	9.	Vous partez dans la soirée?
10.	There are some in the morning.	10.	Il y en a le matin.
11.	The first train for Paris is in the evening.	11.	Le premier train pour Paris est dans la soirée.
12.	Are you leaving for Paris?	12.	Vous partez pour Paris?
13.	Saturday in the evening.	13.	Samedi dans la soirée.
14.	Are there any?	14.	(Est-ce qu') il y en a?
15.	Are there any on Saturday?	15.	(Est-ce qu') il y en a samedi?

5.33

Drill 4

	Questions		Possible answers
1.	Quelle heure est-il?	1.	Il est midi. Il est une heure. Il est midi cinq. etc...
2.	A quelle heure allez-vous déjeuner?	2.	Je vais déjeuner à midi. Je vais déjeuner à midi cinq. Je vais déjeuner à midi dix. Je vais déjeuner à une heure. Je vais déjeuner à une heure cinq. Je vais déjeuner à une heure dix.
3.	Vous partez le matin?	3.	Non. Je pars l'après-midi. Oui, je pars le matin. Non. Je pars dans la soirée.
4.	Est-ce qu'il y a un train pou Paris, l'après-midi?	4.	Oui, il y a un train l'après-midi. Non. Pas l'après-midi. Dans la soirée seulement. Non, pas l'après-midi. Le matin seulement.

Drill 5

Teacher: Il y a un train à huit heures.
Student: Est-ce qu'il y a un train à huit heures?

1. Il y a un train à huit heures.
2. Vous l'avez manqué.
3. C'est le premier.
4. Je pars samedi.
5. Il est midi.
6. Vous allez à côté.
7. Il y en a à dix heures.
8. Vous y allez samedi.
9. Je suis en retard.
10. Je vais déjeuner à midi.

1. Est-ce qu'il y a un train à huit heures?
2. Est-ce que vous l'avez manqué?
3. Est-ce que c'est le premier?
4. Est-ce que je pars samedi?
5. Est-ce qu'il est midi?
6. Est-ce que vous allez à côté?
7. Est-ce qu'il y en a à dix heures?
8. Est-ce que vous y allez samedi?
9. Est-ce que je suis en retard?
10. Est-ce que je vais déjeuner à midi?

INTRODUCTION TO FRENCH PHONOLOGY

Drill 6

Teacher: Il est midi.
Student: Il est midi?

1.	Il est cinq heures.	1.	Il est cinq heures?
2.	Vous avez une minute.	2.	Vous avez une minute?
3.	Il est midi.	3.	Il est midi?
4.	Vous partez samedi.	4.	Vous partez samedi?
5.	Vous y allez souvent.	5.	Vous y allez souvent?
6.	Vous allez déjeuner.	6.	Vous allez déjeuner?

Drill 7

In the following sentence use "Est-ce que" when the inversion is not possible gramatically.

	Teacher		Student
1.	Vous allez souvent à Paris?	1.	Allez-vous souvent à Paris?
2.	Je suis en retard?	2.	Est-ce que je suis en retard?
3.	Je vais à côté?	3.	Est-ce que je vais à côté?
4.	Vous partez dans la soirée?	4.	Partez-vous dans la soirée?
5.	Il y a un train?	5.	Y a-t-il un train?
6.	Vous y allez à une heure?	6.	Y allez-vous à une heure?
7.	Je pars samedi?	7.	Est-ce que je pars samedi?
8.	Vous l'avez manqué?	8.	L'avez-vous manqué?
9.	Je vais déjeuner?	9.	Est-ce que je vais déjeuner?
10.	Vous avez déjeuné?	10.	Avez-vous déjeuné?

Drill 8

Dites en français

1.	That's the first one.	1.	C'est le premier.
2.	That's all.	2.	C'est tout.
3.	There is a train.	3.	Il y a un train.
4.	That's at one o'clock.	4.	C'est à une heure.
5.	That's the train.	5.	C'est le train.
6.	There are some often.	6.	Il y en a souvent.
7.	That's the train.	7.	C'est le train.
8.	That's in the afternoon.	8.	C'est dans l'après-midi.

5.35

Drill 9

Dites en français

1.	It's in the evening.	1.	C'est dans la soirée.
2.	That's the train for Paris.	2.	C'est le train pour Paris.
3.	It's the first train.	3.	C'est le premier train.
4.	It's the train for Paris.	4.	C'est le train pour Paris.
5.	It's at the café.	5.	C'est au café.
6.	That's at the café.	6.	C'est au café.
7.	It's in the train.	7.	C'est dans le train.
8.	It's next door.	8.	C'est à côté.

Drill 10

Conversation dirigée

(Instructor's manual only)

Drill 11

Conversation dirigée

(Instructor's manual only)

Drill 12

Expansion drill

	Teacher		Student
1.	Un train	1.	Un train.
2.	il y a	2.	Il y a un train.
3.	pour Paris	3.	Il y a un train pour Paris.
4.	samedi	4.	Il y a un train pour Paris samedi.
5.	matin	5.	Il y a un train pour Paris samedi matin.
6.	à dix heures	6.	Il y a un train pour Paris samedin matin à dix heures.

5.36

INTRODUCTION TO FRENCH PHONOLOGY

Drill 13

Expansion drill

Teacher	Student
1. le train	1. Le train.
2. vous avez manqué	2. Vous avez manqué le train.
3. premier	3. Vous avez manqué le premier train.
4. pour Paris	4. Vous avez manqué le premier train pour Paris.

Drill 14

Expansion drill

Teacher	Student
1. Un train	1. Un train.
2. il y a	2. Il y a un train.
3. pour Paris	3. Il y a un train pour Paris.
4. dans la soirée	4. Il y a un train pour Paris dans la soirée.
5. à dix huit heures dix	5. Il y a un train pour Paris dans la soirée à dix huit heures dix.

10.

Reading exercises

Lecture

1. Read.

    1. Est-ce que c'est fini?
    2. Est-ce que vous comprenez?
    3. Est-ce qu'il est parti?
    4. Est-ce que nous y allons?
    5. Est-ce qu'il y va aussi?
    6. Est-ce que vous en voulez?

2. Read.

    1. Vous en avez?
    2. Vous en vendez?
    3. Nous en avons.
    4. Nous en vendons.
    5. Nous l'avons manqué?
    6. Vous l'avez fini?

3. Read.

    1. Il y va en auto.
    2. J'y vais en auto.
    3. Nous y allons en auto.
    4. J'habite en Italie.
    5. Il y va en été.
    6. Je suis en avance.

4. Read.

    1. En été nous allons en Scandinavie.
    2. L'autre est dans la cour.
    3. Je vais voir où ils sont.
    4. Il pleut souvent en hiver.
    5. Je crois qu'il est arrivé.
    6. Nous n'en avons pas.

5. Read.

    1. Il est dix heures dix.
    2. Il est trois heures cinq.
    3. Il est six heures dix.
    4. Il y a dix ans.
    5. Il y a trois beaux appartements.
    6. Nos deux enfants sont à l'université.

INTRODUCTION TO FRENCH PHONOLOGY

6. Read.

    1. Quand allez-vous la réparer?
    2. Où avez-vous mis le numéro?
    3. Que voulez-vous qu'il fasse?
    4. A quelle heure vont-ils nous voir?
    5. Quand pouvons-nous la lui montrer?
    6. Quand prenez-vous vos vacances?

7. Read.

    1. canif; loup; loupe; coup; coupe
    2. tardif; le talc; le film; le fil
    3. par; la part; la mare; en vrac
    4. C'est long; le banc; vers
    5. le vert; la verte; le verre; la mer; le fer
    6. bon; le temps; beaucoup, en avril
    7. longtemps; le vin; le pain; le bain
    8. un pain; un saint; un brun; un brin

8. Read.

    1. Est-ce que c'est fini?
    2. C'est fini.
    3. C'est fini?
    4. Quand l'avez-vous fini?
    5. L'avez-vous fini?
    6. Vous l'avez fini?
    7. Nous l'avons fini.
    8. Est-ce que vous l'avez fini?
    9. Il ne l'a pas fini.
    10. Il ne l'a pas fini?
    11. Quand va-t-il le finir?
    12. Est-ce qu'il va le finir ce soir?

9. Dictation.

    1. Vous l'avez manqué.
    2. Vous avez manqué le train.
    3. Le premier train est à cinq heures.
    4. Où déjeunez-vous?
    5. Avez-vous déjeuné à côté?
    6. Vous avez quelques minutes?
    7. Il y en a l'après-midi.
    8. Est-ce qu'il y en a dans la soirée?
    9. A quelle heure allez-vous partir?

10. Je suis souvent en retard.
11. De temps en temps seulement.

12. Il y a un train pour Paris le matin.

Chapter Five, end of Part Two.

Go to lab for Tests 1 to 6.

INTRODUCTION TO FRENCH PHONOLOGY

Chapter Five, Part Three

Tests

Test 1

All of the following sentences have one error. Rewrite them correctly.

Rewrite

1. Je suis en retar.   1._____
2. Vous l'avé manqué.   2._____
3. Il y a un trin.   3._____
4. Il est diz heures.   4._____
5. Je pars samdi.   5._____
6. Où avez-vous déjauné?   6._____
7. Je vai à Paris.   7._____
8. Dan la soirée.   8._____
9. A quelle heure est le premer?   9._____
10. Il est cinq heures dis.   10._____
11. Quelle heure es-til?   11._____
12. Vou zy allez?   12._____
13. Le matin seulment.   13._____
14. Dans quelques minute.   14._____
15. Kand partez-vous?   15._____

Test 2

The following French words have one syllable. Listen to the vowel sound and write it down.

Listen	Write
1. ( )	1. _____
2. ( )	2. _____
3. ( )	3. _____
4. ( )	4. _____
5. ( )	5. _____
6. ( )	6. _____
7. ( )	7. _____
8. ( )	8. _____
9. ( )	9. _____

Test 3

The pronunciation of the following words may be right or wrong. Look, listen and check the appropriate column.

		Right	Wrong
1.	retard ( )	1. ____	____
2.	à midi ( )	2. ____	____
3.	dix heures ( )	3. ____	____
4.	le premier ( )	4. ____	____
5.	cinq heures ( )	5. ____	____
6.	midi dix ( )	6. ____	____
7.	Quand ( )	7. ____	____
8.	seulement ( )	8. ____	____
9.	Il y en a ( )	9. ____	____
10.	un train ( )	10. ____	____

5.42

INTRODUCTION TO FRENCH PHONOLOGY

Test 4

Say the following words.

1.	doux	1.	x( )
2.	dix	2.	x( )
3.	roux	3.	x( )
4.	deux	4.	x( )
5.	six	5.	x( )
6.	fixe	6.	x( )
7.	feux	7.	x( )
8.	paix	8.	x( )
9.	rixe	9.	x( )
10.	taxe	10.	x( )

Test 5

The words you are to listen to are said in pairs. Determine whether they are same or different in each pair. Check the appropriate column.

			Same	Different
1.	( )	1.	____	____
2.	( )	2.	____	____
3.	( )	3.	____	____
4.	( )	4.	____	____
5.	( )	5.	____	____
6.	( )	6.	____	____
7.	( )	7.	____	____
8.	( )	8.	____	____
9.	( )	9.	____	____

5.43

Test 6

Write the number of nasal vowels you hear for each of the following utterances. Stop your machine after each one.

You write:

1. ( )   1._____
2. ( )   2._____
3. ( )   3._____
4. ( )   4._____
5. ( )   5._____
6. ( )   6._____
7. ( )   7._____
8. ( )   8._____
9. ( )   9._____
10. ( ) 10._____

END OF CHAPTER FIVE

INTRODUCTION TO FRENCH PHONOLOGY

Chapter Six

PART 1

Dialogue. (Laboratory)

PART 2

1. Pronunciation of "ill" (billet, bouillir). (Laboratory)
2. Explanation of "s'il vous plaît." (Laboratory)
3. Pronunciation of: "V*i*ent, D*i*eu." (Laboratory)
4. "e" continued. (Il ne sait pas/je ne sais pas). (Laboratory)
5. Numbers: 1, 2, 5, 9, 10, 18, 40, 50, 59. (Laboratory)
6. Review. (Laboratory)
7. Preparation for Class. (Homework)
8. Reading exercises. (Classroom)

PART 3

Tests. (Classroom and laboratory)

Chapter Six

Dialogue

A. Deux billets de première pour Paris, s'il vous plaît.
— Two first class tickets for Paris, please.

B. Aller et retour?
— Round trip?

A. Non, deux allers.
— No, two one way.

B. Voilà Monsieur. C'est cinquante neuf francs quarante.
— Here you are, Sir. It is 59 francs 40.

A. Le train est à l'heure?
— The train is on time?

B. Oui. Il vient d'entrer en gare.
— Yes. It has just pulled into the station.

A. Merci.
— Thank you.

INTRODUCTION TO FRENCH PHONOLOGY

Part One

1. Listen to the following conversation in French.

    A: ( )
    B: (?)
    A: ( )
    B: ( )
    A: (?)
    B: ( )
    A: ( )

2. Listen to the intonation and rhythm of the sentence.

    A: ( )
    B: (?)
    A: ( )
    B: ( )
    A: (?)
    B: ( )
    A: ( )

3. This is the first sentence of the conversation. Listen.

    ( ) ( ) ( )

4. These are the last four words of the sentence. Listen.

    ( ) ( )

5. Listen again to these four words. How many syllables are there?

    ( ) ( )

6. Listen again to these four words and then imitate.

    ( )x ( )x ( )x

7. These four words mean "please." Listen and imitate.

    ( )x ( )x

8. Here are three more words added in front.

    ( ) ( ) ( )

9. The first word has two syllables. Listen.

    ( ) ( )

6.3

10. Listen to the syllable division of that word.

   ( ) ( )

11. This is the wrong way to divide that word into syllables. Listen.

   (W) (W)

12. Listen to the (R)/(W) contrast.

   (R)/(W)   (R)/(W)

13. Which is right? Number one or number 2?

   (1)/(2)   (1)/(2)

(1)

14. Listen to the correct pronunciation and imitate.

   ( )x ( )x ( )x

15. Again.

   ( )x ( )x

16. Look at the word. Listen, then say it.

   Première ( ) ( )   ( )x ( )x ( )x

17. After "première", we will add two words that you know. Listen.

   ( ) ( ) ( )

18. Listen and imitate.

   ( )x ( )x ( )x

19. Listen. How many syllables are there?

   ( ) ( )

(5)

20. Listen again and imitate.

   ( )x ( )x ( )x

21. We need three more words in order to complete the sentence. Here they are in front of "première". Listen.

   ( ) ( ) ( )

INTRODUCTION TO FRENCH PHONOLOGY

22. Listen again.

    ( ) ( ) ( )

23. Listen and imitate.

    ( )x   ( )x   ( )x

24. Imitate again.

    ( )x   ( )x   ( )x

25. Listen. How many syllables are there?

    ( ) ( )

(5)

26. Look at the spelling of these words and listen.

    Deux billets de première. ( ) ( )

27. Look at the spelling again. Notice the pronunciation of the underlined word.

    Deux billets <u>de</u> première. ( ) ( )

28. We'll underline the first word too. Compare its pronunciation with the other underlined word. Listen.

    <u>Deux</u> billets <u>de</u> première.   ( ) ( )

29. We'll call the first word <u>1</u> and the other <u>3</u>. Do they sound alike? Listen.

    <u>Deux</u> billets <u>de</u> première.   ( ) ( )
      1   3

(no)

30. In one of the words, the vowel is very short or not pronounced. Is it word 1 or 3?

    <u>Deux</u> billets <u>de</u> première.   ( ) ( )
      1   3

(3)

31. In word 3 do you hear a "d" or a "t"?

    Deux billets <u>de</u> première.   ( ) ( )

(t)

6.5

202 INTRODUCTION TO FRENCH PHONOLOGY

    32. So this is what you hear. Look, listen and imitate.

          Deux billets t̲ première. ( )x ( )x ( )x

    33. Is this (R) or (W)? Listen.

          ( ) ( )

(W)

    34. Which is (R), number one or two?

          (1)/(2)   (1)/(2)

(2)

    35. Listen and imitate again the correct pronunciation.

          ( )x ( )x ( )x

    36. This sentence is a little longer. Listen. Then imitate.

          ( ) ( )   ( )x ( )x ( )x

    37. Listen again and imitate.

          ( )x ( )x ( )x

    38. Listen to the complete sentence.

          ( ) ( ) ( )

    39. Listen again. How many syllables are there?

          ( ) ( )

(11)

    40. Listen and imitate the first part of the sentence.

          ( )x ( )x ( )x

    41. And now the whole sentence. Listen and then imitate.

          ( ) ( )   ( )x ( )x ( )x

    42. Listen and imitate again.

          ( )x ( )x ( )x

6.6

INTRODUCTION TO FRENCH PHONOLOGY

43. Look at the sentence while imitating your instructor.

    Deux billets de première pour Paris, s'il vous plaît.

    ( )x   ( )x

44. Look at the meaning of that sentence, listen to the French and imitate.

    Two first class tickets for Paris, please.

    (Fr)x   (Fr)x

45. Here is a new sentence. Listen.

    ( )   ( )   ( )

46. Listen again. How many "r" sounds are there?

    ( )   ( )

(2)

47. How many syllables?

    ( )   ( )

(4)

48. Listen and imitate.

    ( )x   ( )x   ( )x

49. Listen to the vowels in syllables 2 and 3. Are they the same?

    (- - - -?)   (- - - -?)
    1 2 3 4   1 2 3 4

(yes)

50. Listen and imitate.

    ( )x   ( )x   ( )x

51. Look at the question, listen and imitate.

    Aller et retour?   ( )x   ( )x   ( )x

52. Notice that the underlined vowel is not pronounced. Look, listen and imitate.

    Aller et r<u>e</u>tour?   ( )x   ( )x   ( )x

6.7

204   INTRODUCTION TO FRENCH PHONOLOGY

53. Look at the meaning of that sentence and imitate.

   Round trip?   (Fr)x   (Fr)x

54. One is (R). Is it number one, two or three?

   (1)   (2)   (3)

(1)

55. Listen and imitate the correct pronunciation again.

   ( )x   ( )x   ( )x

56. Listen to this three-sentence exchange.

   A: ( )
   B: (?)
   A: ( )

57. Listen to the third sentence.

   ( )   ( )   ( )

58. Listen and imitate.

   ( )x   ( )x   ( )x

59. Is this (R) or (W)? Listen.

   ( )   ( )

(W)

60. Which one is right? Number one or two?

   (1)   (2)   (1)   (2)

(1)

61. Imitate again the correct pronunciation.

   ( )x   ( )x   ( )x

62. Look at the spelling. Listen and imitate.

   Non, deux allers.   ( )x   ( )x   ( )x

63. Listen again to the exchange and look at the meaning.

   A: ( ) Two first class tickets for Paris, please.
   B: (?) Round trip?
   A: ( ) No, two one-way.

6.8

INTRODUCTION TO FRENCH PHONOLOGY

64. Answer your instructor.

> Instructor: ( )
> You: _____?
> Instructor: ( )

65. Again.

> Instructor: ( )
> You: _____?
> Instructor: ( )

66. This time you begin the conversation.

> (begin)
> You: _____?
> Instructor: (?)
> You: _____?

67. Again.

> (begin)
> You: _____?
> Instructor: (Q)
> You: _____?

68. The following sentence has two words. Listen.

> ( ) ( ) ( )

69. Listen to the sentence again. Then imitate the last word.

> ( ) ( )   ( )x ( )x

70. Listen again to that word. Are the vowels in both syllables about the same?

> ( ) ( )

(yes)

71. Listen again. Are they the same now?

> ( ) ( )

(no)

72. Listen and imitate the correct pronunciation.

> ( )x ( )x

6.9

INTRODUCTION TO FRENCH PHONOLOGY

73. Imitate the sentence.

    ( )x ( )x

74. Look at the sentence, listen and imitate.

    Voilà Monsieur! ( )x ( )x ( )x

75. Here is the meaning of that sentence. Listen, look at the meaning and imitate.

    ( ) Here you are Sir! ( )x ( )x

76. The same speaker is saying a sequence of two sentences. Listen to the sentence you know followed by the new sentence.

    ( ) ( ) ( )

77. Listen to the new sentence. How many syllables are there?

    ( ) ( )

(7)

78. Listen and imitate the last word of that sentence.

    ( )x ( )x ( )x

79. Which of the following four words is right?

    (1) (2) (3) (4)

(3)

80. Listen again and imitate.

    ( )x ( )x ( )x

81. Now look at the meaning and imitate the French.

    forty ( )x ( )x ( )x

82. Here is the spelling in French. Look and imitate.

    quarante ( )x ( )x ( )x

83. We'll add two words in front. Listen.

    ( ) ( ) ( )

6.10

INTRODUCTION TO FRENCH PHONOLOGY

84. Listen and imitate.

    ( )x ( )x ( )x

85. Imitate again. Be sure to pronounce the "t" at the end.

    ( )x ( )x ( )x

86. Here is a new word. We'll place this word in front of the others. Listen.

    ( ) ( ) ( )

87. Listen again.

    ( ) ( ) ( )

88. Listen. Then imitate.

    ( ) ( )   ( )x ( )x ( )x

89. How many nasal sounds do you hear? Listen.

    ( ) ( )

(4)

90. Listen again and imitate.

    ( )x ( )x ( )x

91. Here is the spelling. Look and listen.

    Cinquante neuf francs quarante. ( ) ( )

92. Now look at the meaning, listen and imitate.

    Fifty nine francs, forty. (Fr)x (Fr)x

93. Here is one more word to complete the sentence. Listen.

    ( ) ( )

94. Listen again. How many syllables do we have now?

    ( ) ( )

(7)

95. Listen again to the sentence. Then imitate.

    ( ) ( )   ( )x ( )x ( )x

6.11

96. Imitate both the rhythm and the pronunciation again.

   ( )x   ( )x   ( )x

97. Here is the sentence again. The pronunciation is correct; the rhythm is not. Listen.

   ( )   ( )

98. This time, the rhythm and pronunciation are correct in one of the following three sentences. Which one is it? Listen.

   (1)   (2)   (3)

(1)

99. Here is the correct pronunciation and rhythm. Listen and imitate.

   ( )x   ( )x   ( )x

100. Now look at the sentence and listen.

   C'est cinquante neuf francs quarante. ( )   ( )

101. Now listen to the sentence, look at the meaning and imitate.

   ( )   ( )   It's 59 francs and 40 cents. ( )x   ( )x   ( )x

102. Do you remember this sentence? Listen.

   ( )   ( )   ( )

103. Listen and imitate.

   ( )x   ( )x   ( )x

104. Here are both sentences now. Listen.

   ( )   ( )   ( )

105. Now listen and imitate.

   ( )x   ( )x   ( )x

106. Listen again and imitate. Be sure to pause a little at the end of the first sentence.

   ( )x   ( )x   ( )x

6.12

INTRODUCTION TO FRENCH PHONOLOGY

107. Let's start from the beginning. Listen to this exchange.

    A: ( )
    B: (?)
    A: ( )
    B: ( )

108. Listen again to the conversation and look at the meaning.

    A: ( ) Two first class tickets for Paris, please.
    B: (?) Round trip?
    A: ( ) No, two one way.
    B: ( ) Here you are Sir! It's 59 francs and 40 cents.

109. Now, answer your instructor.

    Instructor: ( )
    You: _____ ?
    Instructor: ( )
    You: _____

110. Again.

    Instructor: ( )
    You: _____ ?
    Instructor: ( )
    You: _____

111. This time you start the conversation.

    (begin)
    You: _____
    Instructor: (Q)
    You: _____
    Instructor: ( )

112. Again.

    (begin)
    You: _____
    Instructor: (Q)
    You: _____
    Instructor: ( )

113. Now listen to this new sentence.

    ( )   ( )

6.13

210   INTRODUCTION TO FRENCH PHONOLOGY

114. Listen again. It's a question.

( ) ( )

115. Listen and imitate.

( )x ( )x ( )x

116. While looking at the meaning, listen and imitate.

The train's on time? (Fr)x (Fr)x (Fr)x

117. Listen and imitate while looking at the French.

Le train est à l'heure? ( )x ( )x ( )x

118. Here is the answer to that question. Listen.

( ) ( ) ( )

119. Listen again. How many nasal vowels do you hear?

( ) ( )

(3)

120. Listen to the last two words of the sentence.

( ) ( )

121. Listen and imitate.

( )x ( )x ( )x

122. Again.

( )x ( )x ( )x

123. Listen to the first part of the sentence.

( ) ( ) ( )

124. Listen again. How many syllables are there?

( ) ( )

(4)

125. Listen and imitate.

( )x ( )x ( )x

6.14

126. Again.

       ( )x ( )x ( )x

127. Listen to the second part and imitate.

       ( )x ( )x

128. Listen to and imitate the first part of the sentence; then the second.

       (1)x (2)x   (1)x (2)x

129. Here is the full sentence. Listen and imitate.

       ( ) ( )   ( )x ( )x ( )x

130. Imitate again.

       ( )x ( )x ( )x

131. Here is the meaning of that sentence. Look and listen.

       Yes. It has just pulled into the station. (Fr) (Fr)

132. Now, look at the French, listen and imitate.

       Oui. Il vient d'entrer en gare. ( )x ( )x ( )x

133. Answer your instructor.

       Instructor: (Q)
       You:_____

134. Again.

       Instructor: (Q)
       You:_____

135. You ask the question this time.

       (begin)
       You:_____?
       Instructor: ( )

136. Again.

       (begin)
       You:_____?
       Instructor: ( )

6.15

137. Here is a new word. Listen.

    ( ) ( ) ( )

138. This word has two syllables; be sure that they are equally stressed and that the rhythm is even. Listen again, then imitate.

    ( ) ( )   ( )x ( )x

139. Which is right? Number one or number two?

    (1) (2) (1) (2)

(2)

140. This time the rhythm is good, but the pronunciation is wrong. Listen.

    ( ) ( )

141. Of numbers (1), (2) and (3), which one is correct?

    (1) (2) (3)

(1)

142. Listen, look at the writing and imitate.

    ( ) ( ) merci ( )x ( )x ( )x

143. Answer your instructor.

    Instructor: (Q)
    You:_____
    Instructor: ( )

144. Again.

    Instructor: (Q)
    You:_____
    Instructor: ( )

145. You ask the question this time.

    (begin)
    You:_____?
    Instructor: ( )
    You:_____

INTRODUCTION TO FRENCH PHONOLOGY

146. Again.

>   (begin)
>   You: _____?
>   Instructor ( )
>   You: _____

147. Now, listen to the conversation from the beginning.

>   A: ( )
>   B: (?)
>   A: ( )
>   B: ( )
>   A: (?)
>   B: ( )
>   A: ( )

148. Listen to the conversation and imitate.

>   A: ( )x
>   B: (?)x
>   A: ( )x
>   B: ( )x
>   A: (?)x
>   B: ( )x
>   A: ( )x

149. Answer your instructor.

>   Instructor: ( )
>   You: _____?
>   Instructor: ( )
>   You: _____
>   Instructor: (Q)
>   You: _____
>   Instructor: ( )

150. Again.

>   Instructor: ( )
>   You: _____?
>   Instructor: ( )
>   You: _____
>   Instructor: (Q)
>   You: _____
>   Instructor: ( )

6.17

151. Listen to the conversation again.

   A: ( )
   B: (?)
   A: ( )
   B: ( )
   A: (?)
   B: ( )
   A: ( )

152. Begin the conversation.

   (begin)
   You:_____
   Instructor: (Q)
   You:_____
   Instructor: ( )
   You:_____?
   Instructor: ( )
   You:_____

153. Again.

   (begin)
   You:_____
   Instructor: (Q)
   You:_____
   Instructor: ( )
   You:_____?
   Instructor: ( )
   You:_____

154. Practice several times frames 147 to 153.

End of Chapter Six, Part One.

Report to your classroom.

INTRODUCTION TO FRENCH PHONOLOGY

Part Two

1.

Pronunciation of "ill-" (billet, bouillir)

1. Look at the following French word and listen.

    billet ( ) ( )

2. Listen again. Do you hear an "l"?

    ( ) ( )

    Student's answer: No

3. Here is another French word. How do you say it?

    piller x( )

4. With the exception of a limited number of French words, "ll" preceded by "i" is pronounced like the "y" in the English word "yes". Look and listen.

    quille ( ), fille ( ), vrille ( )

5. Here are other French words. Look and listen.

    bailler ( ), fouiller ( )

6. All the underlined parts of each of the following words are pronounced "y" like the "y" in the English word "yes".

    feu_ille_ ( ), fou_ille_ ( ), fa_ille_ ( ), f_ille_ ( )

7. The "ill is always pronounced "y" in the sequence: vowel + ill. Look and listen.

    feu/ille ( ), rou/ille ( ), trava/ille ( )

8. The "ill" is always pronounced "iy" when not preceded by a vowel. Look and listen.

    fille ( ), vrille ( ), famille ( )

6.19

9. Look at the following words. Is the "ill" pronounced "y" or "iy"?

    caille, feuille, maille

    Student's answer: __Y__

10. Say the following words before your instructor does.

    grille x( ), braille x( ), fourmille x( )

11. Now say these.

    piller x( ), maillet x( ), travailler x( ), fouiller x( )

12. How do you say the following words?

    fouler x( ), fouiller x( ), rouler x( ), rouiller x( )

13. The following words are exceptions to the preceding rule. Look and listen.

    a. ville ( ), villa ( ), village ( )
    b. mille ( ), millier ( ), million ( ), milliard ( )
    c. Lille ( ), tranquille (not recorded)

14. This time, look, listen and imitate.

    ville ( )x, mille ( )x, villa ( )x.

15. Look at the following words and say them.

    foule x( )
    fouille x( )
    ville x( )
    fille x( )
    malle x( )
    maille x( )
    travaillons x( )
    ailleurs x( )

6.20

INTRODUCTION TO FRENCH PHONOLOGY 217

2.

Explanation of "s'il vous plaît"

16. Look at the following expression. What does it mean in English?

    s'il vous plaît

    Student's answer: <u>Please</u>

17. Say it in French. Here it is.

    s'il vous plaît x( )

18. In French, the expression "s'il vous plaît" does not begin a sentence. Say the following.

    a. Deux allers, s'il vous plaît. x( )
    b. Oui, s'il vous plaît. x( )
    c. Deux billets, s'il vous plaît. x( )

19. The writing of "s'il vous plaît" is sometimes abbreviated. Look and listen.

    S.V.P. ( )

20. Look at these English sentences and say them in French.

    a. Next door, please.   French x( )
    b. In the evening, please.   x( )
    c. Round trip, please.   x( )

3.

Pronunciation of (vient, Dieu)

21. Say the following English sentence in French.

    The train has just pulled into the station. x( )

22. Look at this word and listen. How many syllables does it contain.

    vient ( )

    Student's answer: <u>1</u>

6.21

23. Listen to the word again. Is the pronunciation right or wrong?

   ( )

   Student's answer: <u>W</u>

24. Here is a different word. How many syllables does it have? Listen.

   ( )

   Student's answer: <u>1</u>

25. Say the following words. Be sure that you are only pronouncing one syllable.

   bien x( ), tien x( ), sien x( )

26. Listen to this word. How many syllables do you hear?

   ( )

   Student's answer: <u>1</u>

27. Here are more words. Look and listen.

   ciel ( ), dieu ( ), tien ( ), rien ( ),
   fier ( ), tier ( ).

28. Now, say these before your instructor does.

   cieux x( ), miel x( ), mieux x( ),
   pied x( ), bien x( ), pion x( )

29. Listen to words 1 and 2. Are they (S) same or (D) different?

   (1)/(2)

   Student's answer: <u>D</u>

30. Listen again. How many syllables does each of them have?

   (1)/(2)

   Student's answer: 1. <u>2</u> 2. <u>1</u>

6.22

INTRODUCTION TO FRENCH PHONOLOGY

31. Look at those two words, listen and imitate.

    piller ( )x, pied ( )x

32. Say the following words.

    milieu   x( )
    mieux   x( )
    adieu   x( )
    pillons x( )
    pion   x( )
    premier x( )
    piano   x( )

4.

"e" continued. (Il ne sait pas/je ne sais pas)

33. Look at the following sentence and listen. Notice that the underlined "e" is not pronounced.

    aller et r<u>e</u>tour? ( )

34. Do you remember these two words? Look and listen.

    sam<u>e</u>di ( ), seul<u>e</u>ment ( )

35. You also know that you may omit the "e" when it is surrounded by only two consonnants. Look at these words and listen.

    mann~~e~~quin ( ), él~~e~~vé ( ).

36. But it is pronounced when it is surrounded by three or more consonnants. Look and listen.

    âp<u>re</u>té ( ), fe<u>rme</u>ture ( ), ca<u>lme</u>ment ( ).

37. Up to now, we have been concerned with isolated words in which the "e" is retained or dropped according to the number of consonnants surrounding it. Look and listen.

    gouve<u>rne</u>ment ( ), habi<u>le</u>té ( ), bre<u>ve</u>té ( )

38. Notice also that the syllable in which the "e" may be omitted is never the first one. Look and listen.

    rapi<u>de</u>ment ( ), bijou<u>te</u>rie ( )

6.23

39. Here are words containing the "e" in the first syllable. Look and listen. Is the "e" of the first syllable pronounced?

    menace ( ), demain ( ), petit ( )

    Student's answer: <u>Yes</u>

40. In lesson three, we also mentioned one-syllable words in which the "e" is retained. Look and listen.

    le ( ), ne ( ), me ( ), de ( )

41. However, listen to "ne" in this phrase.

    Je <u>ne</u> sais pas. ( )

42. Was the "e" in "ne" pronounced? Look and listen again.

    Je <u>ne</u> sais pas. ( )

    Student's answer: <u>No</u>

43. Since French phrases are pronounced as if they were one continuous long word, the rules apply to the entire uninterrupted phrase as they do to isolated words. Listen.

    ne ( )

    but

    je <u>ne</u> sais pas. ( )

44. Would you pronounce the "e" in this phrase?

    Vous ne partez pas.

    Student's answer: <u>No</u>

45. Now listen to the phrase above.

    ( )

46. Here is another phrase. Would the "e" be pronounced?

    Il ne sait pas.

    Student's answer: <u>Yes</u>

6.24

INTRODUCTION TO FRENCH PHONOLOGY

47. Now listen to the phrase.

    ( )

48. Look, listen and imitate.

    a. Je ne sais pas.   ( )x
    b. Il ne sait pas.   ( )x
    c. Les menaces.   ( )x
    d. Il part demain.   ( )x
    e. A demain.   ( )x

49. Look at sentences a, b, and c. Should the underlined "e" be pronounced in all three sentences?

    a. Vous le savez.
    b. Avez-vous le billet?
    c. Vous ne déjeunez pas?

    Student's answer: No

50. In which sentences should the underlined "e" be pronounced?

    a. Pour le matin.
    b. Aller et retour?
    c. Je ne vais pas déjeuner.
    d. Il ne vient pas.

    Student's answer: a, d

51. Say the following sentences before your instructor does.

    a. Vous y allez le samedi?   x( )
    b. Je ne veux pas entrer.   x( )
    c. Il me plait.   x( )
    d. Je pars samedi.   x( )
    e. Est-ce que vous le voulez?   x( )
    f. Je suis en retard.   x( )

5.

Numbers 1, 2, 5, 9, 10, 18, 40, 50, 59

52. Say the following numbers in French.

```
2    x( )
1    x( )
10   x( )
5    x( )
9    x( )
18   x( )
50   x( )
40   x( )
59   x( )
```

53. Now say this in French.

```
It's 10 o'clock.   x( )
It's 5 o'clock.    x( )
It's 2 o'clock.    x( )
It's 1 o'clock.    x( )
```

54. Here are more sentences. Say them in French.

```
Is there a train for Paris at 2 o'clock?   x( )
Is there a train for Paris at 10 o'clock?  x( )
Is there a train for Paris at 1 o'clock?   x( )
Is there a train for Paris at 5 o'clock?   x( )
Is there a train for Paris at 6 o'clock?   x( )
```

55. Your instructor is going to ask you some questions. Answer them according to the following example. Part of your answer is in parenthesis.

```
Question  (Q)   (à une heure)
Answer:         ( )
```

```
a.   (Q)   (à cinq heures)        You:  x( )
b.   (Q)   (dix heures cinq)      You:  x( )
c.   (Q)   (à dix huit heures)    You:  x( )
d.   (Q)   (à midi)               You:  x( )
e.   (Q)   (à deux heures)        You:  x( )
f.   (Q)   (à une heure)          You:  x( )
g.   (Q)   (cinq heures dix)      You:  x( )
```

INTRODUCTION TO FRENCH PHONOLOGY

6.

Review

56. Here is a review. Look at the following words and sentences. Say them before your instructor does.

    a.   J'arrive à midi.   x( )
          Allez-vous à Paris?   x( )
          Partez-vous samedi?   x( )
          Il arrive à Paris.   x( )
          Vous partez mardi.   x( )

    b.   J'ai déjeuné.   x( )
          Avez-vous déjeuné?   x( )
          Je veux leur parler.   x( )
          Il ne veut pas leur parler.   x( )

    c.   Il ne veut pas venir.   x( )
          Deux allers et retours   x( )
            s'il vous plaît.
          Vous ne savez pas tout.   x( )
          Je dois me sauver.   x( )
          Tout le monde est ici.   x( )

    d.   Nous en avons cinq.   x( )
          Vous en avez cent.   x( )
          Ils ont du vin blanc.   x( )
          Le vin blanc est bon.   x( )
          Il en faut cinquante.   x( )

    e.   Il est près de la gare.   x( )
          Il est en face de la gare.   x( )
          L'hôtel est près de la gare.   x( )
          Je dois le faire maintenant.   x( )
          Je viens d'arriver.   x( )
          Je viens de leur parler.   x( )
          J'ai perdu mes billets.   x( )

    f.   Il faut qu'il aille en ville.   x( )
          Il m'en faut mille.   x( )
          Nous devons aller travailler.   x( )
          Ma fille est en ville.   x( )

Report to your classroom.

7.

Preparation

Exercice un

Dites en français

1.	One way	1.	Un aller
2.	The train	2.	Le train
3.	Thanks	3.	Merci
4.	One franc	4.	Un franc
5.	A round trip (ticket)	5.	Un aller et retour
6.	Please	6.	S'il vous plaît
7.	Two tickets	7.	Deux billets
8.	Two round trip (tickets)	8.	Deux aller et retour
9.	One round trip	9.	Un aller et retour
10.	Fifty francs	10.	Cinquante francs
11.	On time	11.	A l'heure
12.	He just came in	12.	Il vient d'entrer
13.	Nine francs	13.	Neuf francs
14.	Forty	14.	Quarante

Exercice deux

Dites en anglais

1.	Je vais souvent à Paris.	1.	I go to Paris often.
2.	Vous y allez samedi?	2.	You are going (there) Saturday?
3.	Avez-vous un aller et retour?	3.	Do you have a round trip (ticket)?
4.	A quelle heure allez-vous à la gare?	4.	At what time are you going to the station?
5.	Il vient d'entrer au café.	5.	He just went in the café.
6.	Il vient de manquer le train.	6.	He just missed the train.
7.	Il vient d'entrer.	7.	He just came in.
8.	Il vient de téléphoner.	8.	He just phoned.
9.	Il vient d'arriver.	9.	He just arrived.
10.	Il vient de déjeuner.	10.	He just had lunch.
11.	Le café est à côté.	11.	The café is next door.
12.	La gare est à côté.	12.	The station is next door.
13.	Le train est à l'heure.	13.	The train is on time.
14.	Je suis en retard.	14.	I'm late.
15.	Je vais à la gare.	15.	I'm going to the station.

INTRODUCTION TO FRENCH PHONOLOGY

Exercice trois

Dites en français

1.	Where is the train?	1.	Où est le train?
2.	The train just came into the station.	2.	Le train vient d'entrer en gare.
3.	What time is the first train for Paris?	3.	A quelle heure est le premier train pour Paris?
4.	Am I on time?	4.	Est-ce que je suis à l'heure?
5.	Here you are Sir.	5.	Voilà Monsieur.
6.	He just entered the café.	6.	Il vient d'entrer au café.
7.	The train has just arrived.	7.	Le train vient d'arriver.
8.	It's nine francs forty.	8.	C'est neuf francs quarante.
9.	There is a train at five.	9.	Il y a un train à cinq heures.
10.	The first train is at two o'clock.	10.	Le premier train est à deux heures.
11.	Did you have lunch?	11.	Avez-vous déjeuné?
12.	The train is often late.	12.	Le train est souvent en retard.
13.	Two one way tickets, please.	13.	Deux allers, s'il vous plaît.
14.	Are you leaving at ten o'clock?	14.	Partez-vous à dix heures?
15.	Two one way (tickets) only.	15.	Deux aller seulement.
16.	Do you have a ticket?	16.	Avez-vous un billet?
17.	It's fifty nine francs ten.	17.	C'est cinquante neuf francs dix.
18.	It's in the evening.	18.	C'est dans la soirée.
19.	One first class ticket, round trip to Paris, please.	19.	Un billet de première aller et retour pour Paris, S.V.P.
20.	It's forty francs.	20.	C'est quarante francs.

Exercice quatre

<u>Questions</u>   <u>Réponses possibles</u>

1. Où allez-vous?   1. Je vais déjeuner.
                                            Je vais au café.
                                            Je vais à côté.

6.29

2. Quand partez-vous?   2. Je pars le matin.
                                 Je pars l'après-midi.
                                 Je pars samedi.
                                 Je pars dans la soirée.
                                 Je pars samedi matin.
                                 Je pars samedi dans la soirée.
                                 Je pars samedi après-midi.

3. Le train est en retard?   3. Oui, il est en retard de
                                    quelques minutes.
                                 Oui, de dix minutes.
                                 Non. Il vient d'entrer en
                                    gare.
                                 Non. Il est à l'heure.

4. Le train est à l'heure?   4. Oui, il vient d'entrer
                                    en gare.
                                 Oui, il est à l'heure.
                                 Non. Il est en retard.
                                 Non. Il est en retard de ...

Exercice cinq

Conversation dirigée

(In instructor's manual only)

Exercice six

Conversation dirigée

(In instructor's manual only)

Excercice sept

Conversation dirigée

(In instructor's manual only)

Exercice huit

Dites en français

1. Where are you going?   1. Où allez-vous?
2. You are leaving?   2. Vous partez?
3. I'm leaving at ten past   3. Je pars à cinq heures dix.
   five.
4. Here you are Sir.   4. Voilà Monsieur.
5. You go there often?   5. Vous y allez souvent?
6. Are there any?   6. Est-ce qu'il y en a?

6.30

INTRODUCTION TO FRENCH PHONOLOGY

7.	Did you miss it?	7.	Vous l'avez manqué?
8.	There are two trains in the afternoon.	8.	Il y a deux trains l'après-midi.
9.	When am I leaving?	9.	Quand est-ce que je pars?
10.	No. Not next door.	10.	Non. Pas à côté.
11.	Yes. Saturday.	11.	Oui. Samedi.
12.	It's for Paris.	12.	C'est pour Paris.
13.	No, not often.	13.	Non. Pas souvent.
14.	I often go to lunch next door.	14.	Je vais souvent déjeuner à côté.
15.	It's next door	15.	C'est à côté.
16.	What time are you leaving?	16.	A quelle heure partez-vous?
17.	You're going to Paris?	17.	Vous allez à Paris?

Exercice neuf

Expansion

	Professeur		Elève
1.	un train	1.	un train.
2.	Il y a	2.	Il y a un train.
3.	pour Paris	3.	Il y a un train pour Paris.
4.	à cinq heures dix huit	4.	Il y a un train pour Paris à cinq heures dix huit.
5.	est-ce que	5.	Est-ce qu'il y a un train pour Paris à cinq heures dix huit?

Exercice dix

Expansion

	Professeur		Elève
1.	le train	1.	le train.
2.	est en retard	2.	Le train est en retard.
3.	de dix heures cinq	3.	Le train de dix heures cinq est en retard.
4.	de cinq minutes	4.	Le train de dix heures cinq est en retard de cinq minutes.

Exercice onze

Expansion

Professeur	Elève
1. samedi	1. samedi.
2. je pars	2. Je pars samedi.
3. après-midi	3. Je pars samedi après-midi.
4. à deux heures	4. Je pars samedi après-midi à deux heures.
5. dix	5. Je pars samedi après-midi à deux heures dix.

Exercice douze

Expansion

Professeur	Elève
1. un billet	1. un billet.
2. vous avez	2. vous avez un billet.
3. de première	3. Vous avez un billet de première.
4. pour Paris	4. Vous avez un billet de première pour Paris.
5. est-ce que	5. Est-ce que vous avez un billet de première pour Paris?

8.

Reading exercices.

1. Read.

    1. quille; mille; bille; ville
    2. fille; villa; piller; billet
    3. maille; malle; caille; taille
    4. rouille; mouillé; fouiller; bouillir
    5. feuille; effeuiller; meilleur; ailleurs

2. Read.

    1. mieux; pied; piller; pilier
    2. tien; mien; pion; lieu
    3. vieux; vieillir; voilier; milieu
    4. Dieu; métier; premier; panier
    5. soulier; souiller; entier; grillé

6.32

3. Read

    1. Nous avons fini.
    2. Nous n'avons pas fini.
    3. Nous avons déjeuné.
    4. Nous n'avons pas déjeuné.
    5. Nous avons compris.
    6. Nous n'avons pas compris.
    7. Nous l'avons fini.
    8. Nous ne l'avons pas fini.
    9. Nous en avons trouvé.
    10. Nous n'en avons pas trouvé.

4. Read.

    1. Ils ont du pain.
    2. Ils n'ont pas de pain.
    3. Ils ont du temps.
    4. Ils n'ont pas de temps.
    5. Ils ont du vin.
    6. Ils n'ont pas de vin.
    7. Ils ont du poisson.
    8. Ils n'ont pas de poisson.
    9. Ils ont du sucre.
    10. Ils n'ont pas de sucre.

5. Read.

    1. Je ne pars pas.
    2. Il ne part pas.
    3. Nous ne partons pas.
    4. Je ne veux pas.
    5. Il ne veut pas.
    6. Nous ne voulons pas.
    7. Je ne vais pas bien.
    8. Il ne va pas bien.
    9. Marie ne va pas bien.
    10. Il ne part pas aujourd'hui.

6. Read.

    1. J'ai un ami d'enfance.
    2. J'ai deux amis américains.
    3. Il a cinq billets.
    4. Ils ont cinq enfants.
    5. Il nous faut neuf places.
    6. Ils ont dix enfants.
    7. Il est une heure dix.
    8. J'ai dix francs.

9. C'est cinquante francs.
10. Il a quanrante ans.
11. Il est dix heures cinq.
12. Elle a dix huit ans.
13. C'est le numéro cinquante neuf.
14. Il a cinq ans.

7. Read.

1. Il y en a beaucoup?
2. Y allez-vous tous les jours?
3. En avez-vous beaucoup?
4. Est-ce qu'il y en a d'autres?
5. Combien en avez-vous?
6. Quand pensez-vous y aller?
7. Y pensez-vous toujours?
8. A quelle heure allons-nous partir?
9. Est-ce qu'il y va souvent?
10. Que vous a-t-on dit?

Chapter Six, end of Part Two.

Go to lab for Test 1 to 4.

INTRODUCTION TO FRENCH PHONOLOGY 231

Chapter Six, Part Three

Tests

Test 1

Rewrite the following sentences and put a slash across any "e" which is not pronounced.

Example: You write:

Je ne veux pas cette liste.   je n/e veux pas cett/e list/e.

1. Je sais ce qu'il veut.   1. _____
2. Il arrive à la gare.   2. _____
3. Voulez-vous le billet?   3. _____
4. Elle ne me dit pas tout.   4. _____
5. Je m'occupe de tout.   5. _____
6. Je pars demain.   6. _____
7. On y va samedi.   7. _____
8. Mercredi ou vendredi?   8. _____
9. Est-ce que vous avez le   9. _____
    numéro?
10. Vous me parlez?   10. _____
11. Il y a beaucoup de cafés   11. _____
    à Paris?
12. C'est à côté de la gare.   12. _____
13. Vous souvenez-vous de son   13. _____
    nom?
14. Il ne le sait pas.   14. _____
15. Je ne le sais pas.   15. _____

Test 2

Look at the following words and listen to the pronunciation. Check whether the pronunciation is right or wrong.

				Right	Wrong
1.	bailler	( )	1.	_____	_____
2.	bouillir	( )	2.	_____	_____
3.	piailler	( )	3.	_____	_____
4.	pallier	( )	4.	_____	_____
5.	paille	( )	5.	_____	_____
6.	malle	( )	6.	_____	_____
7.	maille	( )	7.	_____	_____
8.	mouiller	( )	8.	_____	_____
9.	mille	( )	9.	_____	_____
10.	ville	( )	10.	_____	_____
11.	village	( )	11.	_____	_____
12.	million	( )	12.	_____	_____

Test 3

Listen to the following words. How many syllables do they have?

Number of syllables

1. ( )   1. _____
2. ( )   2. _____
3. ( )   3. _____
4. ( )   4. _____
5. ( )   5. _____
6. ( )   6. _____
7. ( )   7. _____

8. ( )   8. _____
9. ( )   9. _____
10. ( )   10. _____
11. ( )   11. _____
12. ( )   12. _____
13. ( )   13. _____
14. ( )   14. _____
15. ( )   15. _____

Test 4

Listen and write.

1. ( )   1. _____
2. ( )   2. _____
3. ( )   3. _____
4. ( )   4. _____
5. ( )   5. _____
6. ( )   6. _____
7. ( )   7. _____
8. ( )   8. _____
9. ( )   9. _____
10. ( )   10. _____
11. ( )   11. _____
12. ( )   12. _____

END OF CHAPTER SIX

Chapter Seven

PART 1

Dialogue. (Laboratory)

PART 2

1. Pronunciation of final "l." (Laboratory)

2. English meaning of "il." (Laboratory)

3. Pronunciation of written "ch." (Laboratory)

4. Pronunciation of the consonant "g." (Laboratory)

5. The negative form with "ne...pas." (Laboratory)

6. Review. (Laboratory)

7. Preparation for Class (Homework)

8. Reading exercises. (Classroom)

PART 3

Tests. (Classroom and laboratory)

Chapter Seven

Dialogue

A.	Vous êtes toujours à l'hôtel?	-You're still at the hotel?
B.	Oui, mais nous avons enfin un appartement.	-Yes, but we finally have an apartment.
A:	Vous avez de la chance. Comment est-il?	-You're lucky. How is it?
B.	Il n'est pas très grand mais moderne.	-It's not very large but modern.
A.	Vous emménagez bientôt?	-You're moving in soon?
B.	Pas avant la fin du mois.	-Not until the end of the month.

INTRODUCTION TO FRENCH PHONOLOGY

Part One

1. Listen to the following conversation in French.

    A: (?)
    B: ( )
    A: (?)
    B: ( )
    A: (?)
    B: ( )

2. Listen again to the conversation.

    A: (?)
    B: ( )
    A: (?)
    B: ( )
    A: (?)
    B: ( )

3. This is the first sentence of the conversation. Listen.

    ( ) ( ) ( )

4. Here are the last three words of the sentence. Listen.

    ( ) ( ) ( )

5. Listen again. Notice the last syllable.

    ( ) ( ) ( )

6. Here are the three words again. Notice the last consonant.

    ( ) ( ) ( )

7. The final consonant is wrong. Listen.

    (W) (W) (W)

8. This is the right, wrong, right pronunciation of that last consonant. Listen.

    (R) (W) (R)

9. Listen to the correct pronunciation.

    ( ) ( ) ( )

7.3

INTRODUCTION TO FRENCH PHONOLOGY

10. Listen and imitate the French pronunciation.

    ( )x ( )x ( )x

11. Imitate again.

    ( )x ( )x ( )x

12. We'll add one more word to the three that you know. Listen.

    ( ) ( ) ( )

13. Listen and imitate.

    ( )x ( )x ( )x

14. Again.

    ( )x ( )x ( )x

15. Now the sentence is complete. Listen.

    ( ) ( ) ( )

16. Listen again. How many syllables do you hear?

    ( ) ( ) ( )

(7)

17. Look at the sentence while listening again.

    Vous êtes toujours à l'hôtel? ( ) ( ) ( )

18. This time listen and imitate.

    ( )x ( )x ( )x

19. Again.

    ( )x ( )x ( )x

20. Look at the meaning while imitating.

    You're still at the hotel? ( )x ( )x ( )x

21. Repeat No. 20.

22. Is this (R) or (W)?

    ( ) ( )

(W)

7.4

238 INTRODUCTION TO FRENCH PHONOLOGY

23. This is right. Listen.

( ) ( )

24. Which is right No. 1 or No. 2?

(1)/(2)   (1)/(2)

(1)

25. Imitate the correct pronunciation.

( )x ( )x ( )x

26. This is the answer to the sentence you have just repeated. Listen.

( ) ( ) ( )

27. Listen to the last word.

( ) ( ) ( )

28. Listen and imitate.

( ) ( ) ( )x ( )x ( )x

29. We'll add a couple of words. Listen.

( ) ( ) ( )

30. Listen again. How many syllables are there?

( ) ( )

(7)

31. Listen. How many nasal vowels do you hear?

( ) ( ) ( )

(4)

32. How many different kinds of nasals do you hear?

( ) ( ) ( )

(3)

33. Are the vowels in the first and last syllables the same?

( ) ( )

(yes)

7.5

INTRODUCTION TO FRENCH PHONOLOGY 239

34. Listen and imitate. Notice the rhythm.

    ( )x ( )x ( )x

35. Imitate again. Be careful not to pronounce an "n" at the end of the nasal vowels.

    ( )x ( )x ( )x

36. Here are two more words added to the sentence. Listen.

    ( ) ( ) ( )

37. Listen again. How many syllables have a nasal vowel?

    ( ) ( ) ( )

(5)

38. Now listen and imitate.

    ( )x ( )x ( )x

39. Look at the meaning and listen.

    We finally have an apartment. ( ) ( )

40. This is the way it's written in French. Look and listen.

    Nous avons enfin un appartement. ( ) ( )

41. Now listen and imitate.

    ( )x ( )x ( )x

42. This is the complete sentence. Listen.

    ( ) ( ) ( )

43. Listen again. How many syllables are there?

    ( ) ( )

(12)

44. Listen and imitate.

    ( )x ( )x ( )x

7.6

INTRODUCTION TO FRENCH PHONOLOGY

45. Listen carefully to the rhythm of the sentence and imitate.

    ( )x ( )x ( )x

46. Listen to the following exchange while looking at the meaning.

    A: (?) You're still at the hotel?
    B: ( ) Yes, but we finally have an apartment.

47. Listen again.

    A: (?)
    B: ( )

48. Answer your instructor.

    Instructor: (Q)
    You:_____

49. Again.

    Instructor: (Q)
    You:_____

50. This time ask the question then listen to the answer.

    (begin)
    You:_____?
    Instructor: (A)

51. Again.

    (begin)
    You:_____?
    Instructor: (A)

52. Here is another sentence. Listen.

    ( ) ( ) ( )

53. Look at the meaning and listen to the French.

    You're lucky. ( ) ( )

54. Listen again. How many syllables are there?

    ( ) ( ) ( )

(5)

55. Listen to the (W) pronunciation of that sentence.

    (W) (W)

56. And now the (R) and (W) pronunciation.

    (R)/(W) (R)/(W)

57. Listen and imitate.

    ( )x ( )x ( )x

58. Look at the French sentence and listen again.

    Vous avez de la chance. ( ) ( )

59. Imitate again. Be careful not to mispronounce the vowels.

    ( )x ( )x ( )x

60. Is the following (R) or (W)?

    ( )

(W)

61. How about this time? Is it (R) or (W)?

    ( )

(W)

62. Which is right? No. 1 or No. 2?

    (1)/(2) (1)/(2)

(1)

63. Which one is right? No. 1, 2 or 3?

    (1)/(2)/(3)

(3)

64. Imitate the correct pronunciation.

    ( )x ( )x ( )x

65. Look again at the sentence and imitate.

    Vous avez de la chance. ( )x ( )x ( )x

7.8

66. Here is a new sentence. Listen.

    ( )   ( )   ( )

67. Listen carefully to the last syllable.

    ( )   ( )   ( )

68. This is the wrong pronunciation of the last syllable of that sentence. Listen.

    (W)   (W)   (W)

69. This is the right pronunciation.

    (R)   (R)

70. Which one is right? No. 1 or No. 2?

    (1)/(2)   (1)/(2)

(2)

71. Listen to the correct pronunciation and imitate.

    ( )x   ( )x   ( )x

72. Again.

    ( )x   ( )x   ( )x

73. Look at the meaning and imitate the French sentence.

    How is it?   ( )x   ( )x   ( )x

74. And now the French writing; look, listen and imitate.

    Comment est-il?   ( )x   ( )x

75. You remember this sentence. Listen.

    ( )   ( )

76. Listen now to both sentences.

    ( )   ( )   ( )

77. Here is the meaning again. Look and listen.

    You're lucky. How is it?   ( )   ( )

7.9

INTRODUCTION TO FRENCH PHONOLOGY

78. Now listen and imitate.

    ( )x ( )x ( )x

79. Is the following pronunciation correct? Listen.

    ( ) ( )

(no)

80. Here is the correct pronunciation. Listen and imitate.

    ( )x ( )x ( )x

81. Listen carefully to the rhythm and pronunciation and imitate.

    ( )x ( )x ( )x

82. Again.

    ( )x ( )x ( )x

83. Listen to this new sentence.

    ( ) ( ) ( )

84. Listen again. How many syllables are there?

    ( ) ( )

(8)

85. Listen to the last word of the sentence.

    ( ) ( ) ( )

86. Listen to the (R)/(W) pronunciation of that word.

    (R)/(W)   (R)/(W)

87. Which word is (R)? Nos. 1, 2 or 3?

    (1) (2) (3)

(3)

88. Listen to the right pronunciation and say "modern" in French.

    ( )x ( )x ( )x

7.10

89. We'll add one word to the word you know. Listen first.
    Then listen and imitate.

    ( )   ( )   ( )x   ( )x   ( )x

90. Imitate again.

    ( )x   ( )x

91. We'll add three more words. Listen.

    ( )   ( )   ( )

92. Listen again. Which syllable contains a nasal vowel?

    ( )   ( )   ( )

(3)

93. Now listen and imitate.

    ( )x   ( )x   ( )x

94. Listen carefully to the pronunciation and imitate again.

    ( )x   ( )x   ( )x

95. Is the following pronunciation (R) or (W)? Listen.

    ( )   ( )

(R)

96. Listen and imitate.

    ( )x   ( )x   ( )x

97. Is the following pronunciation (R) or (W)? Listen.

    ( )   ( )

(W)

98. Is it right this time?

    ( )   ( )

(no)

99. Listen to the right pronunciation and imitate.

    ( )x   ( )x   ( )x

7.11

INTRODUCTION TO FRENCH PHONOLOGY

100. Here is the complete sentence. Listen.

    ( ) ( ) ( )

101. Listen again. How many syllables are there?

    ( ) ( ) ( )

(8)

102. Listen and imitate.

    ( )x ( )x ( )x

103. Look at the meaning, listen and imitate.

    It's not very large but modern. ( )x ( )x ( )x

104. Now look, listen to the French and imitate.

    Il n'est pas très grand mais moderne. ( )x ( )x ( )x

105. Imitate again.

    ( )x ( )x ( )x

106. Listen to the following exchange.

    A: (?)
    B: ( )
    A: (?)
    B: ( )

107. Listen to each sentence and imitate.

    A: (?)x
    B: ( )x
    A: (?)x
    B: ( )x

108. Again.

    A: (?)x
    B: ( )x
    A: (?)x
    B: ( )x

109. Answer your instructor.

    Instructor: (Q)
    You:_____
    Instructor: (Q)
    You:_____

7.12

246 INTRODUCTION TO FRENCH PHONOLOGY

110. Repeat No. 109.

111. Ask the question this time, then listen to the answer.

    (Begin)
    You:_____?
    Instructor:　(A)
    You:_____?
    Instructor:　(A)

112. Repeat No. 111.

113. Here is another question. Listen.

    ( ) ( ) ( )

114. Listen again. How many nasal vowels do you hear?

    ( ) ( )

(2)

115. How many syllables do you hear?

    ( ) ( )

(7)

116. This is the last word of the question. How many syllables does it have?

    ( ) ( )

(2)

117. Listen to the word. Then imitate it.

    ( ) ( ) ( )x ( )x ( )x

118. Listen to the sentence again.

    ( ) ( )

119. Now listen and imitate.

    ( )x ( )x

120. Again.

    ( )x ( )x

121. Look at the French sentence and listen.

    Vous emménagez bientôt?　( ) ( ) ( )

INTRODUCTION TO FRENCH PHONOLOGY 247

122. Look at the French sentence this time and imitate.

    Vous emménagez bientôt? ( )x ( )x

123. Now look at the meaning, listen and imitate.

    You're moving in soon? (Fr)x (Fr)x

124. This is the answer to the question. Listen.

    ( ) ( ) ( )

125. Listen again. Notice the rhythm of every syllable.

    (.) ( ) ( )

126. How many syllables do you hear?

    ( ) ( )

(7)

127. Do the first four syllables contain the same vowel sound?

    (- - - - - -)   (- - - - - -)
    1 2 3 4 5 6 7   1 2 3 4 5 6 7

(no)

128. Which of the first four is different from the others?

    (- - - - - -)   (- - - - - -)
    1 2 3 4 5 6 7   1 2 3 4 5 6 7

(3)

129. Listen and imitate the sentence.

    ( )x ( )x ( )x

130. Imitate again.

    ( )x ( )x

131. Is this (R) or (W)?

    ( ) ( )

(W)

132. Is it right now?

    ( ) ( )

(R)

7.14

133. How is it this time?

      ( ) ( )

(R)

134. Imitate the correct pronunciation.

      ( )x ( )x ( )x

135. Imitate again while looking at the French sentence.

      Pas avant la fin du mois. ( )x ( )x ( )x

136. Listen again and imitate.

      ( )x ( )x ( )x

137. Listen to the whole conversation.

      A: (?)
      B: ( )
      A: (?)
      B: ( )
      A: (?)
      B: ( )

138. Listen to No. 137.

139. Look at the meaning again and listen to the French (FR).

      A: You're still at the hotel? (Fr)
      B: Yes, but we finally have an apartment. (Fr)
      A: You're lucky. How is it? (Fr)
      B: It's not very large but modern. (Fr)
      A: You're moving in soon? (Fr)
      B: Not until the end of the month. (Fr)

140. Listen to the conversation and imitate each sentence.

      A: (?)x
      B: ( )x
      A: (?)x
      B: ( )x
      A: (?)x
      B: ( )x

141. Answer your instructor.

      Instructor: (Q)
      You:_____
      Instructor: (Q)
      You:_____
      Instructor: (Q)
      You:_____

INTRODUCTION TO FRENCH PHONOLOGY

142. Repeat No. 141.

143. Listen to the conversation again.

        A: (?)
        B: ( )
        A: (?)
        B: ( )
        A: (?)
        B: ( )

144. Now ask the questions. Your instructor will answer you.

    (begin)
    You: _____?
    Instructor: (A)
    You: _____?
    Instructor: (A)
    You: _____?
    Instructor: (A)

145. Repeat No. 144.

146. Practice frames 137 to 145 several times.

End of Chapter Seven, Part One.

Report to your classroom.

Part Two

1

Pronunciation of final "l"

1. Say the following English sentence in French.

    You're still at the hotel? x( )

2. Now look at that sentence and listen. Notice the final "l".

    Vous êtes toujours à l'hôtel? ( )

3. Is the following pronunciation right or wrong?

    l'hôtel ( ) ( )

    Student's answer: <u>W</u>

4. Here are other words ending with "l". Is the pronunciation right or wrong?

    ville( )   foule( )   mal( )   sol( )

    Student's answer: <u>W</u>

5. Of the following words, one is not pronounced correctly. Which one is it?

    1. belle( )   2. cil( )   3. poule( )   4. seul( )

    Student's answer: <u>3</u>

6. Look at the following words and imitate your instructor.

    belle( )x   il( )x   mal( )x   foule( )x

7. Say the following words before your instructor does.

    l'hôpital x( )   l'hôtel x( )   l'ampoule x( )
    Emile x( )   difficile x( )   tilleul x( )

8. Now say these sentences.

    a. Il nous appelle. x( )
    b. Elle m'appelle. x( )
    c. Je l'appelle. x( )
    d. Elle est seule. x( )
    e. Il est seul. x( )

7.17

INTRODUCTION TO FRENCH PHONOLOGY

9. Look at this question and listen.

    Vous êtes toujours à l'hotel? ( )

10. Look at the sentence again and make a question by inverting word 1 and word 2.

    <u>Vous</u> <u>êtes</u> toujours à l'hôtel? x( )
      1   2

11. We'll write what you've said. Is the writing correct?

    Etes vous toujours à l'hôtel?

    Student's answer: <u>No</u>

12. Which sentence is correctly written no. 1 or No. 2?

    1. Etes vous toujours à l'hôtel?
    2. Etes-vous toujours à l'hôtel?

    Student's answer: <u>2</u>

13. Look at the following sentence and change it into a question by inverting the subject and the verb: Il est....

    Il est à l'hôtel. x( )

14. Here are more sentences to change into questions.

    Il est à côté.   x( )
    Il est au café.   x( )
    Il est midi.   x( )
    Il est en retard.   x( )
    Il est cinq heures. x( )

2

<u>Subject pronoun "il" and its English meanings.</u>

15. Translate the following sentences into English.

    a. Il est midi.
    b. Il vient déjeuner.

    Student's answer: a. <u>It's noon.</u>
                            b. <u>He's coming for lunch.</u>

7.18

16. Notice that the subject "il" means he or it. In the following sentence determine whether "il" means "he" or "it".

    Il est dix heures.

    Student's answer: it

17. What is "il" in this sentence?

    Il vient d'emménager à l'hôtel.

    Student's answer: he

18. Here is another sentence. What is "il" this time?

    Il est dans le train.

    Student's answer: it or he

19. Translate the following into French.

    a. He's on the train. x( )
    b. It's on the train. x( )

20. Now translate these into French.

    a. We have an apartment; it's very large. x( )
    b. The train in on time; it has just pulled into the station. x( )

21. Replace the underlined words by the appropriate subject pronoun and end the sentence.

    Le train est en retard. x( )

22. Here are more sentences.

    a. Le café est à côté. x( )
    b. Le train vient d'entrer en gare. x( )
    c. L'appartement est très moderne. x( )
    d. Le premier train est à huit heures. x( )

23. Here are sentences with words that have not been introduced. Replace the underlined words by the subject pronoun "il".

    Son fiancé est américain. x( )
    Mon cousin arrive samedi. x( )
    Le directeur de la compagnie est toujours à l'heure. x( )
    Le téléphone est installé. x( )

INTRODUCTION TO FRENCH PHONOLOGY

24. These are questions. Replace the underlined words by "il".

    Comment est l'appartement?   x( )
    Où est l'hôtel?   x( )
    Où est votre billet?   x( )
    Comment est le café?   x( )

3

Pronunciation of written "ch"

25. Look at the following word and say it.

    chance   x( )

26. Here is the word again. Listen to the right then the wrong pronunciation.

    chance   (R)   chance   (W)

27. How do you say these words?

    chaud x( )   chant x( )   méchant x( )

28. Here are other words with "ch" in different positions. Listen and imitate.

    marche   ( )x   machine   ( )x   chemin   ( )x

29. Now say the following words.

    la mouche   x( )
    les chats   x( )
    chercher   x( )
    chaque   x( )
    séchoir   x( )
    chercheur   x( )
    chiffon   x( )

4

Pronunciation of written "g"

30. Here is a familiar word. Look and listen

    je   ( )

31. How do you say "I" in French?

    x( )

7.20

32. Here is another word. The underlined consonant sounds exactly like "j". Listen to the whole word.

    emménagez ( )

33. Listen and imitate.

    argent ( )x agent ( )x figer ( )x emerger ( )x
    agiter ( )x cageot ( )x

34. Say the following words.

    figer x( ) agir x( ) fugitif x( )

35. When the consonant "g" is immediately followed by the vowels "e" or "i" it is always pronounced "j". Look and listen.

    gens ( ) agent ( ) neige ( ) agile ( )

36. Here "g" is not followed by "i" or "e". Look and listen.

    gare ( ) argot ( ) égout ( ) fatigue ( )

37. Say the following.

    gant x( ) garder x( ) goûter x( ) figure x( )

38. How do you say the following words?

    jardin x( ) l'agent x( ) agilité x( ) cage x( )

39. Notice that the following words have "g" followed by the vowel "u". Listen.

    figure ( ) déguste ( ) augure ( )

40. Look at the following words and listen.

    fatigue ( ) fatigué ( ) guide ( )

41. Listen again to these words. Is the vowel "u" pronounced?

    fatigue ( ) fatigué ( ) guide ( )

    Student's answer: <u>no</u>

42. The "u" has no value as a sound. It looks as if it has been added in front of "e" or "i" to avoid saying the following. Look and listen.

    fatige ( ) fatigé ( ) gider ( )

7.21

INTRODUCTION TO FRENCH PHONOLOGY

43. The words in frame 42 are not French. These are the French words. Look, listen and imitate.

    fatigue ( )x   fatigué ( )   guidé ( )x

44. Here are several words. Say them.

    guichet   x( )
    bague   x( )
    guetter   x( )
    anguille x( )
    figure   x( )
    augure   x( )
    inauguré x( )

45. Say the following words.

    agilité   x( )
    guerre   x( )
    garage   x( )
    géant   x( )
    gens   x( )
    gant   x( )
    goût   x( )
    guide   x( )
    nageoire x( )
    bourgeois x( )
    nage   x( )

5.

The negative marker "ne...pas"

46. Say the following statement in English.

    Il n'est pas très grand.

    Student's answer: <u>It is not very large.</u>

47. It's a negative statement. Look at the underlined words and listen.

    Il <u>n</u>'est <u>pas</u> très grand. ( )

    Student's answer: <u>2</u>

48. Look again at the negative French sentence. How many words are used to make a statement negative?

    Il n'est pas très grand.

    Student's answer: <u>2</u>

7.22

49. Here is the negative statement again. Make it affirmative by omitting "n" and "pas".

    Il n'est pas très grand. x( )

50. Look at the following sentence. Is it right or wrong?

    Vous n'allez pas à Paris.

    Student's answer: <u>R</u>

51. Here is another negative statement. Say it.

    Je ne vais pas à Paris. x( )

52. Here is the sentence again. Be sure not to pronounce the vowel "e" of the second word. Listen and imitate.

    Je ne vais pas à Paris. ( )x ( )x

53. Look at the following sentences and imitate.

    Il n'est pas très grand.   ( )x
    Il n'est pas au café.   ( )x
    Je ne vais pas à Paris.   ( )x
    Je ne suis pas en retard.   ( )x
    Vous n'êtes pas très grand. ( )x

54. Here are three sentences. One is wrong. Which one is it?

    1. Il ne vient pas.
    2. Vous avez de la chance.
    3. Le train n'est à l'heure.

    Student's answer: <u>3</u>

55. If you had to change the following affirmative sentence into a negative sentence, would you use formula 1 or 2?

    Nous avons les billets.

    1. ne + verb + pas
    2. n' + verb + pas

    Student's answer: <u>2</u>

56. Here is another sentence. Make it negative.

    Vous emménagez. x( )

7.23

INTRODUCTION TO FRENCH PHONOLOGY

57. Look at the following negative statements.
    Say them affirmatively before your instructor does.

Il n'est pas midi.	x( )
Il ne vient pas.	x( )
Nous n'avons pas l'heure.	x( )
Il n'est pas très moderne.	x( )
Vous n'êtes pas en retard.	x( )

58. In this exercise you will hear negative statements. Say them in the affirmative form before your instructor does it for you.

    a. ( ) x( )
    b. ( ) x( )
    c. ( ) x( )
    d. ( ) x( )
    e. ( ) x( )
    f. ( ) x( )

59. This time the sentences you will hear are affirmative. Make them negative.

    a. ( ) x( )
    b. ( ) x( )
    c. ( ) x( )
    d. ( ) x( )
    e. ( ) x( )
    f. ( ) x( )

60. Listen to this exchange: question-answer.

    (?) (A)

61. Listen to another question-answer.

    (?) (A)

62. You are going to be asked some questions. Answer each of them negatively before your instructor does.

    a. (?) x( )
    b. (?) x( )
    c. (?) x( )
    d. (?) x( )
    e. (?) x( )
    f. (?) x( )

7.24

258 INTRODUCTION TO FRENCH PHONOLOGY

63. Look at the following English sentences then say them in French before your instructor does.

    I'm not on time.   x( )
    I'm on time.   x( )
    It's five o'clock.   x( )
    It's not five o'clock. x( )
    You're leaving.   x( )
    You're not leaving.   x( )
    The hotel is very modern. x( )
    The hotel is not large. x( )

64. Listen to this sentence. Then say it in English.

    ( )

    Student's answer: <u>Not until the end of the month.</u>

65. Now look at the following phrases and listen.

    pas samedi   ( )
    pas toujours   ( )

66. Say the following in French.

    not Saturday   x( )
    not always   x( )

67. When the negative is applied to words other than verbs only "pas" is used. Look and listen.

    pas samedi   ( )
    pas toujours   ( )
    pas vous   ( )
    pas très grand   ( )
    pas Paris   ( )
    pas le matin   ( )

68. Say the following English sentences in French.

    not the afternoon x( )
    not in the evening x( )
    not you   x( )
    not at noon   x( )

69. To each of the following questions your answer should be "non" followed by a negative statement.

    a. (?) x( )   e. (?) x( )
    b. (?) x( )   f. (?) x( )
    c. (?) x( )   g. (?) x( )
    d. (?) x( )   h. (?) x( )

INTRODUCTION TO FRENCH PHONOLOGY

70. The following questions contain a verb and its subject. When answering with a negative statement, don't forget to begin with "non".

    a. (?) x( )
    b. (?) x( )
    c. (?) x( )
    d. (?) x( )

71. Answer the following questions with a negative statement as you did in frames 69 and 70.

    a. (?) x( )
    b. (?) x( )
    c. (?) x( )
    d. (?) x( )
    e. (?) x( )
    f. (?) x( )
    g. (?) x( )
    h. (?) x( )

6

Review

72. This is a review; look at the following sentences and say them before your instructor does.

    a. Nous n'avons pas de chance.   x( )
        J'ai enfin un appartement.   x( )
        Nous emménageons samedi.   x( )
        Je n'y vais pas très souvent.   x( )

    b. Je ne suis pas fatigué.   x( )
        C'est la fatigue.   x( )
        Au sixième étage.   x( )
        Je voudrais deux billets.   x( )

    c. C'est fermé.   x( )
        Ce n'est pas fermé.   x( )
        C'est l'hôtel.   x( )
        Ce n'est pas l'hôtel.   x( )
        C'est vous.   x( )
        Ce n'est pas vous.   x( )
        C'est le train.   x( )
        Ce n'est pas le train.   x( )

    d. Est-elle seule?   x( )
        Que veut-elle?   x( )
        Comment est-il?   x( )
        Il va à l'hôtel?   x( )
        Où est l'hôtel?   x( )
        Vous allez au bal?   x( )

Report to your classroom.   7.26

7.

Preparation

Exercice un

Dites en français

1.	At the hotel	1.	A l'hôtel
2.	At the café	2.	Au café
3.	At noon	3.	A midi
4.	The hotel	4.	L'hôtel
5.	The apartment	5.	L'appartement
6.	An apartment	6.	Un appartement
7.	The luck	7.	La chance
8.	Always	8.	Toujours
9.	Still	9.	Toujours
10.	One round trip	10.	Un aller et retour
11.	The round trip	11.	L'aller et retour
12.	How	12.	Comment
13.	Large	13.	Grand
14.	Big	14.	Grand
15.	Tall	15.	Grand
16.	Not until	16.	Pas avant
17.	Soon	17.	Bientôt
18.	Often	18.	Souvent
19.	Very tall	19.	Très grand
20.	At last	20.	Enfin
21.	The end	21.	La fin
22.	Two apartments	22.	Deux appartements
23.	Finally	23.	Enfin
24.	Before	24.	Avant
25.	But	25.	Mais

Exercice deux
Dites en anglais

1.	Nous avons de la chance	1.	We're lucky.
2.	Nous n'avons pas de chance.	2.	We're not lucky.
3.	C'est un hôtel moderne.	3.	It's a modern hotel.
4.	Vous n'êtes pas très grand.	4.	You're not very tall.
5.	Comment est le café à côté?	5.	How's the café next door?
6.	Il n'est pas moderne.	6.	It's not modern.
7.	C'est à la gare.	7.	It's at the station.
8.	Je ne suis pas en retard.	8.	I'm not late.

7.27

INTRODUCTION TO FRENCH PHONOLOGY

9. Nous partons très bientôt.
10. Nous avons de la chance.
11. Il n'est pas toujours à l'heure.
12. Nous avons manqué le train.
13. Je ne vais pas déjeuner.
14. Nous n'avons pas déjeuné.
15. L'appartement est grand mais pas moderne.
16. Vous avez un billet?
17. Nous ne partons pas.
18. Le train n'est pas souvent en retard.
19. Je pars à la fin du mois.
20. Pas avant dix heures.

9. We're leaving quite soon.
10. We're lucky.
11. It's (he's) not always on time.
12. We missed the train.
13. I'm not going to have lunch.
14. We did not have lunch.
15. The apartment is large but not modern.
16. You have a ticket?
17. We're not leaving.
18. The train is not often late.
19. I'm leaving at the end of the month.
20. Not (until) before 10 o'clock.

Exercice trois
Dites en français

1. We have two one ways to Paris.
2. I'm at the hotel.
3. It's not very modern.
4. How's the apartment?
5. It's not very large.
6. You're leaving at the end of the month.
7. We have a few minutes, (and) that's all.
8. Where are you?
9. Do you have a round trip?
10. Are you moving in?
11. We're lucky.
12. When are you moving in?
13. When do you move in?
14. Where did you have lunch?
15. I'm going to the hotel.
16. Where is the hotel?
17. We had lunch next door.
18. How's the café next door?
19. I'm leaving soon.
20. You're still at the station?

1. Nous avons deux aller pour Paris.
2. Je suis à l'hôtel.
3. Il n'est pas très moderne.
4. Comment est l'appartement?
5. Il n'est pas très grand.
6. Vous partez à la fin du mois.
7. Nous avons quelques minutes, c'est tout.
8. Où êtes-vous?
9. Avez-vous un aller et retour?
10. Vous emménagez?
11. Nous avons de la chance.
12. Quand emménagez-vous?
13. Quand emménagez-vous?
14. Où avez-vous déjeuné?
15. Je vais à l'hôtel.
16. Où est l'hôtel?
17. Nous avons déjeuné à côté.
18. Comment est le café à côté.
19. Je pars bientôt.
20. Vous êtes toujours à la gare?

7.28

Exercice quatre

	Questions		Réponses possibles
1.	Vous avez un appartement?	1.	Non. Je suis à l'hôtel. Oui, nous avons un appartement.
2.	Vous êtes à l'hôtel?	2.	Non. Nous avons un appartement. Oui, je suis toujours à hôtel. Non. Nous avons de la chance. Nous avons enfin un appartement.
3.	Comment est l'appartement?	3.	Il n'est pas très grand mais moderne. Il est très grand. Il n'est pas très moderne mais très grand. Il est très moderne. Il est très moderne et très grand.
4.	Quand est-ce que vous emménagez?	4.	Très bientôt. Pas avant la fin du mois. A la fin du mois. Samedi. Pas avant samedi.

Exercice cinq

Professeur: Je suis en retard.
Elève: Est-ce que je suis en retard?

1.	Je suis en retard.	1.	Est-ce que je suis en retard?
2.	Nous avons enfin un appartement.	2.	Est-ce que nous avons enfin un appartement?
3.	Je pars avant vous.	3.	Est-ce que je pars avant vous.
4.	Il y en a l'après-midi.	4.	Est-ce qu'il y en a l'après-midi?
5.	Vous y allez à la fin du mois.	5.	Est-ce que vous y allez à la fin du mois?
6.	Je pars bientôt.	6.	Est-ce que je pars bientôt.
7.	Vous êtes toujours au café.	7.	Est-ce que vous êtes toujours au café?
8.	Le train vient d'entrer en gare.	8.	Est-ce que le train vient d'entrer en gare?
9.	Il est moderne.	9.	Est-ce qu'il est moderne?
10.	Vous emménagez avant la fin du mois?	10.	Est-ce que vous emménagez avant la fin du mois?
11.	Je suis à l'heure.	11.	Est-ce que je suis à l'heure?
12.	Il vient d'entrer à l'hôtel.	12.	Est-ce qu'il vient d'entrer à l'hôtel?

7.29

13.	C'est tout.	13.	Est-ce que c'est tout?
14.	Vous êtes en retard.	14.	Est-ce que vous êtes en retard?
15.	Le train est à l'heure.	15.	Est-ce que le train est à l'heure?
16.	Il y en a souvent.	16.	Est-ce qu'il y en a souvent?

Exercice six
Dans l'exercice suivant accepter
une des trois formes interrogatives.

<u>Professeur</u>

Vous êtes en retard.

<u>Elève</u>

Vous êtes en retard?
Etes-vous en retard?
Est-ce que vous êtes en retard?

1.	Vous êtes en retard.	1.	Etes-vous en retard?
2.	Dans la soirée seulement.	2.	Dans la soirée seulement?
3.	Nous avons quelques minutes.	3.	Avons-nous quelques minutes?
4.	Vous y allez à deux heures.	4.	Y allez-vous à deux heures?
5.	Vous partez à une heure.	5.	Partez-vous à une heure?
6.	Le premier est à dix huit heures dix.	6.	Est-ce que le premier est à dix huit heures dix?
7.	Je pars samedi matin.	7.	Est-ce que je pars samedi matin?
8.	Nous avons de la chance.	8.	Avons-nous de la chance?
9.	Samedi après-midi.	9.	Samedi après-midi?
10.	Il vient d'entrer au café.	10.	Est-ce qu'il vient d'entrer au café?
11.	Le train pour Paris.	11.	Le train pour Paris?
12.	Vous avez manqué le train.	12.	Avez-vous manqué le train?
13.	Je vais déjeuner.	13.	Est-ce que je vais déjeuner?
14.	Vous l'avez manqué.	14.	L'avez-vous manqué?
15.	Il y en a l'après-midi.	15.	Est-ce qu'il y en a l'après-midi?
16.	Je suis à l'heure.	16.	Est-ce que je suis à l'heure?
17.	Il est moderne.	17.	Est-il moderne?

Exercice sept
Conversation dirigée
(Instructor's manual only)

Exercice huit
Conversation dirigée
(Instructor's manual only)

Exercice neuf

	Professeur		Elève
1.	pour Paris	1.	Pour Paris.
2.	quelques trains	2.	Quelques trains pour Paris.
3.	Il y a	3.	Il y a quelques trains pour Paris.
4.	l'après-midi	4.	Il y a quelques trains pour Paris l'après-midi.
5.	seulement	5.	Il y a quelques trains pour Paris l'après-midi seulement.

Exercice dix

	Professeur		Elève
1.	téléphoner	1.	Téléphoner.
2.	allez-vous	2.	Allez-vous téléphoner?
3.	à quelle heure	3.	A quelle heure allez-vous téléphoner?
4.	de Paris	4.	A quelle heure allez-vous téléphoner de Paris?

Exercice onze

	Professeur		Elève
1.	les trains	1.	Les trains.
2.	sont à l'heure	2.	Les trains sont à l'heure.
3.	français	3.	Les trains français sont à l'heure.
4.	toujours	4.	Les trains français sont toujours à l'heure.
5.	est-ce que	5.	Est-ce que les trains français sont toujours à l'heure?

Exercice douze

Expansion et correlation

	Professeur		Elève
1.	les trains	1.	Les trains.
2.	français	2.	Les trains français.
3.	sont en retard	3.	Les trains français sont en retard.
4.	pas souvent	4.	Les trains français ne sont pas souvent en retard.

7.31

8.

Reading exercises

Lecture.

1. Read.

    1. Que fait-il?
    2. Que veut-il?
    3. Que dit-il?
    4. Que lit-il?
    5. Que vaut-il?
    6. Que voit-il?

2. Read.

    1. Est-ce qu'il part?
    2. Est-ce que nous partons?
    3. Est-ce que vous avez soif?
    4. Est-ce qu'il veut le numéro?
    5. Est-ce que c'est meilleur?
    6. Est-ce qu'il arrive aujourd'hui?

3. Read.

    1. J'en ai mille.
    2. Un animal.
    3. C'est ma malle.
    4. Il va en ville.
    5. Je ne suis pas tranquille.
    6. Il est toujours seul.

4. Read.

    1. Nous n'avons pas le temps.
    2. Il n'a pas de billet.
    3. Nous ne voulons pas partir.
    4. Il ne veut pas parler.
    5. Il ne veut pas nous le dire.
    6. Nous ne pouvons pas le réparer.

5. Read.

    1. Vous avez la chambre cinq.
    2. Il n'a pas de chance.
    3. Ils ont de la chance.
    4. Voilà la machine à laver.
    5. Il fait très chaud en été.
    6. Ils ne sont pas chez nous.

6. Read.

   1. Le garage est ouvert le dimanche.
   2. C'est un très bon guide.
   3. Je ne voudrais pas vous déranger.
   4. C'est une agence de publicité.
   5. J'ai parlé à des gens intéressants.
   6. C'est la première fois que nous y goûtons.
   7. Les routes sont très glissantes.
   8. C'est chauffé au gaz.

7. Read.

   1. Vous ne voulez pas partir?
   2. Il ne sait pas où c'est.
   3. Quand voulez-vous qu'il parte?
   4. Le lui avez-vous dit?
   5. Vous en avez beaucoup?
   6. Nous n'y pensons pas.
   7. Je ne vais pas la voir.
   8. A quelle heure y allez-vous?
   9. Est-ce que vous y allez souvent?
   10. Nous ne voulons pas le manquer.
   11. Vous les avez manqués.

8. Read.

   1. Il n'y en a pas d'autres.
   2. Est-ce qu'il y en a souvent?
   3. Il y en a tous les jours.
   4. Nous en avons trouvé.
   5. Il n'y en a pas souvent.
   6. Il y a très longtemps.
   7. Mon ami en a beaucoup.
   8. J'ai trouvé un hôtel pas cher.
   9. Ils n'en ont pas demandé.
   10. Il en a trouvé un.

Chapter Seven, end of Part Two.

Go to the lab for Tests 1 through 9.

INTRODUCTION TO FRENCH PHONOLOGY

Chapter Seven, Part Three

Tests

TEST 1

Listen to the following words and write them.

	Listen		Write
1.	( )	1.	_____
2.	( )	2.	_____
3.	( )	3.	_____
4.	( )	4.	_____
5.	( )	5.	_____
6.	( )	6.	_____
7.	( )	7.	_____
8.	( )	8.	_____
9.	( )	9.	_____
10.	( )	10.	_____

TEST 2

The pronunciation of the following words may be right or wrong. Look, listen and check the appropriate column.

			Right	Wrong
1.	L'appartement. ( )	1.	____	____
2.	L'hôtel. ( )	2.	____	____
3.	Bientôt. ( )	3.	____	____
4.	Moderne. ( )	4.	____	____
5.	Grand. ( )	5.	____	____
6.	Enfin. ( )	6.	____	____
7.	La chance. ( )	7.	____	____

7.34

			Right	Wrong
8.	Avant. ( )	8.	_____	_____
9.	Un appartement. ( )	9.	_____	_____
10.	Toujours. ( )	10.	_____	_____

<u>STOP TAPE RECORDER</u>

TEST 3

There is a mistake in each of the following words. Rewrite each word correctly.

	<u>Look</u>		<u>Rewrite</u>
1.	hotel	1.	_____
2.	avand	2.	_____
3.	tougeours.	3.	_____
4.	emménajez	4.	_____
5.	modern	5.	_____
6.	anfin	6.	_____
7.	bientot	7.	_____
8.	coment	8.	_____
9.	grant	9.	_____
10.	samdi	10.	_____

INTRODUCTION TO FRENCH PHONOLOGY

TEST 4

Look at the following sentences then rewrite them using "ne...pas" to make them negative.

	Look		Rewrite
1.	Il est très grand.	1.	_____
2.	Vous emménagez.	2.	_____
3.	Je vais à l'hôtel.	3.	_____
4.	Il vient samedi.	4.	_____
5.	Vous êtes en retard.	5.	_____
6.	Vous partez le matin.	6.	_____
7.	Le premier est à dix heures.	7.	_____
8.	Nous avons les billets.	8.	_____

TEST 5

In each of the following sentences the word which is underlined is incorrectly written. Rewrite it properly.

	Look		Rewrite
1.	Vous y allé souvent?	1.	_____
2.	Quand parter-vous?	2.	_____
3.	Où allé-vous?	3.	_____
4.	Déjeunez-vous a midi?	4.	_____
5.	Vous l'avé manqué.	5.	_____
6.	Je par à la fin du mois.	6.	_____
7.	C'est tou.	7.	_____

	Look		Rewrite
8.	Il est huit heures <u>dis</u>.	8.	_____
9.	<u>Kel</u> heure est-il?	9.	_____
10.	Nous <u>parton</u> samedi.	10.	_____
11.	<u>C'n'est</u> pas le premier.	11.	_____
12.	Je vais <u>déjeunez</u>.	12.	_____
13.	Je <u>n'</u>pars pas.	13.	_____
14.	Dans la soirée <u>seuleument</u>.	14.	_____
15.	Voilà <u>Meusieur</u>.	15.	_____
16.	Il vient d'<u>entrez</u> en gare.	16.	_____
17.	Vous <u>ête</u> toujours à l'hôtel?	17.	_____
18.	Vous avez les <u>biliets</u>?	18.	_____
19.	Nous avons deux aller et <u>retours</u>.	19.	_____
20.	Vous l'avez <u>manké</u>	20.	_____

TEST 6

Look at the following sentences. Check whether the construction is Right or Wrong.

	Look		Check Right	Wrong
1.	Vous allez y souvent?	1.	____	____
2.	Où allez-vous?	2.	____	____
3.	Où avez déjeuné-vous?	3.	____	____
4.	Je suis retard.	4.	____	____

INTRODUCTION TO FRENCH PHONOLOGY

	Look		Check	
			Right	Wrong
5.	Je suis retard.	5.	____	____
6.	Vous avez manqué le.	6.	____	____
7.	De temps à temps seulement.	7.	____	____
8.	Il vient d'entrer la gare.	8.	____	____
9.	A quelle heurè est le premier un?	9.	____	____
10.	Je ne suis pas souvent à l'heure.	10.	____	____
11.	Il est cinq à dix.	11.	____	____
12.	Vous partez bientôt?	12.	____	____

START TAPE RECORDER

TEST 7

Write the number of syllables that you hear in each of the following sentences.

	Listen		Write
1.	( )	1.	_____
2.	( )	2.	_____
3.	( )	3.	_____
4.	( )	4.	_____
5.	( )	5.	_____
6.	( )	6.	_____
7.	( )	7.	_____
8.	( )	8.	_____
9.	( )	9.	_____
10.	( )	10.	_____

7.38

Test 8

Write what you hear. (In order to have enough time to write, stop the machine after each number)

Listen	Write
1. ( )	1. _____
2. ( )	2. _____
3. ( )	3. _____
4. ( )	4. _____
5. ( )	5. _____
6. ( )	6. _____
7. ( )	7. _____
8. ( )	8. _____
9. ( )	9. _____
10. ( )	10. _____

END OF CHAPTER SEVEN:

INTRODUCTION TO FRENCH PHONOLOGY

Chapter Eight

PART 1

    Dialogue. (Laboratory)

PART 2

1. Accents. The accent circonflêxe. (^)

    The accent grave. (ˋ) (Laboratory)

2. The vowel "o" in words like "école." (Laboratory)

3. The "h" in words like: la hauteur. (Laboratory)

4. Pronunciation of "seuil" "rail." (Laboratory)

5. Review. (Laboratory)

6. Preparation for Class. (Homework)

7. Reading exercises. (Classroom)

PART 3

Tests. (Laboratory)

Chapter Eight

Dialogue

A.	Vos filles ne vont pas à l'école?	-Aren't your daughters going to school?
B.	Non. C'est fête. Les écoles sont fermées.	-No. It's a holiday. The schools are closed.
A:	C'est vrai. J'avais oublié que c'était Pâques. Quel âge ont-elles maintenant?	-That's right. I had forgotten it was Easter. How old are they now?
B.	L'une a sept ans et l'autre huit ans et demi.	-One is seven and the other eight and half.
A.	Les enfants grandissent si vite. Notre fils va avoir six ans en octobre.	-Children grow so fast. Our son is going to be six in October.

INTRODUCTION TO FRENCH PHONOLOGY

Part One

1. Listen to the following conversation in French.

    A: (?)
    B: ( )
    A: ( )
    A: (?)
    B: ( )
    A: ( )
    A: ( )

2. Listen again to the conversation.

    A: (?)
    B: ( )
    A: ( )
    A: (?)
    B: ( )
    A: ( )
    A: ( )

3. This is the first sentence of the conversation. Listen.

    ( ) ( ) ( )

4. It's a question, and it's negative. Listen.

    ( ) ( )

5. Listen to the last four words.

    ( ) ( ) ( )

6. Listen to the last four words again. Is the last consonant (R) or (W)?

    ( ) ( )

(W)

7. Which is right No. 1 or No. 2?

    (1) (2)

(1)

8. Listen and imitate the correct pronunciation.

    ( )x ( )x ( )x

9. Imitate again.

    ( )x ( )x ( )x

8.3

10. We'll add two more words to those that you know. Listen.

      ( ) ( ) ( )

11. There are six syllables. One of the syllables has a nasal vowel. Listen.

      (- - - - - -)   (- - - - - -)
      1 2 3 4 5 6   1 2 3 4 5 6

12. Listen again. Which syllable has the nasal vowel?

      (- - - - - -)   (- - - - - -)
      1 2 3 4 5 6   1 2 3 4 5 6

(2)

13. Listen and imitate.

      ( )x ( )x ( )x

14. Again.

      ( )x ( )x ( )x

15. Here is the complete sentence. Listen.

      ( ) ( ) ( )

16. How many syllables do you hear? Listen.

      ( ) ( )

(8)

17. Look at the sentence while listening.

      Vos filles ne vont pas à l'école? ( ) ( ) ( )

18. Now, listen and imitate.

      ( )x ( )x ( )x

19. Again.

      ( )x ( )x ( )x

20. Look at the meaning while imitating.

      Aren't your daughters going to school?

         ( )x ( )x ( )x

21. Repeat No. 20.

8.4

INTRODUCTION TO FRENCH PHONOLOGY

22. Here is the sentence again. Is it (R) or (W)? Listen.

   ( )

(R)

23. Here it is again. Is it (R) or (W)?

   ( )

(W)

24. Imitate the correct pronunciation.

   ( )x   ( )x   ( )x

25. Here are two short phrases. Listen.

   ( )   ( )   ( )

26. Listen to the sentences three times. Then imitate.

   ( )   ( )   ( )   ( )x   ( )x   ( )x

27. Look at the sentence while listening.

   Non. C'est fête.   ( )   ( )

28. Now listen and imitate.

   ( )x   ( )x   ( )x

29. Look at the meaning while imitating.

   No. It's a holiday.   (Fr)x   (Fr)x

30. Imitate again.

   ( )x   ( )x   ( )x

31. Is the following (R) or (W)? Listen.

   ( )   ( )

(W)

32. How about this time? Is it (R) or (W)?

   ( )   ( )

(W)

33. Imitate the correct pronunciation.

   ( )x   ( )x   ( )x

8.5

34. Here is another sentence. Listen.

      ( )   ( )   ( )

35. Listen again. Then imitate.

      ( )   ( )   ( )   ( )x ( )x ( )x

36. Which is right? Number one or two? Listen.

      (1)   (2)

(2)

37. Listen and imitate.

      ( )x ( )x ( )x

38. Look at the sentence in French and listen.

      Les écoles sont fermées. ( )   ( )

39. Look at the meaning and imitate the French.

      Schools are closed. (Fr)x (Fr)x

40. Listen again to the first question of the dialogue and the answer.

      (Q)   (A)   (Q)   (A)

41. Imitate the answer.

      ( )x ( )x ( )x

42. Again.

      ( )x ( )x ( )x

43. Listen to the following exchange.

      A: ( )
      B: ( )

44. Answer your instructor.

      Instructor: (Q)
      You: _____

INTRODUCTION TO FRENCH PHONOLOGY

45. Again.

    Instructor: (Q)
    You: _____

46. Ask the question. Then listen to the answer.

    (begin)
    You: _____?
    Instructor: (A)

47. Again.

    (begin)
    You: _____?
    Instructor: (A)

48. Here is a new sentence. Listen.

    ( ) ( ) ( )

49. Listen again and imitate.

    ( ) ( ) ( )x ( )x ( )x

50. Imitate again.

    ( )x ( )x

51. Listen to these three words.

    ( ) ( ) ( )

52. Listen again. Then imitate.

    ( ) ( ) ( )x ( )x ( )x

53. We'll add two more words in front of the three. Listen.

    ( ) ( ) ( )

54. Now listen and then imitate.

    ( ) ( ) ( ) ( )x ( )x ( )x

55. Imitate the last part of the sentence again.

    ( )x ( )x ( )x

8.7

56. This is the first part of the sentence. Listen.

    ( )   ( )   ( )

57. Listen and imitate.

    ( )x   ( )x   ( )x

58. Again.

    ( )x   ( )x   ( )x

59. Now the complete sentence. Listen.

    ( )   ( )   ( )

60. Listen again. Then imitate.

    ( )   ( )   ( )x   ( )x   ( )x

61. Listen to these two sentences.

    ( )   ( )   ( )

62. Listen again while looking at the writing in French.

    C'est vrai. J'avais oublié que c'était Pâques.   ( )   ( )

63. Look at the writing again. Listen and imitate.

    C'est vrai. J'avais oublié que c'était Pâques.

    ( )x   ( )x   ( )x

64. This time look at the meaning while listening to the French.

    That's right. I had forgotten it was Easter.   (Fr)   (Fr)

65. Listen and imitate again.

    ( )x   ( )x   ( )x

66. This is a new word. Listen.

    ( )   ( )   ( )

67. Listen and imitate this new word.

    ( )x   ( )x   ( )x

8.8

INTRODUCTION TO FRENCH PHONOLOGY

68. Again.

   ( )x   ( )x

69. Now the sentence is complete. Listen.

   ( )   ( )   ( )

70. It's a question. Listen again.

   ( )   ( )   ( )

71. Listen and imitate.

   ( )x   ( )x   ( )x

72. Again.

   ( )x   ( )x   ( )x

73. Look at the writing and listen.

   Quel âge ont-elles maintenant?   ( )   ( )   ( )

74. Now look at the meaning while listening to the French.

   How old are they now?   (Fr)   (Fr)

75. Listen and imitate.

   ( )x   ( )x   ( )x

76. Imitate again while looking at the writing.

   Quel âge ont-elles maintenant?   ( )x   ( )x   ( )x

77. Here are the last three sentences. Listen.

   ( )   ( )   ( )

78. Listen again.

   ( )   ( )   ( )

79. Listen and imitate the first sentence.

   ( )x   ( )x

80. Now imitate the first two sentences.

   ( )x   ( )x   ( )x

8.9

81. Imitate the last sentence.

   ( )x ( )x

82. Imitate the first two sentences.

   ( )x ( )x

83. Imitate the third.

   ( )x

84. Listen to all three sentences and imitate.

   ( ) ( )   ( )x ( )x ( )x

85. Imitate again.

   ( )x ( )x ( )x

86. Listen to the following exchange.

   A: (?)
   B: ( )
   A: (?)

87. Listen again.

   A: (?)
   B: ( )
   A: (?)

88. Now listen and imitate.

   A: (?)x
   B: ( )x
   A: (?)x

89. Again.

   A: (?)x
   B: ( )x
   A: (?)x

90. Answer your instructor.

   Instructor: (Q)
   You: ____A____
   Instructor: (Q)

INTRODUCTION TO FRENCH PHONOLOGY

91. Again.

    Instructor: (Q)
    You: _____ A
    Instructor: (Q)

92. Ask the question this time.

    (begin)
    You: _____?
    Instructor: (A)
    You: _____?

93. Again.

    (begin)
    You: _____?
    Instructor: (A)
    You: _____?

94. Here is a new sentence. Listen.

    ( ) ( ) ( )

95. Listen to the first part of the sentence.

    ( ) ( ) ( )

96. Listen and imitate the first part of the sentence.

    ( )x ( )x ( )x

97. Listen to the second part of the sentence.

    ( ) ( ) ( )

98. Listen again.

    ( ) ( ) ( )

99. Imitate the last four words.

    ( )x ( )x ( )x

100. Again.

    ( )x ( )x ( )x

8.11

101. Listen again to the last part of the sentence. Then imitate.

    ( ) ( ) ( ) ( )x ( )x ( )x

102. Imitate the last part of the sentence.

    ( )x ( )x ( )x

103. Listen to the complete sentence.

    ( ) ( ) ( )

104. We'll divide the sentence in two parts. Listen to the first part and imitate.

    (1st)x (1st)x (1st)x

105. Listen to the second part of the sentence and imitate.

    (2nd)x (2nd)x (2nd)x

106. After listening and imitating the first part of the sentence, listen and imitate the second part.

    (1st part)x (2nd part)x (1st part)x (2nd part)x

107. Again.

    (1st part)x (2nd part)x (1st part)x (2nd part)x

108. This is the complete sentence. Listen and imitate.

    ( )x ( )x ( )x

109. Look at the writing and imitate.

    L'une a sept ans et l'autre huit ans et demi.

    ( )x ( )x ( )x

110. Listen again to the sentence. Is it (R) or (W)?

    ( )

(W)

111. Which one is right? No. 1 or No. 2?

    (1)/(2)

(1)

INTRODUCTION TO FRENCH PHONOLOGY

112. Look at the writing while imitating the correct pronunciation.

    L'une a sept ans et l'autre huit ans et demi.

    ( )x ( )x ( )x

113. Here is the meaning in English. Listen and imitate the French.

    One is seven, and the other eight and a half.

    (Fr)x (Fr)x (Fr)x

114. Listen to the following exchange.

    A: (?)
    B: ( )
    A: (?)
    B: ( )

115. Listen and imitate.

    A: (?)x
    B: ( )x
    A: (?)x
    B: ( )x

116. Again.

    A: (?)x
    B: ( )x
    A: (?)x
    B: ( )x

117. Answer your instructor.

    Instructor: (Q)
    You: _____
    Instructor: (Q)
    You: _____

118. Again.

    Instructor: (Q)
    You: _____
    Instructor: (Q)
    You: _____

8.13

119. Ask the question this time.

    (begin)
    You: _____?
    Instructor: (A)
    You: _____?
    Instructor: (A)

120. Again.

    (begin)
    You: _____?
    Instructor: (A)
    You: _____?
    Instructor: (A)

End of tape one. Part one continues on tape two.

121. Here is a new sentence. Listen.

    ( ) ( ) ( )

122. Imitate the last two words.

    ( )x ( )x ( )x

123. We'll add another word in front of the last two. Listen.

    ( ) ( ) ( )

124. Listen and imitate.

    ( )x ( )x ( )x

125. Listen to the complete sentence.

    ( ) ( ) ( )

126. Listen and imitate the complete sentence.

    ( )x ( )x ( )x

127. Listen and imitate again.

    ( )x ( )x ( )x

128. Imitate again while looking at the writing in French.

    Les enfants grandissent si vite. ( )x ( )x

INTRODUCTION TO FRENCH PHONOLOGY

129. Look at the meaning and imitate the French.

    Children grow so fast.   (Fr)x   (Fr)x

130. This is the last sentence of the dialogue. Listen.

    ( )   ( )   ( )

131. Listen to the last two words and imitate.

    ( )x   ( )x   ( )x

132. In front of the last two words we'll add two. Listen.

    ( )   ( )   ( )

133. Now listen and imitate these four words.

    ( )x   ( )x   ( )x

134. We'll add two more in front of the four that you know. Listen.

    ( )   ( )   ( )

135. Listen and then imitate.

    ( )   ( )   ( )x   ( )x   ( )x

136. Listen to the complete sentence.

    ( )   ( )   ( )

137. Listen and imitate.

    ( )x   ( )x   ( )x

138. Imitate again while looking at the French writing.

    Notre fils va avoir six ans en octobre.   ( )x   ( )x

139. Look at the meaning and imitate the French.

    Our son is going to be six in October.   (Fr)x   (Fr)x

140. Listen again to the last two sentences.

    ( )   ( )

8.15

141. Now listen and then imitate.

   ( )   ( )   ( )x   ( )x   ( )x

142. Imitate again.

   ( )x   ( )x

143. Listen to the whole conversation.

   A: (?)
   B: ( )
   A: (?)
   B: ( )
   A: ( )

144. This time, look at the meaning and listen to the French.

   A: Aren't your daughters going to school? (Fr)
   B: No, it's a holiday. Schools are closed. (Fr)
   A: That's right. I had forgotten it was Easter.
      How old are they now? (Fr)
   B: One is seven and the other eight and a half. (Fr)
   A: Children grow up so fast. Our son is going to
      be six in October. (Fr)

145. Listen to the conversation and imitate each sentence.

   A: (?)x
   B: ( )x
   A: (?)x
   B: ( )x
   A: ( )x

146. Answer your instructor.

   Instructor: (Q)
   You: _____
   Instructor: (Q)
   You: _____
   Instructor: ( )

147. Again.

   Instructor: (Q)
   You: _____
   Instructor: (Q)
   You: _____
   Instructor: ( )

8.16

148. Listen to the conversation again.

    A: (?)
    B: ( )
    A: (?)
    B: ( )
    A: ( )

149. Now begin the conversation with your instructor.

   (begin)
   You: _____?
   Instructor: (A)
   You: _____?
   Instructor: (A)
   You: _____

150. Again.

   (begin)
   You: _____?
   Instructor: (A)
   You: _____?
   Instructor: (A)
   You: _____

151. Practice frames Nos. 143 to 150 several times.

Part Two

1

Accents

    1. The "accent circonflèxe" (^)
    2. The "accent grave"   (˘)

1. The circonflex accent may be used with all French vowels. Look and listen.

    tôt, dû, prêt, âge ( )

2. Words containing vowels with the circonflex accent are limited but quite common. Here are a few. Look and listen.

    hôpital ( )
    pâle   ( )
    dû   ( )
    fête   ( )
    dîner   ( )

3. The (^) accent in connection with the vowel "i" and "u" has no pronunciation value. Look and listen.

    dû/du ( )
    dît/dit ( )

4. Say the following words.

    dû x( ) dit x( ) fît x( ) mûr x( ) mur x( )

5. Some French speakers pronounce "â" differently from "a". Look and listen.

    pâte/patte ( )
    pâle/pale   ( )

6. Since the difference in pronunciation for the vowels â/a is slight, we will not practice it, but we do want you to be aware of it. Look and listen.

    pâte/patte   ( )
    tâche/tache ( )
    pâle/pale   ( )

7. Look at these two words and listen.

    cote ( )
    côte ( )

8.18

INTRODUCTION TO FRENCH PHONOLOGY

8. Listen again. Do they sound same or different?

    cote, côte ( )

    Student's answer: D

9. Listen to the underlined vowels in the following words.

    bat<u>eau</u>.   ( )
    ép<u>au</u>le   ( )
    f<u>au</u>ssaire ( )
    c<u>ô</u>te   ( )
    v<u>ô</u>tre   ( )

10. Listen again. Do the underlined vowels sound the same?

    bat<u>eau</u>, ép<u>au</u>le, f<u>au</u>ssaire, c<u>ô</u>te, v<u>ô</u>tre ( )

    Student's answer: Yes

11. Look at the following vowels or combination of vowels: eau, au, ô. Is it right to assume that they share the same pronunciation?

    Student's answer: Yes

12. Say the following words before your instructor does.

    mauve x( ) nôtre x( ) jaune x( ) côté x( ) maudit x( )

13. Look at these words and listen. Notice the underlined vowels.

    v<u>o</u>s   ( )
    abric<u>o</u>t ( )
    aut<u>o</u>   ( )
    sir<u>o</u>p   ( )
    fard<u>eau</u> ( )

14. Listen again. Do the underlined vowels sound the same?

    aut<u>o</u>   ( )
    sir<u>o</u>p   ( )
    v<u>o</u>s
    abric<u>o</u>t ( )
    fard<u>eau</u> ( )

    Student's answer: Yes

8.19

15. When "o" is the final sound of a word it is pronounced like: au, eau, ô.
    Say the following words.

    côte   x( )
    abricot   x( )
    manteau   x( )
    sauvé   x( )
    beauté   x( )
    sirop   x( )

16. Look at these words and listen.

    rose, j'ose, pose, dose, chose ( )

17. Look at these words again and listen. Is the vowel "o" the final sound?

    rose, j'ose, pose, dose, chose ( )

    Student's answer: <u>Non</u>

18. When the final sound of a word is the sound "z" (written s) the preceding "o" sounds like "eau," "au," "ô," or "o" in final sound position. Look and listen.

    galop, pose, jaunisse, arôme ( )

19. Say the following before your instructor does.

    mauve x( ) dôme x( ) rideau x( ) pavot x( )
    dépose x( )

20. Here are more words for you to say.

    cadeau   x( )
    vélo   x( )
    tableau   x( )
    fantôme   x( )
    diplôme   x( )
    pose   x( )

21. The circonflex accent is also used with the vowel "e."
    Look and listen.

    fenêtre, même ( )

INTRODUCTION TO FRENCH PHONOLOGY

22. Look at the underlined vowels of the following words and listen.

    l<u>ai</u>ne   ( )
    f<u>ai</u>te   ( )
    f<u>ê</u>te   ( )
    m<u>e</u>r   ( )
    m<u>ai</u>re   ( )
    m<u>è</u>re   ( )

23. Here are the same words again. Notice the underlined vowels sound almost alike. Listen and imitate.

    l<u>ai</u>ne   ( )x
    f<u>ai</u>te   ( )x
    f<u>ê</u>te   ( )x
    m<u>e</u>r   ( )x
    m<u>ai</u>re   ( )x
    m<u>è</u>re   ( )x

24. Say the following words before your instructor does.

    nouvelle   x( )
    aile   x( )
    verte   x( )
    ferme   x( )
    sèche   x( )
    rêveur   x( )

25. Now say these.

    enlève   x( )
    empêche   x( )
    précède   x( )
    père   x( )

26. Here are more words. Look, listen and imitate.

    lèvre   ( )x
    pêche   ( )x
    cède   ( )x
    même   ( )x

27. There is not much difference in pronunciation between "è" and "ê." Say the following words.

    la dépêche   x( )
    la première   x( )
    la sève   x( )
    la fenêtre   x( )
    la mère   x( )

8.21

28. All the underlined vowels in the following words sound about the same. Listen and imitate.

    m<u>ai</u>re   ( )x
    m<u>e</u>r   ( )x
    m<u>è</u>re   ( )x
    fr<u>è</u>re   ( )x
    b<u>ê</u>che   ( )x
    qu<u>e</u>l   ( )x
    qu<u>e</u>lle   ( )x

29. Look at words 1, 2, and 3 and listen.

    1. prêt ( )
    2. pré ( )
    3. près ( )

30. Listen again to words 1, 2 and 3 above. Does word 2 sound like 1 and 3?

    (1) (2) (3)

    Student's answer: <u>No</u>

31. Some French speakers pronounce "é" and "è" differently in final position as well as elsewhere. Listen to the contrast of the sounds é/è, ai, ê

    fée/fait ( )
    pré/prêt ( )
    pré/près ( )

32. Other French speakers do <u>not</u> contrast "é" and "è" in final position. Look and listen.

    fée/fait ( )
    pré/prêt ( )
    pré/près ( )

33. As we stated in Chapter One, we will not contrast "é" and "è" in final position. So é = è = ê = ai. Look, listen and imitate.

    déjeun<u>é</u>   ( )x
    déjeun<u>er</u> ( )x
    du l<u>ai</u>t ( )x
    apr<u>è</u>s   ( )x
    c'est pr<u>ê</u>t ( )x

INTRODUCTION TO FRENCH PHONOLOGY

34. Say the following words before your instructor does.

    café x( )   passez x( )   c'est fait x( )   c'est prêt x( )

                                2.

    <u>The vowel "o" in words like "école"</u>

35. Look at the following words and listen.

    l'école ( )   le sol ( )   la note ( )   l'homme ( )

36. Listen to this contrast.

    a. nos/note
    b. vos/vol
    c. nos/noce

37. Up to now we only had one pronunciation for the following underlined vowels. Look and listen.

    mant<u>eau</u> ( )   aussit<u>ôt</u> ( )   rab<u>o</u>t ( )   sir<u>o</u>p ( )   c<u>ô</u>te ( )

38. Here are more words containing the sound "o" as in frame No. 37. Notice that the final consonant is not pronounced. Look and listen.

    s<u>o</u>t ( )   pav<u>o</u>t ( )   tr<u>o</u>p ( )   v<u>o</u>s ( )

39. In the following words the final consonants are pronounced. Look and listen.

    mo<u>ch</u>e ( )   so<u>tt</u>e ( )   mo<u>d</u>e ( )   fo<u>r</u>t ( )

40. Listen and imitate these contrasts.

    a. clos/cloche   ( )x
    b. mot/motte   ( )x
    c. sot/sotte   ( )x

41. Say the following words before your instructor does.

    mauve   x( )
    clos   x( )
    close   x( )
    sotte   x( )
    saute   x( )
    nôtre   x( )
    notre   x( )
    pomme   x( )
    paume   x( )

8.23

42. Should the underlined vowels in the following words sound same or different?

    p<u>o</u>t p<u>o</u>mme

    Student's answer: <u>D</u>

43. In words 1, 2 and 3 which word has a vowel different from the other two?

    1. saute 2. sotte 3. sot

    Student's answer: <u>2</u>

44. Say the following words before your instructor does.

    nord   x( )
    forte   x( )
    pose   x( )
    sauce   x( )
    saut   x( )
    dose   x( )

3.

The "h" in words like: <u>la hauteur</u>

45. In chapter four we stated that there were two kinds of initial "h." Here are words beginning with "h" as introduced in chapter four. Look and listen.

    heure   ( ) l'heure   ( )
    hôpital ( ) l'hôpital ( )

46. In the following words the "h" has no pronunciation value. Look, Listen and imitate.

    leur - l'heure ( )x
    or   - hors   ( )x

47. Here are more words in which the "h" has no pronunciation value. Look, listen and imitate.

    a. hôtel, l'hôtel, hiver, l'hiver ( )x
    b. histoire, l'histoire   ( )x

48. Here are words beginning with a different kind of "h." Look and listen.

    la hauteur ( )
    le homard   ( )

8.24

INTRODUCTION TO FRENCH PHONOLOGY

49. Look at these two words and listen.

    1. hôtel   ( )
    2. homard ( )

50. Listen again to words 1 & 2. Was the "h" pronounced?

    (1)   (2)

    Student's answer: <u>No</u>

51. By looking at words 1 & 2 or by listening to words 1 & 2 is it possible to determine whether the "h" of 1 is different from the "h" of 2? Look again and listen.

    1. hôtel   ( )
    2. homard ( )

    Student's answer: <u>No</u>

52. The only time it is possible to determine whether or not the "h" is different is when the words are preceded by some kind of modifiers such as an article or an adjective. Look and listen.

    1. l'hôtel   2. le homard   ( )

53. Notice that with word 2 the vowel "e" of the preceding article is not replaced by an apostrophe. Here are more words. Look, listen and imitate.

    le homard   ( )x
    l'hôpital   ( )x
    la hache   ( )x
    l'homme   ( )x

54. Here is the word "hôtel" preceded by a different set of articles. Look and listen.

    1. l'hôtel   2. les hôtels   3. un hôtel   ( )

55. The "h" in construction 1, 2, 3 above had no pronunciation value. It was the vowel "o" that you heard at the beginning of "hôtel." Listen to words 1, 2, 3 of frame No. 54.

    (1)   (2)   (3)

56. Now here is the word "homard" preceded by a different set of articles. Look and listen.

    1. le homard   ( )   2. les homards   ( )   3. un homard   ( )

57. Listen again to 1, 2 and 3 of frame No. 56. Does this "h" have any influence on pronunciation?

     (1)   (2)   (3)

     Student's answer: <u>Yes</u>

58. Notice that with the word "homard" there is no linking with the preceding article. Look and listen.

     le homard   ( )
     un homard   ( )
     les homards ( )

59. There are two kinds of initial "h." In isolation it is impossible to distinguish one from the other. Look, listen and imitate.

     hauteur ( )x herbe ( )x heure ( )x hésiter ( )x hibou ( )x

60. Here are more words, this time preceded by an article or an adverb. Listen and imitate.

     le hêtre   ( )x
     là haut   ( )x
     l'hirondelle   ( )x
     les hommes   ( )x
     les hangars   ( )x
     un horizon   ( )x

                          4.

            Pronunciation of "seuil," rail

61. In chapter six you learned how to pronounce the underlined consonants of the following words. Look, listen and imitate.

     boui<u>ll</u>ir ( )x bi<u>ll</u>et ( )x fi<u>ll</u>e ( )x fami<u>ll</u>e ( )x

62. Here are more of the same kind of words containing "ill" + a vowel. Look, listen and imitate.

     pi<u>ll</u>age ( )x roui<u>ll</u>e ( )x veui<u>ll</u>ez ( )x

INTRODUCTION TO FRENCH PHONOLOGY

63. If "ll" of the words above is to be pronounced as the "y" in the English word "yes," the "ll" must be preceded by the vowel "i" and followed by another vowel. Look and listen.

    si<u>ll</u>age   ( )
    fou<u>ill</u>e ( )
    feu<u>ill</u>e ( )

64. Now, look at this set of words and listen.

    rail   ( )
    seuil   ( )
    vermeil ( )

65. In this set of words only one "l" is required to obtain the pronunciation. Look, listen and imitate.

    deuil ( )x   bail ( )x

66. Notice also that all the following words end with an "l" and are preceded by two speech vowels. Here are more words in which we underlined the vowels. Look and listen.

    tr<u>eui</u>l ( )   <u>ai</u>l ( )   rév<u>ei</u>l ( )

67. Here is the same set as above presented differently. Look and listen.

    treu + il = treuil   ( )
    a + il   = ail   ( )
    verme + il = vermeil ( )

68. Look at the following words and say them before your instructor does.

    miel   x( )
    seul   x( )
    seuil   x( )
    aile   x( )
    ail   x( )

69. Here are more words. Say them before your instructor does.

    paille   x( )
    seuil   x( )
    fouille x( )
    rail   x( )
    aile   x( )
    treille x( )
    travail x( )

8.27

5.

Review

70. This is a review, look at the following words or sentences and say them before your instructor does.

   a. J'ai mon billet. x( )
       J'ai le vôtre aussi. x( )
       Nous avons votre numéro. x( )
       Le hazard fait bien les choses. x( )
       Je cherche du travail. x( )

   b. Ils sont à l'école. x( )
       La soupe est bonne. x( )
       Tout est en ordre. x( )
       Elle porte une robe rose. x( )
       La jaune est en solde. x( )

   c. Je crois qu'il est prêt. x( )
       J'habite à côté d'ici. x( )
       La ville est en fête. x( )
       Il est encore en retard. x( )
       Voilà l'arrêt des autobus. x( )

   d. Avez-vous de l'argent? x( )
       Combien d'enfants avez-vous? x( )
       Vous avez trouvé du travail? x( )
       A quelle école vont-ils? x( )
       Est-ce qu'ils vont à l'école? x( )

REPORT TO YOUR CLASSROOM.

INTRODUCTION TO FRENCH PHONOLOGY

6.

Preparation

Exercice un

Dites en français

1.	A daughter	1.	Une fille
2.	A son	2.	Un fils
3.	The children	3.	Les enfants
4.	The child	4.	L'enfant
5.	Our school	5.	Notre école
6.	Our daughter	6.	Notre fille
7.	Our son	7.	Notre fils
8.	The schools	8.	Les écoles
9.	A school	9.	Une école
10.	The school	10.	L'école
11.	Your daughters	11.	Vos filles
12.	The other	12.	L'autre
13.	I had	13.	J'avais
14.	So fast	14.	Si vite
15.	Six years	15.	Six ans.
16.	Closed	16.	Fermé
17.	So big	17.	Si grand
18.	Seven years	18.	Sept ans
19.	Easter	19.	Pâques

Exercice deux

Dites en anglais

1.	Les écoles sont fermées à Pâques.	1.	Schools are closed for Easter.
2.	J'avais oublié que le café était fermé.	2.	I had forgotten the café was closed.
3.	Les enfants sont à l'école.	3.	The children are at school.
4.	Ils ont de la chance.	4.	They're lucky.
5.	J'avais oublié que c'était fête.	5.	I had forgotten it was a holiday.
6.	C'était vrai.	6.	It was true.
7.	Il n'y en a pas.	7.	There isn't any.
8.	L'école vient de fermer.	8.	The school just closed.
9.	Ils ont deux enfants.	9.	They have two children.
10.	Quel âge avez-vous?	10.	How old are you?
11.	Ils n'ont pas d'enfants.	11.	They have no children.

8.29

12.	Ils n'ont pas de chance.	12.	They're not lucky. (they have no luck)
13.	Ils y vont souvent.	13.	They go (there) often.
14.	Ils ont manqué le train.	14.	They missed the train.
15.	La fille n'est pas très grande.	15.	The daughter is not very tall.
16.	Votre fils est très grand.	16.	Your son is very tall.
17.	Pas avant le mois d'octobre.	17.	Not until October.
18.	Vous y allez à une heure?	18.	You go (there) at one?
19.	Notre fille a dix-huit ans et demi.	19.	Our daughter is eighteen and a half.
20.	Je pars en octobre.	20.	I'm leaving in October.

Exercice trois

Dites en français

1.	A girl	1.	Une fille
2.	A daughter	2.	Une fille
3.	The girls	3.	Les filles
4.	It's Easter	4.	C'est Pâques
5.	The school is closed.	5.	L'école est fermée.
6.	The children are going to school.	6.	Les enfants vont à l'école.
7.	The schools are closed.	7.	Les écoles sont fermées.
8.	I had forgotten.	8.	J'avais oublié.
9.	It was Saturday.	9.	C'était samedi.
10.	That's right.	10.	C'est vrai.
11.	That's true.	11.	C'est vrai.
12.	That's not true.	12.	Ce n'est pas vrai.
13.	I had forgotten it was you.	13.	J'avais oublié que c'était vous.
14.	They grow up so fast.	14.	Ils grandissent si vite.
15.	How old is she?	15.	Quel âge a-t-elle?
16.	How old is he?	16.	Quel âge a-t-il?
17.	He's going to be eighteen.	17.	Il va avoir dix-huit ans.
18.	She is forty years old.	18.	Elle a quarante ans.
19.	It was Easter.	19.	C'était Pâques.
20.	He is eight years old.	20.	Il a huit ans.

Exercice quatre

Professeur: C'est fête.
Elève: Ce n'est pas fête.

1.	C'est fête.	1.	Ce n'est pas fête.
2.	C'est vrai.	2.	Ce n'est pas vrai.
3.	C'était grand.	3.	Ce n'était pas grand.
4.	C'était samedi.	4.	Ce n'était pas samedi.
5.	C'est moderne.	5.	Ce n'est pas moderne.
6.	C'est au café.	6.	Ce n'est pas au café.
7.	C'était Pâques.	7.	Ce n'était pas Pâques.
8.	C'est très grand.	8.	Ce n'est pas très grand.
9.	C'est en octobre.	9.	Ce n'est pas en octobre.
10.	C'est très grand.	10.	Ce n'est pas très grand.

Exercice cinq

Professeur: Les enfants vont à l'école?
Elève: Non, ils ne vont pas à l'école.

1. Les enfants vont à l'école?
2. Le train est à l'heure?
3. Votre fille est grande?
4. Les écoles sont fermées?
5. Votre fils est à Paris?
6. Votre fils vient samedi matin?
7. Vous êtes souvent en retard?
8. C'est fête samedi?
9. Les enfants sont à l'école?
10. Vous partez en octobre?

1. Non, ils ne vont pas à l'école.
2. Non, il n'est pas à l'heure.
3. Non, elle n'est pas grande.
4. Non, elles ne sont pas fermées.
5. Non, il n'est pas à Paris.
6. Non, il ne vient pas samedi matin.
7. Non, je ne suis pas souvent en retard.
8. Non, ce n'est pas fête samedi.
9. Non, ils ne sont pas à l'école.
10. Non, je ne pars pas en octobre.

Exercice six
Conversation dirigée
(Manuel du professeur seulement)

Exercice sept

Professeur: Je pars samedi.
Elève: Vous partez samedi?

1. J'y vais souvent.
2. Vous partez en octobre.
3. J'emménage à la fin du mois.

1. Vous y allez souvent?
2. Je pars en octobre?
3. Vous emménagez à la fin du mois?

4.	Je pars samedi.	4.	Vous partez samedi?
5.	Nous avons sept enfants.	5.	Vous avez sept enfants?
6.	Les écoles sont fermées.	6.	Les écoles sont fermées?
7.	Je vais déjeuner à côté.	7.	Vous allez déjeuner à côté?
8.	Il y a un train l'après-midi.	8.	Il y a un train l'après-midi?
9.	Je suis en retard.	9.	Vous êtes en retard?
10.	Vous êtes en retard.	10.	Je suis en retard?
11.	Il est dix heures cinq.	11.	Il est dix heures cinq?
12.	Vous allez déjeuner à midi.	12.	Je vais déjeuner à midi?

Exercice huit

Professeur: Je ne pars pars samedi.
Elève: Vous ne partez pas samedi?

1.	L'autre fille n'est pas à l'école.	1.	L'autre fille n'est pas à l'école?
2.	Je ne pars pas samedi.	2.	Vous ne partez pas samedi?
3.	Vous n'allez pas à Paris.	3.	Je ne vais pas à Paris?
4.	Les enfants ne vont pas à l'école.	4.	Les enfants ne vont pas à l'école?
5.	Vous ne partez pas samedi.	5.	Je ne pars pas samedi?
6.	Je ne suis pas en retard.	6.	Vous n'êtes pas en retard?
7.	Nous n'avons pas les billets.	7.	Vous n'avez pas les billets?
8.	Je ne vais pas déjeuner.	8.	Vous n'allez pas déjeuner?

Exercice neuf

	Professeur		Elève
1.	un billet	1.	Un billet.
2.	vous avez	2.	Vous avez un billet.
3.	de première	3.	Vous avez un billet de première.
4.	pour Paris.	4.	Vous avez un billet de première pour Paris.
5.	est-ce que	5.	Est-ce que vous avez un billet de première pour Paris?

8.32

Exercice dix

	Professeur		Elève
1.	au restaurant	1.	Au restaurant.
2.	déjeuner	2.	Déjeuner au restaurant.
3.	vous allez	3.	Vous allez déjeuner au restaurant.
4.	est-ce que	4.	Est-ce que vous allez déjeuner au restaurant?
5.	samedi	5.	Est-ce que vous allez déjeuner au restaurant samedi?

Exercice onze
Expansion et correlation

	Professeur		Elève
1.	les écoles	1.	Les écoles.
2.	étaient fermées	2.	Les écoles étaient fermées.
3.	j'avais oublié	3.	J'avais oublié que les écoles étaient fermées.
4.	à Pâques	4.	J'avais oublié que les écoles étaient fermées à Pâques.

8.33

INTRODUCTION TO FRENCH PHONOLOGY

7.

Reading exercises

Lecture

1. Read.

    1. La fête commence.
    2. Ne vous en faites pas.
    3. Ils sont très célèbres.
    4. Le Rhône est un fleuve rapide.
    5. Je l'ai déjà vu.
    6. C'est un rôle difficile.

2. Read.

    1. Vous en voulez encore?
    2. Est-ce qu'il est trop fort?
    3. Est-ce que c'est la vôtre?
    4. Vous aimez les roses?
    5. Vous cherchez une bonne?
    6. Vous avez des bottes?

3. Read.

    1. C'est un vieil appartement.
    2. C'est une vieille maison.
    3. C'est un vieil appareil.
    4. Le seuil de la maison.
    5. Nous avons un bail de cinq ans.
    6. Le soleil brille.

4. Read.

    1. A quelle heure vient-il?
    2. Que veut-il faire?
    3. Quel âge ont-ils?
    4. Les écoles sont ouvertes?
    5. Pourquoi ne travaille-t-il pas?
    6. Vous avez pris l'avion?

5. Read.

    1. Je ne vais pas travailler.
    2. Il ne va pas à l'école.
    3. Nicole ne travaille pas.
    4. Elle ne veut pas nous le dire.
    5. Vous ne me dérangez pas.
    6. Nous ne sommes pas à l'hôtel.

8.34

6. Read.

    1. Il y en a un à six heures.
    2. Il n'y en a pas.
    3. Il y en a beaucoup.
    4. Il y en a trois autres.
    5. Il n'y en a pas d'autres.
    6. Il y en a encore un.

7. Read.

    1. Nous avons déjeuné à midi.
    2. Nous avons emménagé samedi.
    3. Vous avez manqué votre train.
    4. Ils ont déjeuné ici.
    5. Il a manqué son train.
    6. Elle a emménagé en octobre.

Chapter Eight, end of Part Two.

Go to lab for Tests 1 through 6.

Chapter Eight, Part Three

Tests

Test 1

Listen to the following words and write them.

Listen	Write
1. ( )	1. _____
2. ( )	2. _____
3. ( )	3. _____
4. ( )	4. _____
5. ( )	5. _____
6. ( )	6. _____
7. ( )	7. _____
8. ( )	8. _____
9. ( )	9. _____
10. ( )	10. _____

Test 2

The pronunciation of the following words may be right or wrong. Look, listen and check the appropriate column.

			Right	Wrong
1.	l'école	1.	____	____
2.	six ans	2.	____	____
3.	en octobre	3.	____	____
4.	c'est fête	4.	____	____
5.	fermé	5.	____	____
6.	ma fille	6.	____	____

8.36

INTRODUCTION TO FRENCH PHONOLOGY

			Right	Wrong
7.	mon fils	7.	_____	_____
8.	j'avais oublié	8.	_____	_____
9.	les enfants	9.	_____	_____
10.	mon fils	10.	_____	_____

STOP TAPE RECORDER

Test 3

Rewrite the following sentences in the negative form.

                                         Rewrite

1. C'est vrai.   1. _____
2. Ils grandissent.   2. _____
3. Elle a sept ans.   3. _____
4. C'est fête.   4. _____
5. Ils vont au café.   5. _____
6. Je pars en octobre.   6. _____
7. C'était Pâques.   7. _____
8. Elles sont à la gare.   8. _____
9. Ils ont les billets.   9. _____
10. Il vient à huit heures.   10. _____

Test 4

Rewrite each of the following words correctly.

                                         Rewrite

1. anfants   1. _____
2. fête   2. _____
3. mintenant   3. _____
4. l'ecôle   4. _____

			Rewrite
5.	Pâque	5.	_____
6.	j'avai	6.	_____
7.	āge	7.	_____
8.	vitte	8.	_____
9.	modèrne	9.	_____
10.	bientot	10.	_____

START TAPE RECORDER

Test 5

Write the number of syllables that you hear in each of these sentences.

Listen		Write the number of syllables
1. ( )	1.	_____
2. ( )	2.	_____
3. ( )	3.	_____
4. ( )	4.	_____
5. ( )	5.	_____
6. ( )	6.	_____
7. ( )	7.	_____
8. ( )	8.	_____
9. ( )	9.	_____
10. ( )	10.	_____

8.38

Test 6

The following sentences may be pronounced with the wrong intonation. Check the appropriate column.

		Right	Wrong
1.	Elles sont fermées. ( )	___	___
2.	C'est vrai. ( )	___	___
3.	J'avais oublié. ( )	___	___
4.	Nous avons un appartement. ( )	___	___
5.	Les enfants grandissent si vite. ( )	___	___
6.	Vous avez de la chance. ( )	___	___
7.	Quelle heure est-il? ( )	___	___
8.	Quand partez-vous? ( )	___	___
9.	Vous l'avez manqué. ( )	___	___
10.	Je vais déjeuner. ( )	___	___

END OF CHAPTER EIGHT

Chapter Nine.

PART 1

Dialogue. (Laboratory)

PART 2

1. The letter "s" between vowels. (Laboratory)
2. The vowel "e." (Laboratory)
3. Numbers: 1-2-3-4-5-6-7-8-9-10-18-40-50-59. (Laboratory)
4. The verb "être" = to be. (Laboratory)
5. The verb "avoir" = to have. (Laboratory)
6. Review. (Laboratory)
7. Preparation for Class. (Homework)
8. Reading exercises. (Classroom)

PART 3

Tests. (Classroom and laboratory)

Chapter Nine

Dialogue

A: Vous désirez Monsieur? — May I help you Sir?

B: Je voudrais deux chambres communicantes. — I would like two connecting rooms.

A: Pour combien de personnes? — For how many persons?

B: Nous sommes quatre. Les enfants, ma femme et moi. — We're a party of four: the children, my wife and I.

A: J'ai exactement ce qu'il vous faut. Combien de temps restez-vous? — I have exactly what you need. How long will you stay?

B: Pas plus de trois jours. — No more than three days.

INTRODUCTION TO FRENCH PHONOLOGY

1. Listen to the following conversation.

    A: (?)
    B: ( )
    A: (?)
    B: ( )
    A: (?)
    B: ( )

2. Listen to the intonation and rhythm of each sentence.

    A: (?)
    B: ( )
    A: (?)
    B: ( )
    A: (?)
    B: ( )

3. This is the first sentence of the conversation. Listen.

    ( ) ( ) ( )

4. The last word of the sentence is familiar to you. Listen again.

    ( ) ( ) ( )

5. Listen. Is this (R) or (W)?

    ( ) ( )

(W)

6. How about this? Is it (R) or (W)? Listen.

    ( ) ( )

(W)

7. Imitate the correct pronunciation.

    ( )x ( )x ( )x

8. Again.

    ( )x ( )x ( )x

9. Here is what it means. Look and listen.

    May I help you Sir? (Fr) (Fr)

10. Look at the French sentence now. Listen and imitate.

    Vous désirez Monsieur? ( )x ( )x ( )x

9.3

INTRODUCTION TO FRENCH PHONOLOGY

11. Repeat frame number 10.

12. Here is another sentence. Listen.

    ( ) ( ) ( )

13. Listen again.

    ( ) ( ) ( )

14. Listen to the last word of that sentence.

    ( ) ( ) ( )

15. Listen again. How many nasal vowels do you hear?

    ( ) ( )

(1)

16. This pronunciation is wrong. Listen.

    ( ) ( )

17. Which is right? Number one or two?

    (1)/(2)   (1)/(2)

(2)

18. Listen again. Is it (R) or (W)?

    ( ) ( )

(W)

19. Which is right? One, two or three?

    (1) (2) (3)

(2)

20. Imitate the correct pronunciation.

    ( )x ( )x ( )x

21. Again.

    ( )x ( )x ( )x

22. Here are two more words added to the one you've said. Listen.

    ( ) ( ) ( )

9.4

23. Listen again.

    ( )   ( )   ( )

24. Listen and imitate.

    ( )x   ( )x   ( )x

25. Again.

    ( )x   ( )x   ( )x

26. Look at the French words, listen and imitate.

    deux chambres communicantes   ( )x   ( )x   ( )x

27. We'll complete the sentence by adding two more words in front of those you know. Listen.

    ( )   ( )   ( )

28. Listen again.

    ( )   ( )   ( )

29. Listen and imitate the first part of the sentence.

    ( )x   ( )x   ( )x

30. Again.

    ( )x   ( )x   ( )x

31. Here is the complete sentence.

    ( )   ( )   ( )

32. Listen and imitate.

    ( )x   ( )x   ( )x

33. Again.

    ( )x   ( )x   ( )x

34. Here is the meaning of that sentence. Look and listen.

    I would like two connecting rooms.   ( )   ( )

INTRODUCTION TO FRENCH PHONOLOGY

35. Look at the French words. Listen and imitate.

    Je voudrais deux chambres communicantes.

    ( )x ( )x

36. Imitate again.

    ( )x ( )x ( )x

37. Listen to the following exchange.

    A: (?)
    B: ( )

38. Listen again.

    A: (?)
    B: ( )

39. Answer your instructor.

    Instructor: (Q)
    You: _____

40. Again.

    Instructor: (Q)
    You: _____

41. This time ask the question and listen to the answer.

    (begin)
    You: _____?
    Instructor: (A)

42. Again.

    (begin)
    You: _____?
    Instructor: (A)

43. Here is another sentence. Listen.

    ( ) ( ) ( )

44. Listen again. How many syllables are there?

    ( ) ( ) ( )

(5)

9.6

45. Listen to the last word of the sentence.

    ( ) ( )

46. Listen again. Notice the pronunciation of the last consonant.

    ( ) ( )

47. Listen and imitate.

    ( )x ( )x ( )x

48. Which is right?

    (1)/(2)   (1)/(2)

(2)

49. Listen and imitate again.

    ( )x ( )x ( )x

50. Here are two more words added in front of the one that you know. Listen.

    ( ) ( ) ( )

51. Listen again. Is it a question?

    ( ) ( ) ( )

(yes)

52. Listen and imitate the question.

    ( )x ( )x ( )x

53. Is this (R) or (W)? Listen.

    ( ) ( ) ( )

(W)

54. Listen to the right pronunciation and imitate.

    ( )x ( )x ( )x

55. We'll add one more word to complete the sentence. Listen.

    ( ) ( ) ( )

INTRODUCTION TO FRENCH PHONOLOGY

56. Listen and imitate.

    ( )x ( )x ( )x

57. Again.

    ( )x ( )x ( )x

58. Look at the meaning of the question and listen.

    For how many persons? (Fr) (Fr)

59. Look at the writing in French. Listen and imitate.

    Pour combien de personnes? ( )x ( )x

60. Listen and imitate again.

    ( )x ( )x

61. Here is a new sentence. Listen.

    ( ) ( ) ( )

62. Listen again.

    ( ) ( )

63. Listen and imitate.

    ( )x ( )x ( )x

64. Again.

    ( )x ( )x ( )x

65. Here is another sentence preceded by the one you have just said. Listen.

    ( ) ( ) ( )

66. Listen again. This time only the new sentence will be said.

    ( ) ( ) ( )

67. Listen to the last two words of the sentence and imitate.

    ( )x ( )x ( )x

9.8

68. We'll add two more words in front of the ones you have said. Listen.

    ( ) ( ) ( )

69. Listen and imitate.

    ( )x ( )x ( )x

70. Again.

    ( )x ( )x ( )x

71. Now listen to the complete sentence.

    ( ) ( ) ( )

72. Listen again.

    ( ) ( )

73. Listen and imitate.

    ( )x ( )x ( )x

74. Again.

    ( )x ( )x ( )x

75. How many nasal vowels do you hear? Listen.

    ( ) ( )

(2)

76. Here are both sentences again. Listen.

    ( ) ( ) ( )

77. Listen to the first sentence (A) and imitate, then to the second (B) and imitate.

    (A)x(B)x   (A)x(B)x   (A)x(B)x

78. Listen and imitate both sentences.

    ( )x ( )x ( )x

79. Here is the meaning of the sentences. Look and listen.

    We are four: the children, my wife and I. (Fr)   (Fr)

INTRODUCTION TO FRENCH PHONOLOGY

80. Look at the writing in French. Listen and imitate.

    Nous sommes quatre. Les enfants, ma femme et moi.

    ( )x   ( )x

81. Imitate again.

    ( )x   ( )x   ( )x

82. Listen to this exchange.

    A: (?)
    B: ( )
    A: (?)
    B: ( )

83. Listen again.

    A: (?)
    B: ( )
    A: (?)
    B: ( )

84. Answer your instructor.

    Instructor: (Q)
    You: _____
    Instructor: (Q)
    You: _____

85. Again.

    Instructor: (Q)
    You: _____
    Instructor: (Q)
    You: _____

86. Now, you begin the conversation.

    (begin)
    You: _____?
    Instructor: (Q)
    You: _____?
    Instructor: (Q)

9.10

87. Again.

>   (begin)
>   You: _____?
>   Instructor: (A)
>   You: _____?
>   Instructor: (A)

88. Here is a new sentence. Listen.

    ( ) ( ) ( )

89. Listen to the last five words of that sentence.

    ( ) ( ) ( )

90. Listen again to these five words. How many syllables do you hear?

    ( ) ( ) ( )

(3)

91. Listen and imitate.

    ( )x ( )x ( )x

92. Again.

    ( )x ( )x ( )x

93. We'll add one more word in front of those you know. Listen.

    ( ) ( ) ( )

94. Now listen again and imitate.

    ( )x ( )x ( )x

95. Imitate again.

    ( )x ( )x ( )x

96. Listen to the complete sentence.

    ( ) ( ) ( )

97. Listen again.

    ( ) ( ) ( )

INTRODUCTION TO FRENCH PHONOLOGY 323

98. Listen and imitate.

    ( )x ( )x ( )x

99. Again.

    ( )x ( )x ( )x

100. Look at the meaning and listen to the French.

    I have exactly what you need. (Fr) (Fr)

101. Look at the writing in French, listen and imitate.

    J'ai exactement ce qu'il vous faut. ( )x ( )x

102. Imitate again.

    ( )x ( )x

103. Here is another sentence. Listen.

    ( ) ( ) ( )

104. Listen again. Is it a question?

    ( ) ( )

(yes)

105. Listen to the last two words.

    ( ) ( ) ( )

106. Now listen and imitate.

    ( )x ( )x ( )x

107. Imitate again.

    ( )x ( )x ( )x

108. Listen to the first part of the sentence.

    ( ) ( ) ( )

109. Listen and imitate.

    ( )x ( )x

9.12

110. Again.

    ( )x ( )x

111. Now, imitate the last part of the sentence.

    ( )x ( )x ( )x

112. Listen to both sentences.

    ( ) ( ) ( )

113. Listen and imitate.

    ( )x ( )x ( )x

114. Look at the meaning of the 2nd sentence and listen.

    How long are you staying? (Fr) (Fr)

115. Look at the writing in French, listen and imitate.

    Combien de temps restez-vous? ( )x ( )x

116. Imitate again.

    ( )x ( )x

117. We'll say the last two sentences again. Listen.

    ( ) ( )

118. Listen again.

    ( ) ( )

119. Listen and imitate sentence (A) and then sentence (B).

    (A)x (B)x   (A)x (B)x   (A)x (B)x

120. Listen and then imitate both sentences.

    ( ) ( )   ( )x ( )x ( )x

121. Imitate again.

    ( )x ( )x ( )x

INTRODUCTION TO FRENCH PHONOLOGY

122. Listen to this exchange.

   A: (?)
   B: ( )
   A: (?)
   B: ( )
   A: (?)

123. Listen again.

   A: (?)
   B: ( )
   A: (?)
   B: ( )
   A: (?)

124. Answer your instructor.

   Instructor: (?)
   You: _____
   Instructor: (?)
   You: _____
   Instructor: (?)

125. Again.

   Instructor: (?)
   You: _____
   Instructor: (?)
   You: _____
   Instructor: (?)

126. This time you start the conversation.

   (begin)
   You: _____ ?
   Instructor: (A)
   You: _____ ?
   Instructor: (A)
   You: _____ ?

127. Again.

   (begin)
   You: _____ ?
   Instructor: (A)
   You: _____ ?
   Instructor: (A)
   You: _____ ?

End of Tape One. Part One continues on Tape Two.

INTRODUCTION TO FRENCH PHONOLOGY

Tape Two, Part One

128. This is the last sentence in the dialogue. Listen.

    ( ) ( ) ( )

129. Listen again. How many syllables are there?

    ( ) ( ) ( )

(5)

130. Listen to the last two word and imitate.

    ( ) ( )   ( )x ( )x ( )x

131. Imitate again.

    ( )x ( )x ( )x

132. We'll add the rest of the sentence in front. Listen.

    ( ) ( ) ( )

133. Listen again and imitate.

    ( ) ( )   ( )x ( )x ( )x

134. Imitate again.

    ( )x ( )x ( )x

135. Look at the meaning in English while listening to the French.

    No more than three days. ( ) ( )

136. Now look at the French, listen and imitate.

    Pas plus de trois jours. ( )x ( )x ( )x

137. Imitate again.

    ( )x ( )x ( )x

138. This is the complete conversation. Listen.

    A: (?)
    B: ( )
    A: (?)
    B: ( )
    A: (?)
    B: ( )

9.15

INTRODUCTION TO FRENCH PHONOLOGY

139. Listen again to the conversation.

        A: (?)
        B: ( )
        A: (?)
        B: ( )
        A: (?)
        B: ( )

140. Listen and imitate each sentence in the conversation.

        A: (?)x
        B: ( )x
        A: (?)x
        B: ( )x
        A: (?)x
        B: ( )x

141. Repeat frame number 140.

142. Answer your instructor.

        Instructor: (?)
        You: _____
        Instructor: (?)
        You: _____
        Instructor: (?)
        You: _____

143. Repeat frame number 142.

144. This time, you begin the conversation.

        (begin)
        You: _____?
        Instructor: (A)
        You: _____?
        Instructor: (A)
        You: _____?
        Instructor: (A)

9.16

145. Again.

>	(begin)
>	You: _____?
>	Instructor: (A)
>	You: _____?
>	Instructor: (A)
>	You: _____?
>	Instructor: (A)

146. For more practice with the conversation review frames number 139 to number 146.

End of Chapter Nine, Part One.

Report to your classroom.

INTRODUCTION TO FRENCH PHONOLOGY

Part Two

1.

The letter "s" between vowels.

1. Look at this French sentence and listen to the underlined consonant in the second word.

    Vous dé<u>s</u>irez Monsieur? ( )

2. Listen again to that sentence above. Is the underlined consonant pronounced as an "s" or "z"?

    ( )

    Student's answer: <u>z</u>

3. An "s" between two vowels is pronounced "z." Look and listen.

    casé   posé   misé   rusé   ( )

4. Here are more words with the "s" sound in final position. Look and listen.

    case   pose   mise   ruse   ( )

5. Now look, listen and imitate.

    a. brise - brisé   ( )x
    b. aise - aisé   ( )x
    c. cause - causé   ( )x
    d. muse - musé   ( )x

6. Say the following words before your instructor does.

    musique   x( )
    amusant   x( )
    rasoir   x( )
    saisi   x( )

7. Here are more words with "s" between vowels. Look and listen.

    décision   asiatique   fusion   vision   ( )

8. Now look, listen and imitate.

    occasion ( )x
    révision ( )x
    casier   ( )x
    plusieurs ( )x

9. Say the following words before your instructor does.

    décision x( )
    plusieurs x( )
    occasion x( )
    asiatique x( )

10. Here are more words. Say them before your instructor does.

    valise   x( )
    fusillé x( )
    vision   x( )
    résidu   x( )

11. You remember "s" in a linking position (liaison) which we discussed in chapter two. Here are a few examples. Say them before your instructor does.

    les enfants   x( )
    vous arrivez   x( )
    nous y allons x( )
    ils en font   x( )

12. Say the following words before your instructor does.

    des amis   x( )
    les voisins x( )
    le réseau   x( )
    une infusion x( )
    la brise   x( )

13. When the letter "s" is surrounded by a consonant and a vowel or a vowel and a consonant, it is pronounced "s." Look and listen.

    l'espace l'absence l'esprit brusque ( )

INTRODUCTION TO FRENCH PHONOLOGY

14. Look at the following words and say them before your instructor does.

    l'averse   x( )
    cousin   x( )
    les course x( )
    la pose   x( )
    la poste   x( )
    la valise x( )

15. Here are more words for you to say.

    désespoir   x( )
    des amis   x( )
    la crise   x( )
    l'instant   x( )
    vision   x( )

16. The "s" at the beginning of a word is always pronounced "s." Look, listen and imitate.

    la souris   ( )x
    le sous   ( )x
    les saints   ( )x
    le système   ( )x

17. One "s" in the following words is pronounced "z." In which word is it?

    1. liste   2. crise   3. crispé   4. arsenic

    Student's answer: <u>2</u>

18. Which of the following words have the letter "s" pronounced "z"?

    1. des hôtels   2. la salle   3. dessert
    4. desert   5. poison

    Student's answer: <u>1, 4, 5</u>

2.

The vowel "e"

19. We stated in Chapter Three, Part Two that in order to avoid a cluster of three consonants, the vowel "e" is inserted between two of them. Look and listen.

    doublement ( )   parsemer ( )   vastement ( )
    12 3   12 3   12 3

9.20

20. Notice that the following words have 2 consonants preceding the "e" and one following it. Look and listen.

   gouve‿rnement ( )   parve‿nir ( )   propre‿té ( )
   ‾2‾ ‾1‾   ‾2‾ ‾1‾   ‾2‾ ‾1‾

21. Since French phrases are pronounced as if they were one continuous long word, the rule applies to entire uninterrupted phrases just as it does to isolated words. (Chapter six). Look and listen.

   Il‿ ne part‿ pas.   ( )
   ‾1‾ ‾2‾ ‾3‾

   Je n/ pars‿ pas.   ( )
   ‾1‾ ‾2‾

22. Notice that when two consonants precede the "e" and one follows it, the "e" is pronounced.

   Il‿ ne part‿ pas.   ( )
   ‾2‾ ‾1‾

   Un sac‿ de farine   ( )
        ‾2‾ ‾1‾

   Pour‿ demain.   ( )
   ‾2‾ ‾1‾

23. However the "e" may be dropped when preceded by one consonant and followed by two. Look and listen.

   pas l/ grand.   ( )
   ‾1‾ ‾2‾

   ça m/ plaît.   ( )
   ‾1‾ ‾2‾

   c'est l/ train.   ( )
   ‾1‾ ‾2‾

24. In which sentence should the "e" be pronounced.

   a. Il ne vient pas.
   b. Vous le voulez?
   c. Vous n'avez pas de chance.

   Student's answer: _a_

9.21

INTRODUCTION TO FRENCH PHONOLOGY

25. Say the following before your instructor does.

    Vous n'allez pas le trouver. x( )
    Je ne sais pas ce qu'il a. x( )
    C'est le bras droit. x( )
    La porte blanche. x( )

        3.

    Numbers: 1-2-3-4-5-6-7-8-9-10-
              18-40-50-59

26. Say the following numbers in French.

    9   x( )
    7   x( )
    5   x( )
    1   x( )
    2   x( )
    8   x( )
    6   x( )
    4   x( )
    3   x( )
    10 x( )

27. Now say these.

    40 x( )
    50 x( )
    59 x( )
    18 x( )

28. Your instructor is going to ask you questions. Answer them according to the following example. Part of your answer is underlined.

	Instructor		Answer
(Q)	à une heure		( )
a.	(Q) quatre heures	You:	( )
b.	(Q) à dix huit heures dix	You:	( )
c.	(Q) cinq heures dix	You:	( )
d.	(Q) sept ans	You:	( )
e.	(Q) huit ans et demi	You:	( )
f.	(Q) à trois heures cinq	You:	( )

9.22

INTRODUCTION TO FRENCH PHONOLOGY

29. Say the following numbers in French.

    9   x( )
    10   x( )
    8   x( )
    6   x( )
    2   x( )
    3   x( )
    1   x( )
    7   x( )
    4   x( )
    5   x( )

30. Listen to the following numbers.

    neuf ( )
    cinquante-neuf ( )
    neuf enfants ( )
    cinquante-neuf jours ( )

31. Look at the numbers in frame 30 again and listen. Is the "f" at the end of "neuf" pronounced?

    Student's answer: <u>Yes</u>

32. This time "neuf" is followed by the words "heure" and "ans." Look and listen.

    cinquante-neuf ans ( )
    neuf heures ( )

33. Here again is "neuf" followed by "heure" or "ans." Look at the underlined consonant and listen. Does it sound like an "f"?

    neu<u>f</u> ans ( )
    neu<u>f</u> heures ( )

    Student's answer: <u>no</u>

    What does it sound like?

    Student's answer: <u>v</u>

34. The "f" of "neuf" always sounds like a "v" when followed by either "ans" or "heure." Say the following phrases.

    neuf jours   x( )
    neuf enfants   x( )
    cinquante neuf ans   x( )
    neuf heures   x( )
    neuf écoles   x( )

INTRODUCTION TO FRENCH PHONOLOGY

35. Answer the questions according to the following example. Part of your answer is underlined.

	Instructor		Answer
(Q)	<u>8</u>		( )
a.	(Q)	<u>7</u>	You: x( )
b.	(Q)	<u>10</u>	You: x( )
c.	(Q)	<u>3</u>	You: x( )
d.	(Q)	<u>9</u>	you: x( )
e.	(Q)	<u>6</u>	You: x( )
f.	(Q)	<u>7</u>	You: x( )
g.	(Q)	<u>1</u>	You: x( )
h.	(Q)	<u>8</u>	You: x( )

4.

The verb "être" = to be

36. You know all of the different persons of the verb "to be" in the present tense. Look at the following English sentences and say them in French.

a.	It's a holiday.	x( )
b.	They're closed.	x( )
c.	Am I late?	x( )
d.	It's five past ten.	x( )
e.	We are four.	x( )
f.	You're still at the hôtel?	x( )

37. Look at the following sentences then say them using the negative form "ne...pas."

a.	Je suis en retard.	x( )
b.	Nous sommes à l'heure.	x( )
c.	L'hôtel est très moderne.	x( )
d.	C'est fête.	x( )
e.	Vous êtes en retard.	x( )

38. Look at the following sentences then say them in French.

a.	It's noon.	x( )
b.	I'm next door.	x( )
c.	You're on time.	x( )
d.	We're at the hôtel.	x( )
e.	The schools are closed.	x( )

9.24

39. Your instructor is going to ask you questions. Answer them according to the following example. Part of your answer is underlined.

		Instructor		Answer
(Q)		très grand et moderne	You:	( )
a.	(Q)	quatre	You:	x( )
b.	(Q)	à l'école	You:	x( )
c.	(Q)	à côté	You:	x( )
d.	(Q)	dix heures dix	You:	x( )

5.

The verb "avoir" = to have

40. You know all the different forms of the verb "to have" in the present tense. Look at the following English sentences and say them in French.

    a. We finally have an apartment.   x( )
    b. How old are they?   x( )
    c. I have exactly what you need.   x( )
    d. My daughter is seven.   x( )
    e. You missed it.   x( )

41. All the following sentences will contain the negative form "ne...pas". Listen. Then say them omitting the "ne...pas."

    a. ( ) x( )
    b. ( ) x( )
    c. ( ) x( )
    d. ( ) x( )
    e. ( ) x( )

42. The statements you're going to hear are in the affirmative form. Listen to them, then say them in the negative form.

    a. ( ) x( )
    b. ( ) x( )
    c. ( ) x( )
    d. ( ) x( )
    e. ( ) x( )

9.25

INTRODUCTION TO FRENCH PHONOLOGY

43. Say the following English sentence in French.

    a. She is lucky.   x( )
    b. He is nine years old.   x( )
    c. You are lucky.   x( )
    d. We have an apartment.   x( )
    e. I don't have the tickets. x( )

44. Say the following sentences in French before your instructor does.

    a. Do you have an apartment?   x( )
    b. No, I'm at the hotel.   x( )
    c. Do you have connecting rooms?   x( )
    d. Yes. How many days are you staying? x( )
    e. No more than two days.   x( )

45. Here are more sentences. Say them in French before your instructor does.

    a. I have exactly one hour.   x( )
    b. I have more than three hours.   x( )
    c. We have exactly what you need.   x( )
    d. We are at the hotel.   x( )
    e. We are lucky.   x( )

6.

Review

46. This is a review. Look at the following sentences and say them before your instructor does.

    a. Nous ne sommes pas en retard. x( )
        Ils n'ont pas de chambres. x( )
        Pas avant trois mois. x( )
        C'est exactement ce qu'il nous faut. x( )

    b. Vous désirez quelque chose? x( )
        Que désirez-vous? x( )
        Il n'a pas encore dix ans? x( )
        Quand va-t-il avoir six ans? x( )

    c. Pourquoi l'école est-elle fermée? x( )
        Les trains sont très rapides. x( )
        Ils ne sont pas toujours à l'heure. x( )
        Voulez-vous voir l'appartement? x( )

d. Je n'aime pas le costume bleu. x( )
    Nous partons dans l'après-midi. x( )
    Ils grandissent très vite. x( )
    C'est la saison chaude. x( )

Report to your classroom.

INTRODUCTION TO FRENCH PHONOLOGY

7.

Preparation

Exercice un

Dites en français

1.	For three days	1.	Pour trois jours
2.	Exactly	2.	Exactement
3.	How long	3.	Combien de temps
4.	Two persons	4.	Deux personnes
5.	We are	5.	Nous sommes
6.	Sir	6.	Monsieur
7.	Connecting	7.	Communicantes
8.	The other bedroom	8.	L'autre chambre
9.	I have	9.	J'ai
10.	How long	10.	Combien
11.	Me	11.	Moi
12.	One child	12.	Un enfant
13.	Three days	13.	Trois jours
14.	I would like	14.	Je voudrais
15.	The bedrooms	15.	Les chambres
16.	What you need	16.	Ce qu'il vous faut
17.	My wife	17.	Ma femme

Exercice deux

Dites en anglais

1.	Ils ont deux enfants.	1.	They have two children.
2.	C'est mon fils.	2.	He is my son.
3.	Ce n'est pas mon fils.	3.	He is not my son.
4.	C'est mon train.	4.	It's my train.
5.	Nous avons ce qu'il vous faut.	5.	We have what you need.
6.	C'est pour quatre personnes.	6.	It's for a party of four.
7.	Ils n'ont pas d'enfants.	7.	They have no children.
8.	Vous avez de la chance.	8.	You're lucky.
9.	Vous n'avez pas de chance.	9.	You're not lucky.
10.	Nous n'avons pas de chambres communicantes.	10.	We don't have any connecting rooms.
11.	Mon fils et ma fille grandissent très vite.	11.	My son and my daughter grow up fast.
12.	Il y a une école à côté.	12.	There's a school next door.
13.	Il n'y a pas d'école à côté.	13.	There is no school next door.
14.	Ma fille grandit.	14.	My daughter grows up very fast.

15.	Il vous faut deux chambres communicantes.	15.	You need two connecting rooms.
16.	C'est ma fille.	16.	She is my daughter.
17.	Combien de jours avez-vous?	17.	How many days do you have?
18.	Il vous faut plus de trois jours.	18.	You need more than three days.
19.	Combien de chambres désirez-vous?	19.	How many rooms do you want?
20.	Nous n'y allons pas souvent.	20.	We don't go (there) often.

Exercice trois

Dites en français

1.	He is our son.	1.	C'est notre fils.
2.	He is not our son.	2.	Ce n'est pas notre fils.
3.	She is my daughter.	3.	C'est ma fille.
4.	She is not my daughter.	4.	Ce n'est pas ma fille.
5.	We are four: my wife, the children and I.	5.	Nous sommes quatre: ma femme, les enfants et moi.
6.	He is our son.	6.	C'est notre fils.
7.	It's our train.	7.	C'est notre train.
8.	Where are you moving to?	8.	Où emménagez-vous?
9.	How old is she?	9.	Quel âge a-t-elle?
10.	How old are you?	10.	Quel âge avez-vous?
11.	She is fifty years old.	11.	Elle a cinquante ans.
12.	He is twelve.	12.	Il a douze ans.
13.	He is going to be six years old in October.	13.	Il va avoir six ans en octobre.
14.	It's a holiday.	14.	C'est fête.
15.	It's not a holiday.	15.	Ce n'est pas fête.
16.	She is my wife.	16.	C'est ma femme.
17.	How many children do you have?	17.	Combien d'enfants avez-vous?
18.	It's a large apartment.	18.	C'est un grand appartement.
19.	She has five children.	19.	Elle a cinq enfants.
20.	It's the hotel next door.	20.	C'est l'hôtel à côté.

Exercice quatre

Professeur	Vous
Les enfants sont en retard?	Oui, ils sont en retard.

1.	Vous avez un billet?	1.	Oui, j'ai un billet.
2.	Vous êtes en retard?	2.	Oui, je suis en retard.
3.	Vous allez déjeuner?	3.	Oui, je vais déjeuner.
4.	Les enfants sont en retard?	4.	Oui, ils sont en retard.

INTRODUCTION TO FRENCH PHONOLOGY

5. Les écoles sont fermées.
6. J'ai de la chance?
7. Vous partez samedi?
8. Je suis en retard?

5. Oui, elles sont fermées.
6. Oui, vous avez de la chance.
7. Oui, je pars samedi.
8. Oui, vous êtes en retard.

Exercice cinq

(fill in the blanks)

1. Il est à l'hôtel; il a la chambre quarante.
2. Je suis à l'hôtel; _____
3. Nous sommes à l'hôtel; _____
4. Ils sont à l'hôtel; _____
5. Elle est à l'hôtel; _____
6. Je suis à l'hôtel; _____
7. Elles sont à l'hôtel; _____
8. Il est à l'hôtel; _____

Exercice six

(Fill in the blanks)

1. Ils ne sont pas à l'hôtel; ils ont enfin un appartement.
2. Je ne suis pas à l'hôtel; _____
3. Elles ne sont pas à l'hôtel; _____
4. Il n'est pas à l'hôtel; _____
5. Nous ne sommes pas à l'hôtel; _____
6. Elle n'est pas à l'hôtel; _____
7. Ils ne sont pas à l'hôtel; _____
8. Je ne suis pas à l'hôtel; _____
9. Vous n'êtes pas à l'hôtel; _____

Exercice sept

Professeur	Vous
Je suis en retard.	Je ne suis pas en retard.
1. Les enfants vont à l'école.	1. Les enfants ne vont pas à l'école.
2. Je vais déjeuner.	2. Je ne vais pas déjeuner.
3. Nous sommes quatre.	3. Nous ne sommes pas quatre.
4. Le train est à l'heure.	4. Le train n'est pas à l'heure.
5. C'était Pâques.	5. Ce n'était pas Pâques.
6. Il est très grand.	6. Il n'est pas très grand.
7. C'est vrai.	7. Ce n'est pas vrai.
8. Je suis en retard.	8. Je ne suis pas en retard.
9. Il vient.	9. Il ne vient pas.
10. Je pars samedi.	10. Je ne pars pas samedi.

Exercice huit

Professeur	Vous
Vous partez en octobre.	Vous ne partez pas en octobre.

Professeur	Vous
1. Il est au café.	1. Il n'est pas au café.
2. Il sont à l'heure.	2. Ils ne sont pas à l'heure.
3. Nous avons les billets.	3. Nous n'avons pas les billets.
4. Les enfants sont à l'école.	4. Les enfants ne sont pas à l'école.
5. Ils vont à Paris.	5. Il ne vont pas à Paris.
6. Vous emménagez samedi.	6. Vous n'emménagez pas samedi.
7. Je vais à la gare.	7. Je ne vais pas à la gare.
8. Vous partez en octobre.	8. Vous ne partez pas en octobre.

Exercice neuf

Conversation dirigée

(Manual du professeur seulement)

Exercice dix

Professeur	Elèves
1. pour Paris	1. Pour Paris.
2. quelques trains	2. Quelques trains pour Paris.
3. il y a	3. Il y a quelques trains pour Paris.
4. l'après-midi	4. Il y a quelques trains pour Paris l'après-midi.
5. seulement	5. Il y a quelques trains pour Paris l'après-midi seulement.

Exercice onze

Professeur	Elèves
1. téléphoner	1. Téléphoner.
2. nous avons	2. Nous avons téléphoné.
3. à l'ambassade	3. Nous avons téléphoné à l'ambassade.
4. à une heure	4. Nous avons téléphoné à l'ambassade à une heure.
5. américaine	5. Nous avons téléphoné à l'ambassade américaine à une heure.

9.31

Exercice douze

	Professeur		Elèves
1.	il vient	1.	Il vient.
2.	d'emménager	2.	Il vient d'emménager.
3.	dans un appartement	3.	Il vient d'emménager dans un appartement.
4.	moderne	4.	Il vient d'emménager dans un appartement moderne.
5.	à côté de la gare	5.	Il vient d'emménager dans un appartement moderne à côté de la gare.

Exercice treize

	Professeur		Elèves
1.	un billet	1.	Un billet.
2.	de première	2.	Un billet de première.
3.	Vous avez	3.	Vous avez un billet de première.
4.	aller et retour	4.	Vous avez un billet de première aller et retour.
5.	est-ce que	5.	Est-ce que vous avez un billet de première aller et retour.
6.	pour Paris	6.	Est-ce que vous avez un billet de première aller et retour pour Paris?

8.

Reading exercises

Lecture

1. Read.

    1. Vous désirez, Monsieur?
    2. Vous partez, Madame?
    3. Vous voulez l'adresse, Monsieur?
    4. Vous avez l'adresse, Mademoiselle?
    5. Vous cherchez vos amis, Monsieur?
    6. Vous connaissez la route, Madame?

2. Read.

    1. Nous cherchons un taxi.
    2. Nous restons jusqu'à samedi.
    3. Nous avons de la chance.
    4. Nous déménageons samedi.
    5. Nous fermons à six heures.
    6. Nous préférons des chambres communicantes.

3. Read.

    1. Combien de personnes y a-t-il?
    2. Combien de jours voulez-vous?
    3. Combien de valises emportez-vous?
    4. Combien de mois faut-il?
    5. Combien de chambres leur faut-il?
    6. Combien d'enfants avez-vous?

4. Read.

    1. Il a de la chance.
    2. Il n'a pas de chance.
    3. Ils ont des billets.
    4. Ils n'ont pas de billets.
    5. Nous avons des enfants.
    6. Nous n'avons pas d'enfants.

5. Read.

    1. Vous ne partez pas.
    2. Nous partons
    3. Vous ne savez pas.
    4. Nous savons.
    5. Vous ne restez pas.
    6. Nous restons.

9.33

6. Read.

    1. J'ai les billets.
    2. Nous n'avons pas les billets.
    3. Ils ont un appartement.
    4. Il a dix huit ans.
    5. Vous avez de la chance.
    6. Elle n'a pas le temps.

7. Read.

    1. Les enfants grandissent trop vite.
    2. Ma fille grandit trop vite.
    3. Ils finissent leur déjeuner.
    4. Nous finissons notre déjeuner.
    5. Je ne brunis pas facilement.
    6. Vous brunissez facilement.

8. Read.

    1. Ils grandissent.
    2. Ils glissent.
    3. Ils tombent.
    4. Ils parlent.
    5. Ils arrivent.
    6. Ils restent.
    7. Ils partent.
    8. Ils déjeunent.
    9. Ils emménagent.
    10. Ils entrent.

Chapter Nine, end of Part Two.

Go to lab for Test 1 through 8.

INTRODUCTION TO FRENCH PHONOLOGY

Chapter Nine, Part Three

Tests

Test 1

Listen to the following words and write them.

1. ( )   1. _____
2. ( )   2. _____
3. ( )   3. _____
4. ( )   4. _____
5. ( )   5. _____
6. ( )   6. _____
7. ( )   7. _____
8. ( )   8. _____
9. ( )   9. _____
10. ( )   10. _____

Test 2

The pronunciation of the following words may be right or wrong. Look, listen and check the appropriate column.

		Right	Wrong
1.	exactement	1. ____	____
2.	communicantes	2. ____	____
3.	deux chambres	3. ____	____
4.	j'ai	4. ____	____
5.	personne	5. ____	____
6.	ma femme	6. ____	____
7.	les enfants	7. ____	____
8.	moi	8. ____	____

INTRODUCTION TO FRENCH PHONOLOGY

			Right	Wrong
9.	mon fils	9.	_____	_____
10.	monsieur	10.	_____	_____

Test 3

There is a mistake in each of the following words. Rewrite each word correctly.

1. meusieur   1. _____
2. conbiem   2. _____
3. exactment   3. _____
4. lécole   4. _____
5. toujour   5. _____
6. premiére   6. _____
7. l'enfent   7. _____
8. ma famme   8. _____

Test 4

Fill in the blanks using the verb "être" (to be)

1. Les enfants _____ à l'école.
2. Ma fille _____ toujours en retard.
3. Ils _____ au café.
4. Le train _____ à l'heure.
5. C' _____ très moderne.
6. Ce n' _____ pas ce qu'il faut.
7. Je _____ à l'hôtel.
8. Il _____ dix heures cinq.
9. Nous _____ cinq.
10. Vous _____ très grand.

9.36

Test 5

Fill in the blanks using the verb "avoir" (to have)

1. Notre fille _____ huit ans et demi.
2. Quel âge _____ les enfants?
3. Ils _____ deux chambres communicantes.
4. Est-ce que vous _____ les billets?
5. Vous _____ manqué le train.
6. Il _____ manqué le train.
7. J'_____ un grand appartement.
8. Nous _____ de la chance.

Test 6

Fill in the blanks using "avoir" or "être."

1. Je ne _____ pas en retard.
2. Nous _____ enfin un appartement.
3. Les enfants _____ à l'école.
4. Vous _____ deux chambres communicantes?
5. Ma fille _____ sept ans et demi.
6. Où _____ vos enfants?
7. Notre fils va _____ huit ans en octobre.
8. Notre fille _____ à Paris.
9. Nous _____ en retard.
10. C' _____ tout.

9.37

INTRODUCTION TO FRENCH PHONOLOGY

Test 7

Look at the following sentences. Check in the appropriate column whether their construction is right or wrong.

		Right	Wrong
1.	j'avais oublié c'était Pâques.	_____	_____
2.	Je voudrais chambres communicantes.	_____	_____
3.	Nous avons quatre enfants.	_____	_____
4.	Combien temps restez-vous?	_____	_____
5.	J'ai exactement qu'il vous faut.	_____	_____
6.	Notre fils va avoir six en octobre.	_____	_____
7.	Il vous faut plus de trois jours.	_____	_____
8.	Ils sont en retard de quelques minutes.	_____	_____
9.	Vous allez souvent?	_____	_____
10.	Avez-vous déjeuné à côté?	_____	_____

Test 8

Write the number of syllables that you hear in each of the following sentences.

Write

1. ( )   1. _____
2. ( )   2. _____
3. ( )   3. _____
4. ( )   4. _____
5. ( )   5. _____
6. ( )   6. _____
7. ( )   7. _____
8. ( )   8. _____

END OF CHAPTER NINE.

9.38

Chapter Ten

PART 1

    Dialogue. (Laboratory)

PART 2

1. The consonant "ʕ." (Laboratory)
2. The verb "aller" to go. (Laboratory)
3. Verbs ending in "er" like "déjeuner." (Laboratory)
4. Past tense, "passé composé." (Laboratory)
5. Review. (Laboratory)
6. Preparation for Class. (Homework)
7. Reading exercises. (Classroom)

PART 3

    Tests. (Classroom and laboratory)

Chapter Ten

Dialogue

A: Quelle belle journée! —What a beautiful day?

B: En effet. Il fait vraiment beau ces temps-ci. —Yes indeed. It's really nice lately.

A: Pourvu que ça dure. —Hope it'll last.

B: Vous avez fait des projets pour le week-end? —Have you made any plans for the week-end?

A: Oui. Nous allons au bord de la mer. Et vous? —Yes. We're going to the seaside, and you?

B: Nous aussi peut-être. Ça va dépendre du temps. —Maybe we ('ll go) too. It'll depend on the weather.

A: Ne soyez pas si pessimiste; voyons! —(Come on!) Don't be so pessimistic.

Part One

1. Listen to the following conversation in French.

    A: (!)
    B: ( )
    A: ( )
    B: (?)
    A: (?)
    B: ( )
    A: (!)

2. Listen again to the conversation.

    A: (!)
    B: ( )
    A: ( )
    B: (?)
    A: (?)
    B: ( )
    A: (!)

3. Listen to the first sentence of the conversation.

    ( ) ( ) ( )

4. The sentence has three words. Listen to the last two.

    ( ) ( ) ( )

5. Listen again. Notice the rhythm and intonation.

    ( ) ( ) ( )

6. Listen again and imitate.

    ( )x ( )x ( )x

7. Imitate again.

    ( )x ( )x ( )x

8. Now listen to the full sentence.

    ( ) ( ) ( )

9. Listen and again notice the rhythm and intonation.

    ( ) ( ) ( )

INTRODUCTION TO FRENCH PHONOLOGY

10. This time, listen and imitate.

    ( )x ( )x ( )x

11. Listen again to the sentence. Is it (R) or (W)?

    ( ) ( )

(W)

12. Which one is (R), number 1 or 2?

    (1) (2)

(1)

13. Look, listen and imitate.

    Quelle belle journée! ( )x ( )x

14. This time, listen and imitate.

    ( )x ( )x ( )x

15. Look at the meaning and imitate the French.

    What a beautiful day! (Fr)x (Fr)x

16. Imitate again.

    ( )x ( )x

17. Here is another sentence. Listen.

    ( ) ( )

18. There are two words in this sentence. Listen and imitate.

    ( )x ( )x ( )x

19. Is this (R) or (W)?

    ( ) ( )

(W)

20. Which is right? 1 or 2?

    (1) (2)

(2)

21. Listen again and imitate.

    ( )x ( )x ( )x

10.4

22. Listen to this sentence.

    ( )   ( )   ( )

23. Listen to the last three words of the sentence.

    ( )   ( )   ( )

24. Listen again and imitate.

    ( )x   ( )x   ( )x

25. Now listen to the full sentence.

    ( )   ( )

26. These are the first four words. Listen.

    ( )   ( )   ( )

27. Listen and imitate.

    ( )x   ( )x   ( )x

28. Imitate again.

    ( )x   ( )x   ( )x

29. Here is the whole sentence again. Listen.

    ( )   ( )

30. Listen and imitate the 1st part of the sentence, then the second part.

    (1st part)x (2nd part)x (1st part)x (2nd part)x

31. Again.

    (1st part)x (2nd part)x (1st part)x (2nd part)x

32. Listen to the full sentence again.

    ( )   ( )

33. Now listen and imitate.

    ( )x   ( )x   ( )x

34. Again.

    ( )x   ( )x

10.5

INTRODUCTION TO FRENCH PHONOLOGY

35. Up to this point you have learned three sentences. Let's listen to the last two.

     ( )   ( )   ( )

36. Listen again.

     ( )   ( )

37. Now listen and imitate.

     ( )x   ( )x   ( )x

38. Imitate again.

     ( )x   ( )x

39. Look at the sentences and listen.

    En effet. Il fait vraiment beau ces temps-ci. ( ) ( )

40. This time look, listen and imitate.

    En effet. Il fait vraiment beau ces temps-ci.

     ( )x   ( )x

41. This is what the two sentences mean in English. Look at the meaning while imitating the French.

    Yes indeed. It is really nice lately.   (Fr)x   (Fr)x

42. Listen and imitate again.

     ( )x   ( )x

43. Listen to this exchange.

    A: (!)
    B: ( )

44. Answer your instructor.

    Instructor: (!)
    You: _____

45. Again.

    Instructor: (!)
    You: _____

10.6

356   INTRODUCTION TO FRENCH PHONOLOGY

46. This time, say the first sentence and then listen to your instructor.

    (begin)
    You: _____!
    Instructor: ( )

47. Again.

    (begin)
    You: _____!
    Instructor: ( )

48. Here is another sentence. Listen.

    ( ) ( ) ( )

49. Look at the meaning of this sentence and listen to the French.

    Hope it'll last. (Fr) (Fr)

50. Listen again. How many syllables are there?

    ( ) ( )

(4)

51. Listen and imitate.

    ( )x ( )x ( )x

52. Imitate again.

    ( )x ( )x

53. Look at the French sentence, listen and imitate.

    Pourvu que ça dure. ( )x ( )x

54. Imitate again.

    ( )x ( )x

55. Here is another sentence. Listen.

    ( ) ( ) ( )

56. Listen again. How many syllables are there?

    ( ) ( )

(11)

10.7

INTRODUCTION TO FRENCH PHONOLOGY

57. Listen to the last four words of this sentence.

    ( ) ( )

58. Listen and imitate.

    ( )x ( )x ( )x

59. Again.

    ( )x ( )x

60. Listen to the last six words of the sentence.

    ( ) ( ) ( )

61. Now listen and imitate.

    ( )x ( )x ( )x

62. Imitate again.

    ( )x ( )x ( )x

63. Listen again to the whole sentence.

    ( ) ( )

64. Listen and imitate this part of the sentence.

    ( )x ( )x ( )x

65. Imitate again.

    ( )x ( )x ( )x

66. Listen, and imitate the complete sentence.

    ( )x ( )x ( )x

67. Listen to the sentence. How many syllables are there?

    ( ) ( )

(11)

68. Look at the French sentence and imitate.

    Vous avez fait des projets pour le week-end?

    ( )x ( )x

69. Repeat frame No. 68.

10.8

70. Look at the English meaning and listen to the French.

   Have you made any plans for the week-end?

   ( )x ( )x

71. Listen to the sentence and imitate.

   ( )x ( )x

72. Imitate again.

   ( )x ( )x

73. Listen to this exchange.

   A: (')
   B: ( )
   A: ( )
   B: (?)

74. Listen, and imitate each sentence.

   A: (!)x B: ( )x A: ( )x B: (?)x

75. Repeat No. 74.

76. Answer your instructor.

   Instructor: (!)
   You: _____
   Instructor: ( )
   You: _____ ?

77. Repeat No. 76.

78. This time you begin the conversation with your instructor.

   (begin)
   You: _____ !
   Instructor: ( )
   You: _____
   Instructor: (?)

79. Repeat No. 78.

80. Here is another sentence. Listen

   ( ) ( ) ( )

10.9

INTRODUCTION TO FRENCH PHONOLOGY

81. Listen again. How many syllables are there?

    ( ) ( )

(11)

82. Listen to the last part of the sentence.

    ( ) ( )

(7)

83. Listen again. How many syllables are there?

    ( ) ( )

(7)

84. Listen and imitate.

    ( )x ( )x ( )x

85. Again.

    ( )x ( )x

86. The sentence has two more words in front. Listen.

    ( ) ( )

87. Listen to the first two repetitions and then imitate.

    ( ) ( ) ( )x ( )x

88. Imitate again.

    ( )x ( )x ( )x

89. Listen again to the complete sentence, this time with the word "oui" in front.

    ( ) ( )

90. Listen and imitate.

    ( )x ( )x

91. Look at the French, listen and imitate.

    Oui. Nous allons au bord de la mer. Et vous?

    ( )x ( )x

92. Repeat No. 91.

10.10

93. Look at the meaning in English while listening to the French.

   Yes. We're going to the seaside, and you?   (Fr)   (Fr)

94. This time listen and imitate.

   ( )x   ( )x

95. Listen to the whole sentence. Is the intonation (R) or (W)?

   ( )   ( )

(W)

96. Which one is (R)? Number 1 or 2?

   (1)   (2)

(2)

97. Listen and imitate.

   ( )x   ( )x

98. Listen to this exchange.

   A: (!)
   B: ( )
   A: ( )
   B: (?)
   A: (?)

99. Listen again to number 98.

100. Answer your instructor.

   Instructor: (!)
   You: _____
   Instructor: ( )
   You: _____ ?
   Instructor: (?)

101. Repeat No. 100.

102. This time you begin the conversation with your instructor.

   (begin)
   You: _____ !
   Instructor: ( )
   You: _____
   Instructor: (?)
   You: _____ ?

10.11

INTRODUCTION TO FRENCH PHONOLOGY

103. Repeat No. 102.

104. Here is another sentence. Listen.

    ( ) ( ) ( )

105. Listen again.

    ( ) ( )

106. Listen to the last three words.

    ( ) ( ) ( )

107. Listen and imitate.

    ( )x ( )x ( )x

108. Again.

    ( )x ( )x ( )x

109. We'll add two more words in front of the first three. Listen.

    ( ) ( ) ( )

110. Listen and imitate.

    ( )x ( )x ( )x

111. Again.

    ( )x ( )x

112. This is the first part of the sentence. Listen.

    ( ) ( )

113. Listen, and imitate the first part of the sentence.

    ( )x ( )x ( )x

114. Imitate the second part.

    ( )x ( )x ( )x

115. Imitate the first part; then the second part.

    (1st part)x (2nd part)x (1st part)x (2nd part)x

10.12

116. Again.

   (1st part)x (2nd part)x (1st part)x (2nd part)x

117. Listen to the full sentence and imitate.

   ( )x   ( )x   ( )x

118. Again.

   ( )x   ( )x

119. Look at the French sentence and imitate again.

   Nous aussi pent-être, ça va dépendre du temps.

   ( )x   ( )x

120. Listen and imitate.

   ( )x   ( )x

121. Look at the meaning in English and listen to the French.

   Maybe we('ll go) too. It'll depend on the weather.

   (Fr)   (Fr)

122. Now say this same sentence in French.

   ( )x   ( )x

123. Here is a new sentence. Listen.

   ( )   ( )   ( )

124. Listen to the last word of this sentence and imitate.

   ( )x   ( )x   ( )x

125. Here are two more words added to the one you have just said. Listen.

   ( )   ( )   ( )

126. Now listen and imitate.

   ( )x   ( )x   ( )x

10.13

INTRODUCTION TO FRENCH PHONOLOGY

127. Listen to this. Is it (R) or (W)?

      ( ) ( )

(W)

128. How is it this time? Is it (R) or (W)?

      ( ) ( )

(W)

129. Which is right? number 1 or 2?

      (1) (2)

(2)

130. Listen to the right pronunciation and imitate.

      ( )x ( )x

131. Again.

      ( )x ( )x

132. Listen to the first part of that long sentence.

      ( ) ( ) ( )

133. Listen again and imitate.

      ( )x ( )x

134. Imitate the first part again.

      ( )x ( )x

135. Now listen and imitate the 2nd part.

      ( )x ( )x

136. Listen to the complete sentence.

      ( ) ( )

137. Listen, and imitate the 1st part and then the 2nd part.

      (1st part)x (2nd part)x (1st part)x (2nd part)x

138. Again.

      (1st part)x (2nd part)x (1st part)x (2nd part)x

10.14

139. This is the whole sentence. Listen and imitate.

    ( )x   ( )x

140. Look at the French sentence and imitate.

    Ne soyez pas si pessimiste; voyons!   ( )x   ( )x

141. Look at the meaning in English and listen to the French.

    Come on! Don't be so pessimistic.   (Fr)   (Fr)

142. Listen, and imitate the French again.

    ( )x   ( )x

143. Listen to the whole conversation.

    A: (!)
    B: ( )
    A: ( )
    B: (?)
    A: (?)
    B: ( )
    A: (!)

144: Listen again to frame 143.

145. Listen to the conversation and imitate each sentence.

    A: (!)x
    B: ( )x
    A: ( )x
    B: (?)x
    A: (?)x
    B: ( )x
    A: (!)x

146. Answer your instructor.

    Instructor: (!)
    You: _____
    Instructor: ( )
    You: _____ ?
    Instructor: (?)
    You: _____
    Instructor: (!)

10.15

INTRODUCTION TO FRENCH PHONOLOGY

147. Repeat frame 146.

148. Listen to the conversation again.

        A: (!)
        B: ( )
        A: ( )
        B: (?)
        A: (?)
        B: ( )
        A: (!)

149. Now, you begin the conversation with your instructor.

      (begin)
      You: _____!
      Instructor: ( )
      You: _____
      Instructor: (?)
      You: _____?
      Instructor: ( )
      You: _____!

150. Repeat from 149.

151. Practice frames 143 to 150 several times.

        End of Chapter Ten, Part One.

        Report to your classroom.

Part Two

1.

The consonant "ç".

1. The mark which looks like an up side down question mark and is attached to the letter "c" is called "cédille" in French. Look and listen.

    ça - garçon - leçon - reçu ( )

2. Notice that "ç" is pronounced "s". Look, listen and imitate.

    façon -façade ( )x

3. The letter "c" (without cédille) followed by "e" or "i" is pronounced "s." Look, listen and imitate.

    cinéma - cela - race ( )x

4. Now look at the following words and say them before your instructor does.

    facile   x( )
    façade   x( )
    reçu   x( )
    puce   x( )
    leçon   x( )

5. Now say these.

    morceau x( )
    farci   x( )
    cascade x( )
    perçu   x( )
    glaçon   x( )
    glacé   x( )

2.

The verb "aller" = to go

6. You know all of the different persons of the verb "to go" in the present tense. Look at the following English sentences and say them in French.

    a. We're going to the sea side. x( )
    b. Our son is going to be six.   x( )

10.17

INTRODUCTION TO FRENCH PHONOLOGY

    c. Where are you going? x( )
    d. I'm going to lunch. x( )
    e. Aren't the children going to school? x( )
    f. Do you go there often? x( )

7. Your instructor is going to ask you some questions. Answer them according to the following examples. Listen to the examples.

    Example 1: (?)   ( )
    Example 2: (?)   ( )

    Listen   Answer

    a. (?)   ( )
    b. (?)   ( )
    c. (?)   ( )
    d. (?)   ( )
    e. (?)   ( )
    f. (?)   ( )

8. In the sentences below replace the verb "être" with the appropriate form of the verb "aller".

    a. Je suis à côté.   x( )
    b. Je ne suis pas à l'école.   x( )
    c. Sont-ils au bord de la mer?   x( )
    d. Où êtes-vous?   x( )
    e. Elle n'est pas à la gare.   x( )
    f. Ils sont toujours à Paris.   x( )

9. Look at the following sentences. Then say them in French.

    a. He goes there often.   x( )
    b. Are you going to the café?   x( )
    c. The children are going next door.   x( )
    d. I'm going to the station.   x( )
    e. We go there often.   x( )
    f. She is going next door.   x( )

10. Look at the following sentences, then say them in French.

    a. He goes to the station.   x( )
    b. He is late.   x( )
    c. He has a round-trip ticket.   x( )
    d. There is a train in the morning.   x( )
    e. The train is always on time.   x( )

11. Here are more sentences. Say them in French.

    a. We're going to the hôtel.   x( )
    b. We have two connecting rooms.   x( )
    c. The rooms are very modern.   x( )
    d. The hôtel is not large.   x( )
    e. We are lucky.   x( )

                        3.

    Verbs like: "déjeuner" = to have lunch.

12. Here are verbs like "déjeuner" that were introduced in chapters 1 through 10. Look, listen and imitate.

    déjeuner ( )x   manquer x( )   entrer ( )x   emménager x( )
    fermer ( )x   oublier ( )x   désirer ( )x   rester x( )
    'urer x( )

13. Here are more verbs like those above. In the infinitive form they all end in "er". Look and listen.

    téléphoner   ( )
    danser   ( )
    exporter   ( )
    refuser   ( )

14. Look at the following verbs and say them in French before your instructor does.

    to move in   x( )
    to last   x( )
    to forget   x( )
    to stay   x( )

15. "er" ending verbs are easy to conjugate. Say this in French.

    Are you moving in soon? x( )

16. How would you say this one?

    Yes, we're moving in soon. x( )

17. Say the following sentences before your instructor does.

    a. Nous emménageons   x( )
    b. nous restons   x( )
    c. nous déjeunons.   x( )

INTRODUCTION TO FRENCH PHONOLOGY

18. With the exception of four verbs, all verb endings are predictable. Look and listen.

    <u>Vous désirez</u>   ( )
    <u>Nous désirons</u> ( )

19. What should be the ending of a verb if its subject is "vous"? Write your answer.

    Student's answer: <u>Vous   ez</u>

20. What should the ending be if the subject is "nous"?

    Student's answer: <u>Nous   ons</u>

21. Here are some verbs that you already know. Say them using "nous" or "vous" as the subjects.

	Student	
déjeuner	Vous _____	x( )
déjeuner	Nous _____	x( )
oublier	Vous _____	x( )
entrer	Nous _____	x( )

22. This phrase demonstrates another ending form of "er" verbs. Look and listen.

    ça dure ( )

    What does it mean in English?

    Student's answer: <u>It lasts</u>

23. Here is the verb "durer" again, this time with a different subject pronoun. Does it mean: It lasts, he lasts or both?

    il dure

    Student's answer: <u>both</u>

24. Now, look and listen to the following subject verb constructions.

    a. Il dure   ( )
    b. Elle dure ( )
    c. ça dure   ( )
    d. Je dure   ( )

10.20

INTRODUCTION TO FRENCH PHONOLOGY

25. Was any one verb of the preceding four examples pronounced differently from the other three?

    Student's answer: <u>no</u>

26. Are the two construction below, pronounced correctly?

    Elle déjeune ( )
    Je déjeune ( )

    Student's answer: <u>yes</u>

27. How about these constructions? Are they correctly written and pronounced?

    J'oublie ( )
    Il oublie ( )

    Student's answer: <u>yes</u>

28. Look at the following constructions and say them in French before your instructor does.

    a. She's having lunch. x( )
    b. I'm moving in.   x( )
    c. He's staying.   x( )
    d. I'm going in.   x( )

29. Now say these in French.

    a. We're staying in Paris.   x( )
    b. When do you close?   x( )
    c. May I help you Sir?   x( )
    d. You're forgetting that it's Easter. x( )

30. Look at the following construction. What does it mean in English?

    Ils déjeunent à côté.

    Student's answer: <u>They are having lunch next door.</u>

31. Here is the same construction again. Look and listen.

    Ils déjeunent à côté. ( )

32. Look at construction "a" and "b" and listen. Do they sound alike?

    a. Il déjeune.   ( )
    b. Ils déjeunent. ( )

    Student answer's: <u>yes</u>

10.21

INTRODUCTION TO FRENCH PHONOLOGY

33. Say the following before your instructor does.

    a. Il déjeune. Ils déjeunent. x( )
    b. Il reste. Ils restent. x( )
    c. Il ferme. Ils ferment. x( )

34. For practical purposes "il + verb" differs from "ils + verb" in writing only. Say the following.

    a. Il ferme. x( )
    b. Ils déjeunent. x( )
    c. Elles durent. x( )
    d. Elle ne reste pas. x( )

35. This is the same verb with different subjects. Should the verbs in a, b, c, d, or e be pronounced differently?

    a. ça ferme
    b. Ils ferment
    c. Elle ferme
    d. Il ferme
    e. Je ferme

    Student's answer: no

36. Listen and imitate.

    J'entre.   ( )x
    Il entre.   ( )x
    Ils entrent. ( )x

37. Now say these before your instructor does.

    Il entre.   x( )
    Ils entrent. x( )
    J'entre.   x( )

38. Now say these.

    Il oublie.   x( )
    Ils oublient. x( )
    J'oublie.   x( )

39. Say the following French sentences before your instructor does.

    a. Qu'oubliez-vous? x( )
    b. J'oublie toujours. x( )
    c. Nous oublions que c'est Pâques. x( )
    d. Ils entrent au café. x( )

10.22

e. Nous entrons?   x( )
f. Ils n'oublient pas.   x( )

40. Look at the following English constructions and say them in French.

    a. I don't forget.   x( )
    b. They're not coming in.   x( )
    c. He's not coming in.   x( )
    d. She's moving in Saturday.   x( )
    e. They forget.   x( )

4.

Past tense = passé composé.

41. This sentence is from the conversation in Chapter Two.

    Où avez-vous déjeuné?

    In the above construction, how many verbs are there? One or two?

    Student's answer: __2__

42. In order to refer to the past using the "passé composé" we need two verbs. One is conjugated. Which one is it? Number 1 or 2?

    Où <u>avez-vous</u> <u>déjeuné</u>?
           1   2

    Student's answer: __1__

43. Here is that sentence again. Notice the pronunciation of the underlined verb.

    Où avez-vous <u>déjeuné</u>? ( )

44. The underlined verb in frame 43 is called a past participle. Listen to it again and also to its infinitive form.

    déjeuné   ( )
    déjeuner   ( )

45. Here they are again. Do they sound same or different?

    déjeuner   ( )
    déjeuné   ( )

    Student's answer: __S__

INTRODUCTION TO FRENCH PHONOLOGY

46. In order to form the past participle of any "er" verb, the final "r" is dropped and an "accent aigu" is placed above the final "e". Look, listen and imitate.

    a. téléphoner - téléphoné   ( )x
    b. importer   - importé   ( )x
    c. armer   - armé   ( )x

47. Here is a French sentence. Say it in English.

    Nous avons oublié.

    Student's answer: **We forgot**

48. Here is an English sentence. Say it in French.

    You forgot. x( )

49. Here is another English sentence. Say it in French.

    We forgot. x( )

50. Look at this English sentence and listen to the French.

    We have forgotten. (Fr)

51. Here is another English sentence. Listen to the French.

    We forgot. (Fr)

52. In English there are two ways of saying the following French construction. Say both English constructions.

    Vous avez oublié.

    Student's answer: 1. **You forgot**
                        2. **You have forgotten**

53. Say the following English sentences in French.

    a. He forgot.   x( )
    b. They forgot.   x( )
    c. I have forgotten.   x( )

54. Notice that in order to form the past tense the verb "to have" is the only one that is conjugated. Look and listen.

    a. Nous avons déjeuné. ( )
    b. Ils ont déjeuné.   ( )
    c. Vous avez déjeuné. ( )

10.24

INTRODUCTION TO FRENCH PHONOLOGY

55. The verb "avoir," which is the one that changes according to its subject, is called an auxiliary verb. Look at the following constructions and listen.

	Subject	Auxiliary verb	Past participle of verb	
a.	vous	avez	déjeuné	( )
b.	j'	ai	oublié	( )
c.	il	a	emménagé	( )
d.	nous	avons	téléphoné	( )
e.	ils	ont	dansé	( )

56. In the following construction, which is the auxiliary verb 1, 2 or 3?

    En avez-vous oublié?
     1   2   3

    Student's answer: <u>1</u>

57. Which is the auxiliary verb in this construction.

    Ils ont fermé les écoles.
     1 2   3

    Student's answer: <u>2</u>

58. Here are two sentences. Which one is the passé composé? 1 or 2?

    1. Nous allons déjeuner.
    2. Nous avons déjeuné.

    Student's answer: <u>2</u>

59. In order to form the "passé composé" we conjugate the verb "avoir" and add the infinitive form of any verb. Is that statement right or wrong?

    Student's answer: <u>W</u>

60. Look at the following sentence. Is the past participle correctly written?

    Ils ont oublier.

    Student's answer: <u>No</u>

10.25

INTRODUCTION TO FRENCH PHONOLOGY

61. Say the following sentences before your instructor does.

    a. J'ai oublié.   x( )
    b. Nous avons téléphoné.   x( )
    c. Ils ont accepté.   x( )
    d. Elle a refusé.   x( )

62. Here are a few more sentences, this time in the negative form. Notice that "ne...pas" surrounds the auxiliary verb. Listen and imitate.

    Nous n'avons pas déjeuné.   ( )x
    Ils n'ont pas oublié.   ( )x
    Il n'a pas accepté.   ( )x

63. Look at the following sentences and then say them in the negative form before your instructor does.

    a. Nous avons téléphoné.   x( )
    b. Il a déjeuné.   x( )
    c. J'ai oublié.   x( )
    d. Ils ont refusé.   x( )

64. Say the following sentences in French.

    a. Where did she have lunch?   x( )
    b. What did you forget?   x( )
    c. Did they miss the train?   x( )

65. Look at the following sentences and say them in the past tense.

    a. Où déjeunent-ils?   x( )
    b. Vous oubliez vos billets.   x( )
    c. Je refuse.   x( )

66. Now say these in the past tense.

    a. Je n'oublie pas.   x( )
    b. Nous ne déjeunons pas.   x( )
    c. Ils n'emménagent pas samedi.   x( )

67. The verb "to be" (être) is also used to form the passé composé with not more than 20 verbs. Look and listen.

    a. Je suis allé à Paris.   ( )
    b. Il est resté.   ( )

10.26

376   INTRODUCTION TO FRENCH PHONOLOGY

68. Look at the following sentences and say them before your instructor does.

    a. Nous sommes allés au café.   x( )
    b. Ils sont arrivés samedi.   x( )
    c. Est-ce que vous êtes resté?   x( )

69. In later chapters, you'll learn all the verbs requiring the auxiliary "être" to form the passé composé. For the time being we'll concern ourselves with the auxiliary "avoir" only. Say the following in French:

    a. What did you forget?   x( )
    b. I forgot the tickets.   x( )
    c. Where did they have lunch?   x( )
    d. They had lunch next door.   x( )

5.

Review

70. This is a review: look at the following words or sentences and say them before your instructor does.

    a. Vous l'avez manqué.   x( )
        Vous l'avez oublié.   x( )
        Vous y avez déjeuné.   x( )
        Nous y avons déjeuné.   x( )

    b. Ils sont allés au café.   x( )
        Ils y sont allés.   x( )
        Elle est allée au café.   x( )
        Elle y est allée.   x( )

    c. Ça va dépendre du temps.   x( )
        Ça va dépendre de vous.   x( )
        Ça va dépendre de la saison.   x( )
        Çc va dépendre des enfants.   x( )

    d. Qu'avez-vous fait pendant le week-end?   x( )
        Nous sommes allés au bord de la mer.   x( )
        Vous avez oublié quelque chose?   x( )
        'J'ai oublié mon passport.   x( )

    e. Ils ne parlent pas français.   x( )
        On parle anglais.   x( )
        J'emménage ce week-end.   x( )
        Ça ne va pas durer.   x( )

Report to your classroom.

6.

Préparation

Exercice un

Dites en français

1.	For the week-end	1.	Pour le week-end
2.	For me	2.	Pour moi
3.	Really	3.	Vraiment
4.	The week-end	4.	Le week-end
5.	Plans	5.	Des projets
6.	The plans	6.	Les projets
7.	The sea	7.	La mer
8.	By the seaside	8.	Au bord de la mer
9.	The side	9.	Le bord
10.	A nice week-end	10.	Un beau week-end
11.	Bedrooms	11.	Des chambres
12.	To depend	12.	Dépendre
13.	The bedrooms	13.	Les chambres
14.	Indeed	14.	En effet
15.	It lasts	15.	Ça dure
16.	Me too	16.	Moi aussi
17.	Us	17.	Nous
18.	Lately	18.	Ces temps-ci
19.	Perhaps	19.	Peut-être
20.	My wife and I	20.	Ma femme et moi

Exercice deux

Dites en anglais

1.	Ne soyez pas en retard	1.	Don't be late
2.	Soyez optimiste, voyons!	2.	Come on! Be optimistic
3.	Quel beau matin!	3.	What a beautiful morning!
4.	Quelle belle soirée!	4.	What a beautiful evening!
5.	Vraiment?	5.	Really?
6.	Nous n'avons pas de projets.	6.	We have no plans.
7.	Je n'ai pas fait de projets.	7.	I haven't made any plans.
8.	Soyez à l'école à neuf heures.	8.	Be at school at nine.
9.	Vous allez être en retard.	9.	You're going to be late.
10.	Soyez moderne.	10.	Be modern.
11.	Il fait vraiment beau.	11.	The weather is really nice.

10.28

12.	Il ne fait pas beau ces jours-ci.	12.	The weather is not nice lately.
13.	Ils sont en retard de dix minutes.	13.	They're ten minutes late.
14.	Où est-ce que vous êtes?	14.	Where are you?
15.	Il fait beau ce matin.	15.	The weather is nice this morning.
16.	Quelle belle femme!	16.	What a beautiful women!
17.	Ça va dépendre de vous.	17.	It's going to depend on you.
18.	C'est ma femme.	18.	She is my wife.
19.	Soyons à l'heure.	19.	Let's be on time.
20.	Pourvu qu'il emménage avant la fin du mois.	20.	Hope he moves in before the end of the month.

Exercice trois

Dites en français

1.	It's not going to depend on me.	1.	Ça ne va pas dépendre de moi.
2.	We are five minutes late.	2.	Nous sommes en retard de cinq minutes.
3.	Do you have any tickets?	3.	Avez-vous des billets?
4.	Do you have the tickets?	4.	Avez-vous les billets?
5.	Do you have tickets?	5.	Avez-vous des billets?
6.	How many tickets do you have?	6.	Combien de billets avez-vous?
7.	The train just pulled into the station.	7.	Le train vient d'entrer en gare.
8.	How much time does he have?	8.	Combien de temps a-t-il?
9.	He just came in.	9.	Il vient d'entrer.
10.	He does not have the tickets.	10.	Il n'a pas les billets.
11.	The weather is not nice lately.	11.	Il ne fait pas beau ces temps-ci.
12.	She is lucky.	12.	Elle a de la chance.
13.	How long are you staying?	13.	Combien de temps restez-vous?
14.	It's not our train.	14.	Ce n'est pas notre train.
15.	She is not my daughter.	15.	Ce n'est pas ma fille.
16.	She is my daughter.	16.	C'est ma fille.
17.	How many trains are there?	17.	Combien de trains y a-t-il?
18.	I had forgotten it was Saturday.	18.	J'avais oublié que c'était samedi.
19.	At what time are we going to the café?	19.	A quelle heure allons-nous au café?
20.	We have exactly what you need.	20.	Nous avons exactement ce qu'il vous faut.

INTRODUCTION TO FRENCH PHONOLOGY

Exercice quatre

(Fill in the blanks)

1. Je ne suis pas toujours en retard. De temps en temps je suis à l'heure.
2. Il n'est pas toujours en retard. _____
3. Nous ne sommes pas toujours en retard. _____
4. Elle n'est pas toujours en retard. _____
5. Je ne suis pas toujours en retard. _____
6. Ils ne sont pas toujours en retard. _____
7. Vous n'êtes pas toujours en retard. _____
8. Elles ne sont pas toujours en retard. _____

Exercice cinq

Dites en français

1. He is very tall.
2. How old is she?
3. Where are the children going?
4. There is a train in the evening.
5. The first train is at six.
6. My wife is next door.
7. I'm on time.
8. We're lucky.
9. He is forty years old.
10. Where is the railway station?
11. It's true.
12. He is lucky.

1. Il est très grand.
2. Quel âge a-t-elle?
3. Où vont les enfants?
4. Il y a un train dans la soirée.
5. Le premier train est à six heures.
6. Ma femme est à côté.
7. Je suis à l'heure.
8. Nous avons de la chance.
9. Il a quarante ans.
10. Où est la gare?
11. C'est vrai.
12. Il a de la chance.

10.30

Exercice six

Dites en français

1. Our hotel is very modern.
2. I don't have the tickets.
3. The children have connecting rooms.
4. She is lucky.
5. Where are you going Saturday?
6. How much time do we have?
7. They have children.
8. Do you have connecting rooms?
9. The children are in school.
10. He is going next door.

1. Notre hôtel est très moderne.
2. Je n'ai pas les billets.
3. Les enfants ont des chambres communicantes.
4. Elle a de la chance.
5. Où allez-vous samedi?
6. Combien de temps avons-nous?
7. Ils ont des enfants.
8. Avez-vous des chambres communicantes?
9. Les enfants sont à l'école.
10. Il va à côté.

Exercice sept

Professeur	Vous
Je suis toujours à l'hôtel.	Vous êtes toujours à l'hôtel?
1. Vous allez à Paris.	1. Je vais à Paris?
2. J'emménage bientôt.	2. Vous emménagez bientôt?
3. Le train est à l'heure.	3. Le train est à l'heure?
4. Je vais souvent au café à côté.	4. Vous allez souvent au café à côté?
5. Vous partez dans trois jours.	5. Je pars dans trois jours?
6. Je n'ai pas les billets.	6. Vous n'avez pas les billets?
7. Je suis toujours à l'hôtel.	7. Vous êtes toujours à l'hôtel?
8. Vous avez de la chance.	8. J'ai de la chance?
9. J'y vais souvent.	9. Vous y allez souvent?
10. Vous êtes en retard.	10. Je suis en retard?

Exercice huit

Professeur	Vous
Vous êtes à l'heure?	Oui, je suis toujours à l'heure.
1. Je suis pessimiste?	1. Oui, vous êtes toujours pessimiste.
2. Vous avez de la chance?	2. Oui, j'ai toujours de la chance.
3. Vous déjeunez à midi?	3. Oui, je déjeune toujours à midi.
4. Les trains sont à l'heure?	4. Oui, ils sont toujours à l'heure.
5. Vous êtes à l'heure?	5. Oui, je suis toujours à l'heure.
6. Vous partez à dix heures?	6. Oui, je pars toujours à dix heures.

Exercice neuf

Dites en français

1.	She is still in Paris.	1.	Elle est toujours à Paris.
2.	He is always on time.	2.	Il est toujours à l'heure.
3.	You are still at the hotel?	3.	Vous êtes toujours à l'hôtel?
4.	You're still leaving at the end of the month?	4.	Vous partez toujours à la fin du mois?
5.	We always go to the ocean.	5.	Nous allons toujours au bord de la mer.
6.	I always leave in the morning.	6.	Je pars toujours le matin.
7.	We're always late.	7.	Nous sommes toujours en retard.
8.	I always have lunch next door.	8.	Je déjeune toujours à côté.
9.	It's always in the evening.	9.	C'est toujours dans la soirée.
10.	You're always lucky.	10.	Vous avez toujours de la chance.

Exercice dix

Dites en anglais

1.	Combien de temps le voyage a-t-il duré?	1.	How long did the trip last?
2.	Il a duré un mois.	2.	It lasted one month.
3.	Avez-vous téléphoné à la police?	3.	Did you call the police?
4.	Oui. Elle vient.	4.	Yes, they're on their way.
5.	Ont-ils oublié mon adresse?	5.	Did they forget my address?
6.	Non, ils ne l'ont pas oubliée.	6.	No they didn't forget it.
7.	Ils ont visité la capitale.	7.	They visited the capital.
8.	J'ai oublié mon passeport.	8.	I forgot my passport.
9.	Combien de personnes avez-vous invité?	9.	How many people did you invite?
10.	Nous avons visité la capitale.	10.	We visited the capital.

Exercice onze

Dites en français

1.	When did you move in?	1.	Quand avez-vous emménagé?
2.	We moved in Saturday.	2.	Nous avons emménagé samedi.
3.	Did I miss the train?	3.	Est-ce que j'ai manqué le train?
4.	Oui, vous l'avez manqué.	4.	Yes, you missed it.
5.	Where did she have lunch?	5.	Où a-t-elle déjeuné?
6.	She had lunch next door.	6.	Elle a déjeuné à côté.
7.	Did you forget it was Easter?	7.	Avez-vous oublié que c'était Pâques?
8.	No, I didn't forget.	8.	Non, je n'ai pas oublié.
9.	Did it last more than three days?	9.	Ça a duré plus de trois jours?
10.	Yes, it lasted four days.	10.	Oui. Ça a duré quatre jours.

Exercice douze

Professeur	Vous
Les écoles sont fermée?	Oui, elles sont fermées.
1. Les écoles vont fermer?	1. Oui, elles vont fermer.

10.33

2. Les écoles sont fermées? 2. Oui, elles sont fermées.
3. Les écoles ont fermé? 3. Oui, elles ont fermé.
4. Avez-vous oublié? 4. Oui, j'ai oublié.
5. Allez-vous déjeuner? 5. Oui, je vais déjeuner.
6. Avez-vous déjeuné? 6. Oui, j'ai déjeuné.
7. Avez-vous téléphoné? 7. Oui, j'ai téléphoné.
8. Allez-vous téléphoner? 8. Oui, je vais téléphoner.
9. Avez-vous emménagé à côté? 9. Oui, J'ai emménagé à côté.
10. Allez-vous emménager à la fin du mois? 10. Oui, je vais emménager à la fin du mois.

Exercice treize

Professeur | Vous

Je n'ai pas déjeuné à midi. | Je ne déjeune pas à midi.

1. Ils n'ont pas oublié Paris. | 1. Ils n'oublient pas Paris.
2. Ils ont réservé deux chambres. | 2. Ils réservent deux chambres.
3. Ça a duré quelques minutes. | 3. Ça dure quelques minutes.
4. Nous avons visité la capitale. | 4. Nous visitons la capitale.
5. Je n'ai pas déjeuné à midi. | 5. Je ne déjeune pas à midi.
6. Je n'ai pas oublié que c'était Pâques. | 6. Je n'oublie pas que c'est Pâques.
7. Elle a téléphoné à la gare. | 7. Elle téléphone à la gare.
8. Ils ont accepté. | 8. Ils acceptent.
9. Nous n'avons pas déjeuné à l'ambassade. | 9. Nous ne déjeunons pas à l'ambassade.
10. Il n'a pas insisté. | 10. Il n'insiste pas.

Exercice quatorze

Questions générales

Questions | Réponses possibles

1. Les enfants vont à l'école à Pâques. | 1. Non, l'école est fermée.
Non, ils ne vont pas à l'école.
2. Est-ce que les écoles sont fermées à Pâques? | 2. Oui, elles sont fermées.
3. Comment est votre appartement? | 3. Il est (très) grand et moderne.
Il n'est pas moderne.
Il n'est pas (très) grand.
Il n'est pas (très) beau.
Il est (très) beau.

10.34

4.	A quelle heure avez-vous déjeuné samedi?	4.	J'ai déjeuné à midi. J'ai déjeuné à une heure.
5.	A quelle heure allez-vous déjeuner?	5.	Je vais déjeuner à une heure.
6.	Les écoles sont fermées le weekend?	6.	Oui, elles sont fermées.
7.	Est-ce qu'il fait beau ces temps-ci?	7.	Oui, il fait vraiment beau ces temps-ci.
8.	Allez-vous souvent au bord de la mer?	8.	Non, je ne vais pas souvent au bord de la mer. Non, je n'y vais pas souvent.
9.	Avez-vous visité l'Europe?	9.	Oui, j'ai visité l'Europe. Non, je n'ai pas visité l'Europe.

Exercice quinze

Dites en français

1.	When are you leaving?	1.	Quand partez-vous?
2.	Do the children have lunch at school?	2.	(Est-ce que) les enfants déjeunent à l'école?
3.	We have two daughters.	3.	Nous avons deux filles.
4.	One is at school.	4.	L'une est à l'école.
5.	The other is here.	5.	L'autre est ici.
6.	I'm not always late.	6.	Je ne suis pas toujours en retard.
7.	How many trains are there in the afternoon?	7.	Combien de trains y a-t-il l'après-midi?
8.	How long are you staying?	8.	Combien de temps restez-vous?
9.	How old are you?	9.	Quel âge avez-vous?
10.	I missed the train.	10.	J'ai manqué le train.
11.	Are there any in the afternoon?	11.	(Est-ce qu') Il y en a l'après-midi?
12.	Do you go there often?	12.	Vous y allez souvent?
13.	It doesn't last.	13.	Ça ne dure pas.
14.	I go there once in a while.	14.	J'y vais de temps en temps.
15.	We have what we need.	15.	Nous avons ce qu'il nous faut.
16.	It's going to depend on the weather.	16.	Ça va dépendre du temps.
17.	It was Easter and the school was closed.	17.	C'était Pâques et l'école était fermée.
18.	How long is he staying?	18.	Combien de temps reste-t-il?
19.	Don't be late.	19.	Ne soyez pas en retard.

Exercice seize

	Professeur		Vous
1.	les écoles	1.	Les écoles.
2.	sont fermées	2.	Les écoles sont fermées.
3.	à Pâques	3.	Les écoles sont fermées à Pâques.
4.	toujours	4.	Les écoles sont toujours fermées à Pâques.

Exercice dix-sept

	Professeur		Vous
1.	durer	1.	durer.
2.	ça va	2.	Ça va durer.
3.	est-ce que	3.	Est-ce que ça va durer?
4.	combien de jours	4.	Combien de jours est-ce que ça va durer?

Exercice dix-huit

	Professeur		Vous
1.	huit-heures	1.	Huit-heures.
2.	et demie	2.	Huit-heures et demie.
3.	avant	3.	Avant huit-heures et demi.
4.	à la gare	4.	A la gare avant huit-heures et demie.
5.	soyez	5.	Soyez à la gare avant huit heures et demie.

Exercice dix-neuf

Expansion et correlation

	Professeur		Vous
1.	bord de la mer	1.	Bord de la mer.
2.	nous allons	2.	Nous allons au bord de la mer.
3.	à Pâques	3.	Nous allons au bord de la mer à Pâques.

10.36

Exercice vingt

	Professeur		Vous
1.	emménager	1.	Emménager.
2.	vous allez	2.	Vous allez emménager.
3.	est-ce que	3.	Est-ce que vous allez emménager?
4.	quel jour	4.	Quel jour est-ce que vous allez emménager?

Exercice vingt et un

Expansion et corrélation

	Professeur		Vous
1.	Paris	1.	Paris.
2.	rester	2.	Rester à Paris.
3.	vous allez	3.	Vous allez rester à Paris.
4.	est-ce que	4.	Est-ce que vous allez rester à Paris?
5.	Combien de mois	5.	Combien de mois est-ce que vous allez rester à Paris?

INTRODUCTION TO FRENCH PHONOLOGY

7.

Reading exercises

Lecture

1. Read.

    1. Nous préférons déjeuner plus tôt.
    2. Elles préfèrent partir maintenant.
    3. Nous changeons de train à Paris.
    4. On ne parle pas anglais.
    5. Ils parlent lentement.
    6. Ça ne dure pas longtemps.

2. Read.

    1. Je vais au bureau à neuf heures.
    2. Je commence à deux heures.
    3. Je termine à six heures.
    4. Je rentre à cinq heures et demie.
    5. Elle va à l'école à côté.
    6. Nous allons en ville.

3. Read.

    1. Nous avons des enfants.
    2. Nous n'avons pas d'enfants.
    3. Nous avons fait des projets.
    4. Nous n'avons pas fait de projets.
    5. Vous avez de la chance.
    6. Vous n'avez pas de chance.

4. Read.

    1. C'est un enfant.
    2. Ce sont des enfants.
    3. C'est ma fille.
    4. Ce sont mes filles.
    5. C'est le billet.
    6. Ce sont les billets.

5. Read.

    1. J'y suis allé ce matin.
    2. Ils y sont allés samedi.
    3. Nous y allons plus tard.
    4. Je n'y vais pas.
    5. Ils y vont ce week-end.
    6. Il y est allé.

6. Read.

   1. Où avez-vous déjeuné?
   2. Où allez-vous déjeuner?
   3. Avez-vous emménagé?
   4. Allez-vous emménager?
   5. A-t-il téléphoné?
   6. Va-t-il téléphoner?

7. Read.

   1. Vous les avez manqués.
   2. Ils vous ont téléphoné.
   3. On nous a invités.
   4. Il n'en a pas trouvé.
   5. Ils nous en ont parlé.
   6. J'y ai déjeuné avec des amis.

8. Read.

   1. Combien d'argent avez-vous dépensé?
   2. Combien de personnes avez-vous invité?
   3. Qu'avez-vous décidé?
   4. Où les avez-vous rencontrés?
   5. Quand l'avez-vous commencé?
   6. Combien de jours y avez-vous passé?

Chapter Ten, End of Part Two.

Go to the lab for Tests 1 through 10.

INTRODUCTION TO FRENCH PHONOLOGY

Chapter Ten, Part Three

Tests

Test 1

Listen to the following words and write them.

Listen	Write
1. ( )	1. _____
2. ( )	2. _____
3. ( )	3. _____
4. ( )	4. _____
5. ( )	5. _____
6. ( )	6. _____
7. ( )	7. _____
8. ( )	8. _____
9. ( )	9. _____
10. ( )	10. _____

Test 2

The pronunciation of the following words may be right or wrong. Look, listen and check the appropriate column.

		Right	Wrong
1. journée ( )	1.	____	____
2. vraiment ( )	2.	____	____
3. Nous allons ( )	3.	____	____
4. en effet ( )	4.	____	____
5. pessimiste ( )	5.	____	____
6. voyons ( )	6.	____	____
7. pourvu ( )	7.	____	____

3. combien ( )   8. _____ _____

9. personne ( )   9. _____ _____

10. exactement ( ) 10. _____ _____

STOP TAPE RECORDER

Test 3

There is a mistake in each of the following words. Rewrite each word correctly.

	Look		Rewrite
1.	journé	1.	_____
2.	seulment	2.	_____
3.	projé	3.	_____
4.	bort	4.	_____
5.	conbien	5.	_____
6.	pouvus	6.	_____
7.	famme	7.	_____
8.	voyon	8.	_____
9.	dépandre	9.	_____
10.	ausi	10.	_____

START TAPE RECORDER

Test 4

You're going to hear "vous" or "nous" followed by a verb in the present tense. Check whether the "nous" or "vous" + verb is right or wrong.

	Listen		Right	Wrong
1.	( )	1.	_____	_____
2.	( )	2.	_____	_____
3.	( )	3.	_____	_____

INTRODUCTION TO FRENCH PHONOLOGY

			Right	Wrong
4.	( )	4.	_____	_____
5.	( )	5.	_____	_____
6.	( )	6.	_____	_____
7.	( )	7.	_____	_____
8.	( )	8.	_____	_____
9.	( )	9.	_____	_____
10.	( )	10.	_____	_____

Test 5

In each of the following sentences one word is incorrectly written. Rewrite the complete sentence correctly.

	Look		Rewrite
1.	Où avez-vous déjeuner?	1.	_____
2.	Nous avez déjeuné à côté.	2.	_____
3.	Il ont emménagé samedi.	3.	_____
4.	Vous reste trois jours.	4.	_____
5.	Ils a manqué le train.	5.	_____
6.	Nous étons en retard.	6.	_____
7.	Vous partons à six heures.	7.	_____
8.	Ils déjeune à l'hôtel.	8.	_____
9.	Elle déjeunent au café.	9.	_____
10.	Nous êtes à Paris.	10.	_____

Test 6

Look at the following sentences. Check whether their construction is right or wrong.

	Look		Check
			Right Wrong
1.	Vous avez téléphoné?	1.	____ ____
2.	Je déjeuné au café.	2.	____ ____
3.	J'ai déjeune au café.	3.	____ ____
4.	Ils ont oublient.	4.	____ ____
5.	Il a oublié.	5.	____ ____
6.	Pourvu ça dure.	6.	____ ____
7.	Ils ne pas déjeunent.	7.	____ ____
8.	Vous avez n'oublié pas.	8.	____ ____
9.	Combien chambres désirez-vous?	9.	____ ____
10.	Ils vont au bord de la mer.	10.	____ ____

Test 7

Listen to the following sentences. Check whether they are grammatically right or wrong.

	Listen		Check
			Right Wrong
1.	( )	1.	____ ____
2.	( )	2.	____ ____
3.	( )	3.	____ ____
4.	( )	4.	____ ____
5.	( )	5.	____ ____
6.	( )	6.	____ ____

7. ( )   7. _____ _____

8. ( )   8. _____ _____

9. ( )   9. _____ _____

10. ( )   10. _____ _____

Test 8

Write what you hear.

    Listen   Write

1. ( )   1. _____

2. ( )   2. _____

3. ( )   3. _____

4. ( )   4. _____

5. ( )   5. _____

6. ( )   6. _____

7. ( )   7. _____

8. ( )   8. _____

9. ( )   9. _____

10. ( )   10. _____

Test 9

Look at the following sentences then rewrite them, changing them from the present tense to the "passé composé."

    Look   Passé composé

1. Nous déjeunons à une heure.   1._____

2. Ils oublient la date.   2._____

3. Ça ne dure pas.   3._____

4. J'emménage samedi.   4._____

5. Vous oubliez quelque   5._____
    chose?

10.44

6.	Elle déjeune avec nous.	6.	_____
7.	Quand emménagent-ils?	7.	_____
8.	Nous téléphonons de la gare.	8.	_____
9.	Je n'oublie pas.	9.	_____
10.	Ils refusent.	10.	_____

Test 10

Check whether the following sentences are "passé composé" or not.

Listen		Check	
		Passé composé	Not passé composé
1.	( )	1. _____	_____
2.	( )	2. _____	_____
3.	( )	3. _____	_____
4.	( )	4. _____	_____
5.	( )	5. _____	_____
6.	( )	6. _____	_____
7.	( )	7. _____	_____
8.	( )	8. _____	_____
9.	( )	9. _____	_____
10.	( )	10. _____	_____

END OF CHAPTER TEN

END OF "INTRODUCTION TO FRENCH PHONOLOGY"